D0758444

DATE DUE

DEMCO 38-296

Teodoro Moscoso and

Puerto Rico's Operation Bootstrap

Teodoro Moscoso
and Puerto Rico's
Operation Bootstrap

A. W. MALDONADO

University Press of Florida

Gainesville Tallahassee Tampa Boca Raton

Pensacola Orlando Miami Jacksonville

Riverside Community College
Library
4800 Magnolia Avenue
Riverside, CA 92506

HC 154.5 .M34 1997

Maldonado, A. W.

Teodoro Moscoso and Puerto
 Rico's Operation Bootstrap

Copyright 1997 by the Board of Regents of the State of Florida
Printed in the United States of America on acid-free paper

All rights reserved

02 01 00 99 98 97 6 5 4 3 2 1

Library of Congress Cataloging-in-Publication Data

Maldonado, A. W.
Teodoro Moscoso and Puerto Rico's Operation Bootstrap / A. W. Maldonado.
 p. cm.
Includes bibliographical references and index.
ISBN 0-8130-1501-4 (alk. paper)
 1. Puerto Rico—Economic policy. 2. Puerto Rico—Economic conditions—1952– . 3.
Moscoso, Teodoro, 1910– . I. Title.
HC154.5.M34 1997
338.97296—dc21 96-49822

The University Press of Florida is the scholarly publishing agency for the State University
System of Florida, comprised of Florida A & M University, Florida Atlantic University,
Florida International University, Florida State University, University of Central Florida,
University of Florida, University of North Florida, University of South Florida, and
University of West Florida.

University Press of Florida
15 Northwest 15th Street
Gainesville, FL 32611

1934
". . . that place is hopeless, *hopeless* . . ."
FRANKLIN D. ROOSEVELT

1953
"It is not too much to say that a transformation is in process [in Puerto Rico] which for a long time will be one of the wonders of human history."
REXFORD TUGWELL

Contents

Acknowledgments

The original idea of writing the largely untold story of Teodoro Moscoso's role in Puerto Rico's economic miracle—as the "father" of Operation Bootstrap—belongs to Guillermo Martínez, the chairman of the GM Group. Martínez gave the author a grant to conduct a year-long series of recorded interviews with Moscoso.

William Díaz of the Ford Foundation supported the project with a Ford grant. The bulk of the research and writing was financed by another grant from the Chase Manhattan Bank. Terrence Wadsworth, vice president and general manager of Chase in Puerto Rico, made this project possible through his support and faith.

José Alberto Morales, president of Sacred Heart University of Puerto Rico, and his successor, José Jaime Rivera, enthusiastically embraced the project, offering office, logistic, and research support, generously provided mostly by the staff of the university's library.

Members of the Moscoso family, his widow, Gloria, his daughter, Margarita, and his son, José Teodoro, were all cooperative in providing and verifying material.

Finally, Carmen Casellas-Marcou carried out much of the research, performed interviews, and did very helpful editing. This book is as much the work of Carmen Casellas-Marcou as of the author.

Prologue

San Ciriaco was more than a killer hurricane: Father Juan Perpiñá y Pibernat, the Spanish-born capitular vicar of the Catholic Diocese of Puerto Rico, was convinced that it was an evil omen.

Born in Africa on August 2, 1899, the monstrous tropical storm crossed the Atlantic in five days, tore into the West Indies, cut a highway of destruction through the length of Puerto Rico, turned north toward the Bahamas, smashed into Florida on August 13, continued up the East Coast of the United States, veered and crossed the Atlantic again, passing south of the Azores to finally die in the Mediterranean.[1]

Alone and bewildered in the diocese's main office in Old San Juan, Father Perpiñá y Pibernat attempted to understand what had happened. In his twenty-eight years in the Antilles, the Spanish priest had experienced tropical storms but none like this. The reports of death and destruction from the clergy throughout the island overwhelmed him. Two-thirds of the churches and chapels were demolished. As he attempted to write, his hand trembled. He described the horror of whole families trapped in their wooden homes, swept by the raging floods, terrified children crying out desperately for help, the houses collapsing, entire families disappearing in the water, the unearthing of hundreds of bodies of men, women, and children who sought shelter in buildings they considered safe, now buried under gigantic mud slides. Days after the hurricane, he wrote, ships entering Ponce harbor still found bodies floating in the bay.

Father Perpiñá y Pibernat added the deaths reported by the priests and other religious sources and determined that San Ciriaco had taken 8,000 souls. The actual count was 3,369 people killed,[2] most by drowning. Many poor souls, he thought, perished celebrating what they believed was the end of the storm; abandoning the shelters, they attempted to return to their homes, lured by the treacherous calm of the storm's eye.

But the purpose of the twenty-seven-page letter was not to describe what had happened but to explain why.

In Latin America, it was long the custom to name hurricanes after the saints of the Catholic Church. August 8, the day the storm hit Puerto Rico, belonged to the martyr San Ciriaco.[3] It was also Church custom during the months of August and September for priests to recite a special prayer at every mass to ward off storms: "Ad repellendas tempestasdes." Why did God choose this particular time to ignore the prayers with such a furious, brutal, murderous hurricane? What did it mean?

Father Perpiñá y Pibernat believed the answer was evident: the huge storm was "God's punishment." The cruelty of San Ciriaco, he said, could only be explained and understood by the gravity of Puerto Rico's sins. And most sinful, he wrote, was the attitude of Puerto Ricans after the "change in nationality": most "shameful" was how the Puerto Ricans embraced the Americans and turned their backs on the Mother Country, Spain.[4]

It could not be a coincidence that San Ciriaco had punished Puerto Rico almost exactly on the first anniversary of the American invasion of the island, July 25, 1898. Three months later, on October 18, 1898, in a solemn ceremony at La Fortaleza, the sixteenth-century governor's palace, the Spanish flag was lowered and the American flag raised, ending four hundred years of Spanish rule.

The reaction of the Puerto Ricans, Father Perpiñá y Pibernat wrote, was disgraceful: "They have not only rejected the Mother Country, but in that moment of acute pain for all her sons and daughters, of humiliation before the world, down at her knees before victors, the Puerto Ricans have lent themselves to the campaign of defamation and insults against the history, the legacy of Spanish rule, in Puerto Rico." The priest's strongest attack was directed against those Puerto Ricans, "cowardly sons of the Mother Country," who had become accomplices of the American determination to separate Church and State, not only in their statements and writings but also with their "shameful silence." The Americans had ended the government's funding of the Catholic Church, forcing scores of priests to return to Spain. "So there you have a sin of this nation, Puerto Rico," Father Perpiñá y Pibernat concluded, "that God did not wait to have purified in the other world, that He proceeds to punish in this world, with hurricanes, epidemics and hundreds of other public calamities."

The Puerto Ricans, by embracing the Americans, by not defending their own Spanish blood and the glorious legacy of Spanish rule in Puerto Rico, and by not defending the Church, had forced God to send San Ciriaco, the terrible "emissary."

Was Puerto Rico cursed? So it seemed. This beautiful island had remained mired in social and economic stagnation for the four centuries following

Christopher Columbus's landing in 1493 and Juan Ponce de León's coloni-
zation. Nothing seemed to work on the island, not the Spanish dominion
nor the arrival of the Americans in 1898 promising the "blessings" of American democracy and prosperity and not, three decades later, the extraordinary efforts of President Franklin Delano Roosevelt to extend the New Deal
to this "disgrace to the American flag." The supremely confident Roosevelt
could lift his nation from the Great Depression and was about to lead the
free world in defeating the scourge of fascism, but he too felt defeated by
Puerto Rico's problems.

"As for Puerto Rico," Roosevelt told the director of the Division of Terri-
tories and Island Possessions, Ernest Gruening, "that place is hopeless, *hopeless*," raising his arms above his head for emphasis and in resignation.[5]

The hopelessness existed in the minds of Puerto Ricans and Americans,
but it was grounded in the island's realities. Puerto Rico possessed none of
the conditions considered indispensable for economic development.

When the Americans arrived in 1898, the 3,435-square-mile island was
already critically overcrowded with 899,820 people: its population density
was five times that of Cuba and the Dominican Republic. Only 25 percent
of the land was suitable for modern, mechanized agriculture. There were no
exploitable minerals. The island's geographic location, a thousand miles
from the U.S. mainland and sixteen hundred miles from New York, was
ideal for a naval base but patently absurd for large-scale industrialization.
The infrastructure that existed was primitive, roads were inadequate, electric power scarce and costly.

The Puerto Rican workforce was poorly educated, untrained and unskilled.
Puerto Rico's Hispanic, rural, "mañana" culture was seen as another insurmountable obstacle to economic development, as was the nature of Puerto
Rican politics—at times idealistic, at times vicious, personalistic, and destructive.

By the 1950s an economic miracle was taking place in Puerto Rico. For it
was indeed a remarkable economic transformation. From a centuries-old
rural-agricultural country with all its traditional socioeconomic character-
istics, within a generation and within a democratic framework, Puerto Rico
became a modern urban-industrial society. In practically all economic and
social indices—from per capita income to life expectancy—Puerto Rico joined
the ranks of the "developed countries" of the world.

The credit went to Luis Muñoz Marín, the extraordinary leader who carried out a "democratic revolution" on the island. In 1948 he was described
as the "Bard of Bootstrap" on the cover of *Time*. In the words of Abe Fortas,
quintessential Washington insider for a half-century who served on the U.S.

Supreme Court in the 1960s, Muñoz was a "spectacularly great figure."[6] But he was not the originator of or the force behind Operation Bootstrap, the industrialization program that actually lifted Puerto Rico from the long centuries of extreme poverty. Bootstrap was the work of Teodoro Moscoso.

Born into a wealthy family, educated to carry on the family business, Moscoso dedicated his life to public service in Puerto Rico and the United States. He was influenced principally by three men—Rexford Tugwell, the professor of economics who formed part of Roosevelt's "brain trust," who first recruited Moscoso into public service; Muñoz Marín, Puerto Rico's first elected governor and its principal leader for forty years, who led and inspired Moscoso throughout his life; and John F. Kennedy, who placed enormous trust and responsibility on him.

Moscoso created and ran Fomento, Puerto Rico's Economic Development Administration, "the most successful government development corporation in the Western Hemisphere."[7] He pioneered the craft of aggressive industrial promotion. Fomento's organization and techniques were imitated by state governments on the U.S. mainland and in foreign countries from Ireland to Taiwan. He converted Puerto Rico into a laboratory of Third World development for over ten thousand foreign visitors under President Harry S. Truman's Point Four program.

Moscoso was relentless, driven, in a breathless race against time. His impatience "set teeth grinding" in San Juan and later in Washington. He took risks at times amazing to those below and above him. He earned lifelong loyalty and respect, but he moved through life so fast that even his closest associates felt that his core as a human being had escaped their grasp. He was creative. David Ogilvy, the British-born U.S. advertising "genius," wrote that Moscoso was the most inspiring man with whom he had ever worked.

Moscoso's impact on Puerto Rico was second only to that of Muñoz. Moscoso covered the island with huge signs announcing, "This is another Fomento plant." Every Fomento employee proudly wore a Fomento pin that made him or her a member of the "elite" in the Puerto Rican government. He created and ran a multimillion-dollar communications strategy that transformed the image of Puerto Rico throughout the United States and the world. From Beardsely Ruml, the outspoken New Dealer and originator of the "pay-as-you-go" income tax mechanism who went on to a successful business career in Macy's and other large businesses, to Conrad Hilton, whose hotel in San Juan launched Hilton International, to David Ogilvy and David Rockefeller, Moscoso created a network of admirers in corporate America always willing to come to Puerto Rico's aid.

In Moscoso's eyes the greatest tribute to Operation Bootstrap appeared in an article by economist Kenneth E. Boulding, published in June 1961 by the Center for the Study of Democratic Institutions: "There is a type of revolution which does not fit into any type of . . . category and which may be the most important of all in the long run. I call it the Fomentarian Revolution . . . in honor of a remarkable institution in Puerto Rico which embodies it, known as 'Fomento.'" The democratic transformation in Puerto Rico, Boulding wrote, the intriguing mixture of strong government direction and incentives for private capital may prove the best model for economic and social change in the world.

The Fomentarian Revolution, Boulding continued, required two kinds of leadership: "The charismatic but unrealistic leader may awake the people out of their apathy and give them a sense of identity and purpose. For the revolution to be accomplished, however, a new type of leadership may be necessary—more sober, less dramatic, and with a clearer and more realistic vision." The Fomentarian Revolution was Moscoso's revolution.

In 1961 President John F. Kennedy, aware of the global implications of what had been accomplished in Puerto Rico, recruited Moscoso to play a central role in a dramatically new U.S. policy toward Latin America. First the president named Moscoso ambassador to Venezuela to help Rómulo Betancourt become the first elected head of state to complete his term in office in the country's history. Then Kennedy brought Moscoso to Washington to organize and run the Alliance for Progress.

It was in 1940 that Kenneth Boulding's "two kinds of leadership" essential for democratic development came together. Luis Muñoz Marín, the "charismatic but unrealistic leader," met for the first time a young pharmacist from Ponce who was desperately seeking a cause to which he could dedicate his life and enormous energy. That meeting changed Teodoro Moscoso's life and became a turning point in Puerto Rico's history. For it was the ensuing Fomentarian Revolution that turned Father Juan Perpiñá y Pibernat's prophecy of the San Ciriaco "curse" into the "blessings" of Puerto Rico's golden era and the period of its economic miracle.

Part

One

Liberation

I was conscious that I had met a superior person
. . . and everything from then on I was to assess in
my mind had to be weighed against the standards
that this extraordinary man had set for me in that
conversation which lasted a couple of hours.

Moscoso describing his first meeting
with Luis Muñoz Marín, 1990

Chapter 1
Moscoso's Conversion

On November 5, 1940, Teodoro Moscoso spent the day packing his car with as many *jíbaros*—Puerto Rican farm workers—as would fit and driving them to the polling precincts. It was a race against time. At two in the afternoon the voting was scheduled to start and the doors to the precincts would close. Police officers would be posted to prevent anyone from entering. Only those already inside and identified as registered voters were allowed to vote, ensuring that no one could vote more than once.

Moscoso's wife, Gloria Sánchez Vilella, was nine months pregnant with their second child, José Teodoro. The first, Margarita, was born in 1938. Gloria had set up a sandwich assembly line for the jíbaro voters. As the day wore on the tension and expectation mounted.

Finally, in the early evening, the results started to trickle in. Puerto Rico, at that time, elected its legislature, mayors, and municipal assemblies, and its resident commission in Washington, a member of Congress with voice but no vote. The governor was named by the president of the United States. At the beginning it seemed that the conservative Republican-Socialist Coalition—that strange alliance of the Republican Party, controlled by the island's sugar barons, and the Socialist Party, representing the labor unions—had been returned to power. It led Luis Muñoz Marín's new party, the Popular Democratic Party, in total voting. What was crucial, however, was the vote distribution, as it determined the legislative composition. The following day the newspapers reported tentatively: "Everything Indicates Populares Dominate the Senate, Coalition the House."[1] This was only half right. The Populares won the senate by one vote, while the House was evenly divided between the Coalition and the Populares, with the splinter group, the Triparty Unification, controlling three votes that initially swung to the Populares.

There was nothing tentative, however, about Muñoz's reaction to the election result. He declared that he and his party had received a mandate to carry out to the letter the sweeping economic and social reforms promised in the campaign. Muñoz went further. The election, he said, changed the fundamental power structure in Puerto Rico. Through the "electoral mandate," power had been transferred from a conservative elite to "the people." Muñoz was determined to make November 5, 1940, second only to July 25, 1898—the landing of American troops on the island—in historical importance and thereby mark the beginning of the island's "peaceful revolution."

Moscoso had decided only a few months before the election that he wanted to be part of that revolution. He became a Popular in the summer of 1940, following a meeting with Muñoz that took place in an isolated wooden house at a coffee farm up in the Adjuntas Mountains.

Dr. José Gándara, a physician married to one of Gloria's sisters and a new member of the Popular Party, came by the Moscoso pharmacy one afternoon and invited Moscoso to accompany him to Adjuntas. Gándara had been summoned to treat Muñoz, who had suspended his campaigning due to a bad cold and high fever. When they arrived at the house, they were told that Muñoz was unable to get out of bed. Gándara went inside to treat his patient. When Gándara emerged he told Moscoso to go inside for a few moments to greet Muñoz.

Muñoz was unshaven and clearly worn down, but he asked Moscoso to sit down. Despite the illness he seemed eager to talk. Moscoso was struck by a sensation of authenticity. Muñoz was the only son of Puerto Rico's greatest nineteenth-century political leader, Luis Muñoz Rivera. But unlike the island's traditional *políticos,* he was natural, down to earth; there was in him no posturing, no trace of ego-inflation. Muñoz seemed confident and spoke with deep conviction. Politics was clearly no game for him. The younger Muñoz, dubbed *El Vate,* the poet, had turned into a controversial politician, intensely feared by some, adulated by others.

In the farmhouse, stretched out in a jíbaro hammock, dressed in simple clothes, Muñoz seemed totally in his element. Moscoso saw immediately how radically different he was from the island's traditional leaders, stiff and formal men, always dressed in jackets and ties, who gave long speeches punctuated by obscure words that only a few could grasp. The jíbaros called them *picos de oro,* men with golden tongues, for they were seen essentially as entertainers playing the role of "political leaders." They seemed to take themselves very seriously and often referred to their "patriotism" and "sacrifice." But the jíbaros saw all of this as only a contest between machos, a thrilling cockfight at which bets were made. Most jíbaros sold their votes for two dollars. If the jíbaro was lucky enough to have backed the winning party, the vote could pay off with a job for himself or a favor for his family. But the candidates' promises and programs remained meaningless to the jíbaros. Forty years of insular partisan politics and elections had changed nothing in their lives, and there was no reason for them to believe that it ever would.

Muñoz was different, Moscoso thought, not only in what he was saying, but in another way. They were speaking in Spanish, of course, but Moscoso felt that he was communicating with a man thinking, organizing, and presenting his ideas in a way—including the sense of humor—that was typically American.

Instead of the usual sweeping, evident generalizations, Muñoz described concrete, specific social reform projects. Moscoso became excited; he too wanted to talk about specific reforms. He wanted Muñoz to believe that while he was certainly from one of Ponce's elite Republican families, he abhorred the inhumane social and economic injustice on the island, that he had touched and smelled the inequality in the horrid slums of Ponce.

Gándara looked into the room to see why Moscoso was taking so long. Muñoz waved for him to come in and join the discussion that he was obviously relishing. Muñoz went on to describe his campaign, *Verguenza Contra Dinero*—shame versus money—the seemingly quixotic attempt to convince the jíbaros not to sell their votes. How would he do it? Simple, Muñoz answered: by convincing them that their votes are worth much more than the two dollars the parties paid for them. Muñoz would draft a series of specific economic and social reform bills. Then he would have all the Popular candidates publicly raise their right hands at a giant public rally and swear that if elected, they were going to vote for each one of the bills. This was a binding contract, Muñoz declared, that would give the people "real power" for the first time in island history.

A half-century later, Moscoso recalled: "I am sorry to say that coming back from that farm to my house my memory is blurred, principally because I was so emotionally enthralled by the experience. I was conscious that I had met a superior person, a superior human being, a superior mentality, and everything from then on that I was to assess in my mind had to be weighed against the standards that this extraordinary man had set for me in that conversation which lasted a couple of hours. The standards were so high, the demands were so great—for integrity, for honesty, for striving, for becoming involved in the problems of the community, of the city, of the island—that you had to rearrange your values."[2] He did.

*   *   *

It was a decision bound to disturb Moscoso's father. Muñoz and his party represented everything the elder Moscoso detested. The poet-turned-politician was a danger, a demagogue who fomented a destructive class war to win jíbaro votes. The senior Moscoso argued that even if Muñoz was not a rabid anti-American with a Communist agenda, his followers certainly were. Thank God, his father declared, that the Americans still governed; they would not permit Muñoz and his leftist ideas to ruin the island. How could his son be attracted to this man and this party that were out to destroy the Moscosos' world?

Moscoso, in fact, was already caught between conflicting family loyalties. While his own family was solidly conservative Republican, Gloria's family was liberal and now strongly backed the Populares. Gloria's father, the successful merchant Luis Sánchez Frasquieri, was elected to the House of Representatives as a Popular. Her older brother, Roberto Sánchez Vilella, had also joined the party and was to be recruited into Muñoz's new government.

For Moscoso, however, it was not a matter of politics. He had never thought of participating in the futile game of partisan politics. The sterile status debate reminded him very much of the obsession his father, a former seminarian, had with theology: mental constructions that were irrelevant to reality, to the day-to-day life of the Ponce poor. He accepted without much thought his father's insistence that Puerto Rico would eventually become a state of the United States. It seemed evident to him that for an island so poor and overcrowded, independence from the United States was economic suicide.

*   *   *

But personal independence was exactly what Moscoso desperately longed for, independence from his father. The elder Moscoso, a native of Carolina, Puerto Rico, had married Alejandrina Mora Fajardo, a tall, imposing woman born in Soller, in the Balearic island of Majorca, Spain. In 1909, while living in Ponce, Alejandrina convinced her husband to allow the family, which included Carmen, the firstborn, to spend a long sojourn in Barcelona, the Catalonian capital. The elder Moscoso, by then a successful pharmacist, agreed and made arrangements to travel as frequently as possible between Puerto Rico and Spain.

Three-year-old Teodoro Moscoso as a Spanish clown with his six-year-old sister, Carmen. Moscoso, in his own words, grew up as a "wandering Jew." Born in Barcelona, his mother was originally from Majorca, Spain, and his father was Puerto Rican. Young Moscoso spent his early years living in Spain, the U.S. mainland, and Puerto Rico.

Teodoro Moscoso was born at the family's Barcelona apartment on Rambla de Catalonia on November 26, 1910. Now the father had what he most wanted: a son who, within two decades, could help him to accomplish his dream of a chain of pharmacies with branches in Puerto Rico, New York, and even South America. Four years later, a second son, José, was born in Puerto Rico.

Teodoro's education was carefully planned and implemented; he attended school in New York, where he became proficient in English, and graduated from Ponce High School. He was then sent to the Philadelphia School of Pharmacy. But after three years, in 1931, Moscoso insisted on transferring to the University of Michigan, which offered the liberal arts courses he wanted. He graduated in 1932 and returned to Ponce to work at the Farmacia Moscoso, as predetermined by his father.

He was bored and restless. Moscoso simply hated drugstore work. The marriage to Gloria was the only saving grace. Despite his sense of guilt and filial duty, he wanted to escape from the role assigned to him by his father.

Luckily, an exit soon appeared, an opening leading to public service: clearing slums and making public housing available to the poor. It all came about in circuitous fashion. A $2 million grant from the U.S. Housing Authority to the city of Ponce was about to be lost because no one in the municipal government had the skills or the time needed to fill out the mountain of forms requested by Washington. Moscoso's father was approached by the Ponce Housing Authority. Might his son, known for his command of English, be able to help? The father owed some favors to the board member making the request, banker Pedro Juan Rosaly. Yes, his son could take a leave of absence from the family pharmacy.

Within weeks Moscoso was in Washington. Completing the forms was the easy part; now he wanted to talk to the persons in charge of the U.S. Housing Authority about changing the agency's philosophy in order to accommodate it to Puerto Rico's desperate plight. Instead of building only a few housing units with the $2 million grant, Moscoso suggested a totally radical approach. The island agencies would provide the essential infrastructure: roads, water and sewer, and electric power. Then the slum-dwellers would transport their existing dwellings—mostly shacks—to the developed parcels and hook up to the utilities. Once in the clean, orderly environment, Moscoso argued, the people would begin to improve their homes. The cost to the Ponce Housing Authority would be $400 per unit instead of the anticipated $2,000 for an entirely new dwelling.

The first three officials to whom Moscoso spoke were unconvinced, even shocked; they dismissed him. Undaunted, on November 5, 1939, he went to see Director of Housing Nathan Straus, a member of New York's liberal "Jewish aristocracy," who had been considered as a Democratic gubernatorial candidate. Moscoso gave him the first promotional sales talk of his public life. He talked breathlessly about saving lives, about upgrading the cesspool-like conditions in which thousands lived, worse than anything found in the U.S. mainland. What was important was quick action, basic sanitation; complying with exact building codes could come later, Moscoso explained.

"Go ahead, try it. I'll take care of the objections," said Straus.

Moscoso came back to Ponce and quickly went to work. Soon six hundred families were moved to the innovative housing project. All in all,

Moscoso's Housing Authority built five projects, a total of nearly one thousand units.

* * *

Moscoso's experiences clearing Ponce slums from 1937 to 1941 awakened his passion for social justice and consequently his interest in Muñoz's new political party. It also increased his contempt for the island's traditional politicians. What mattered, he thought, was rescuing real people from real slums, which he had been able to do with American money and American know-how. Why weren't the island's leaders, so prone to giving speeches, as interested in clearing the Ponce slums as Nathan Straus, the head of U.S. Housing?

Moscoso considered himself a liberal. He believed that government had the obligation to step in and correct the malfunctions and social injustices of the capitalist system. Like Muñoz, he had read George Bernard Shaw and admired the Fabian Socialists. But he was not doctrinaire; he was uninterested in grand ideological schemes. He knew that he had inherited from his mother a need to reach out and help others, that he was at heart a "do-gooder." He was exhilarated by being able to change things; he was attracted to innovation. He also wanted to move in the high circles of economic and political power. His experiences in Washington, especially with Nathan Straus, had convinced him that this was the life for which he was searching.

But Moscoso's conversion was also a substitution. In Muñoz he found a person who could inspire him, the person his own father could never be. Muñoz widened Moscoso's vision of Puerto Rico; he put the island's problems within the context of movements and ideas that had already changed other societies; he magnified the challenges and rewards on the island. Muñoz was "bigger" than anyone whom Moscoso had met in Puerto Rico. Moscoso had already tasted the satisfaction of winning a battle for social justice in Ponce. If he followed Muñoz, Moscoso could wage the battle island-wide.

But how could he support a man then so passionately determined to lead Puerto Rico toward political independence, a status that the Moscosos considered tantamount to economic suicide? At the 1940 meeting with Muñoz, up in the coffee-farm house, Moscoso was struck by a contradiction: this *independentista* leader was at the same time highly Americanized. Not only did Muñoz speak perfect English, but he understood American politics and democracy as no other Puerto Rican leader ever had. Raised as much in the United States as on the island, Muñoz had seen American democracy function from up close. His teenage years overlapped his father's work in Congress. Luis Muñoz Rivera was a member of the U.S. House of Representatives as Puerto Rico's Resident Commissioner in Washington.

Writing of his electoral victory in 1940, Muñoz recognized that he was, indeed, a product of American political culture: "The appearance of the Popular Democratic Party, the entry of the people on the political stage, is dramatic evidence of another cultural influence. The very fact that the person that writes this—to a great extent formed in the democratic climate of the United States—is part of the leadership of this new PDP movement, points to the importance of this. The Popular Democratic Party is the first party that achieves power in Puerto Rico whose leadership comes fundamentally from the generation most under American democratic influences."[3]

This is what made Muñoz different; his belief in independence was not driven by "anti-Americanism." This was the bridge that allowed Moscoso to cross over their otherwise huge ideological differences as to Puerto Rico's political relation to the United States. They both gave economic and social reform priority over political status. They both believed in the liberalism embodied by U.S. President Franklin Roosevelt's New Deal. These were bonds much stronger than their status ideologies. Moscoso was placing his trust in Muñoz's natural, deeply bred faith in an American-style democracy.

The test came soon. On November 17, 1940, a Saturday night, Moscoso and Gloria awaited Muñoz's victory speech on the radio. Puerto Rico would learn if Muñoz and the Popular Party meant what they had said in the campaign. Had Muñoz cynically convinced the jíbaros not to sell their votes for two dollars, giving them instead a false promise? That was precisely what the Republican-Socialist Coalition argued, and what many of the Populares' own *independentista* leaders wanted to believe: that forgoing the status issue and concentrating instead on social and economic change was a promise that Muñoz would not keep.

But Moscoso's instinctive trust in Muñoz was right. In his victory speech Muñoz forcefully reiterated that he would not break his vow to the jíbaros, that he would rigorously honor his promise that a vote for him and his party would not be interpreted as a vote for independence or any other status.[4]

It was a long, disorganized speech, held together by one fundamental theme—that "the people in Puerto Rico, in the country and in the towns, have learned the lesson of democracy." The deepest meaning of the election, Muñoz declared, was that the people were finally "liberated" from bad politics and partisan tribalism. Those who voted against the Populares were as "liberated" as the winners, he declared, for there would be no persecution of public employees nor anyone else for partisan reasons. Muñoz struck close to Moscoso's home when he referred to a friend, Pedro Juan Serrallés, a member of the Ponce elite, owner of the island's largest rum distillery, producers of Don Q rum, to dramatize the political transformation that had begun. Serrallés, a Republican, had run for reelection to the senate; the millionaire, Muñoz pointed out with pride, was defeated by a *público* car driver. "As a man and as a citizen," Muñoz said referring to the Ponce industrialist, "he will receive from us the same legitimate and profound respect that the Popular Democratic Party has for all men equal before God and before democracy; and his legitimate rights . . . will be safeguarded as the legitimate rights of all equal men before God and democracy." Muñoz added that Serrallés was also "liberated" for he was now politically equal to all the 500,000 voters, both jíbaros and members of the elite. Clearly, Moscoso thought, there would be no class war in Puerto Rico; his father was wrong.

Moscoso also thought of the voters whom he had shuttled in his car to the polling precincts, of how their lives would be changed. He was now a Popular, a *Muñocista*. He looked forward to breaking out of the small world of a Ponce druggist and to becoming part of a socioeconomic movement that could, indeed, fill his life. Like the jíbaros and Serrallés, as he heard Muñoz's speech, Teodoro Moscoso hoped that he too was about to be liberated.

Chapter 2

Rexford Tugwell's Call

The radical but democratic economic and social changes promised in the Popular Party campaign soon began to take shape. The first line of attack was massive land reform. The tool was enforcing federal legislation dating back to 1900 that limited the size of corporate land holdings to five hundred acres. The law had been widely ignored by the sugar companies, most of which were absentee-owned. As of 1929, four American sugar companies owned and operated 68 percent of the land devoted to sugar, a total of 170,675 acres.[1] Muñoz deeply believed that the economic control exercised by the sugar interests lay at the root of the jíbaros' poverty and of the social injustice that victimized them.

Enforcing the Five-Hundred Acre Law meant not only breaking up the large, mostly American-owned sugar plantations but also unraveling the island's entire economic base. Under Republican administrations Washington had shown little interest in taking that action. But under the Roosevelt administration, Muñoz's land reform plans gained the support of the New Dealers, including Secretary of Agriculture Henry Wallace and Assistant Secretary of Agriculture Rexford G. Tugwell.

Eleanor Roosevelt made helping Puerto Rico—the miserable island that had already awakened the nation's liberal conscience and had been labeled a "disgrace to the American Flag"—one of her personal crusades. Helping to ignite this conscience and the First Lady's interest was a close friend, Ruby Black, a Washington journalist. Black was the Washington correspondent for Muñoz's newspaper, *La Democracia,* and functioned for years as his loyal eyes and ears in the nation's capital.

In 1934 the Washington New Dealers encouraged the drafting of a massive land reform and economic reconstruction program, later called the Chardón Plan after one of its authors, Carlos Chardón, a noted Puerto Rican agronomist and educator. The plan's proposals, however, had more in common with the Mexican agrarian reform than with the American experience.

The government would form a public corporation to acquire all the lands in excess of five hundred acres and redistribute them among the small sugar farmers and workers.

Even among New Dealers the Chardón Plan was seen as too radical. It had become the target of acrimonious attacks in Washington as well as in Puerto Rico. The insular legislature, controlled by the Republican-Socialist Coalition until Muñoz's 1940 election upheaval, had succeeded in paralyzing it.

In March 1941, former Assistant Secretary of Agriculture Tugwell was sent to Puerto Rico by President Roosevelt to study the effect of the enforcement of the Five-Hundred Acre Law on the island's economy. Pushed by Senator Muñoz, the insular attorney general, Benigno Fernández García, had taken a sugar corporation to court for violation of the law. In July 1938, after a two-year court battle, he finally won.

No one in Roosevelt's group of advisors was more interested in agricultural reform than Tugwell. An original member of FDR's brain trust, the outspoken and controversial Tugwell had gained the sobriquet "Red Rex" and became the lighting rod attracting the ire of the anti-New Dealers.

*   *   *

It was another hot and humid southern Puerto Rico afternoon. Moscoso was behind the counter at his father's pharmacy, where he was required to work during his time off from the Ponce Housing Authority. Suddenly four obviously American-looking men walked in from the scorching heat. One of them seemed to Moscoso as handsome as a Hollywood star, a man in his late forties or early fifties, dressed in a seersucker suit. Moscoso recognized him: Rexford Tugwell. He was accompanied by several men; Moscoso recognized one of them, Leon Henderson, director of the Commodity Credit Corporation.

Tugwell and his group had just arrived after the long, hot drive from the Guánica sugar mill. They had been touring the island as part of the land ownership study. The group was clearly pleased to have found this cool oasis in the middle of the Ponce plaza, with the high ceilings and big electric fans. As they sat around one of the tables they began a relaxed conversation about the conditions back in Washington and about the war in Europe. Tugwell and Henderson complained about the agonizing slowness in the nation's preparation for war. The old "reactionaries," the industrialists whom the President had allowed to return to power in Washington, Tugwell commented, were too busy fighting among themselves, interested only in maximizing their profits. Then the conversation turned to Hitler, how everybody had underestimated him, how the American media had deliberately played down his monstrous military buildup. Tugwell reminded everyone that for years he had been warning about the German threat.

Tugwell looked up and noticed the young man standing nearby, taking it all in. Tugwell asked him to join them at the table. He identified himself as Teodoro Moscoso. Speaking surprisingly good English, Moscoso told Tugwell that he had read something about him in a magazine; he had also read several of his articles on social and economic planning. Tugwell was flattered and began asking Moscoso about the situation in Ponce, especially the area's sugar industry. But Moscoso was more interested in talking about Washington. Turning to Henderson, he said that he was familiar with the Commodity Credit Corporation's programs for stabilizing corn, wheat, and other grain prices: it was, he added enthusiastically, "one of the greatest New Deal organizations." Henderson, who never recalled hearing that before, asked Moscoso how a drugstore owner in Ponce could be so well informed about events in Washington. Moscoso turned and pointed to the magazine rack. One of the magazines, he commented, had an excellent article on the U.S. Housing Authority, a topic of personal interest to him; another article described the national debate over a topic of great interest to Tugwell, the creation of the National Resource Planning Board, which the National Association of Manufacturers and the U.S. Chamber of Commerce strongly opposed. Tugwell's eyes widened even more when Moscoso revealed that he knew the details of their academic backgrounds, including that Tugwell and Henderson had both studied economics at the University of Pennsylvania's Wharton School.

It was embarrassing, Moscoso confessed, that he probably knew more about what was happening in the United States than about the sugar industry in Ponce, although the big sugar plantations came right up to the east and west boundaries of the city. Tugwell said that since Moscoso had such an interest in national affairs, if he gave him an address, he would send him articles and other material on issues related to social and economic planning. It was a delight, Tugwell commented, to find a bright young man in Ponce who understood that economic and social planning was not synonymous with Communism. No, Moscoso smiled, it's the "fourth power," Tugwell's own phrase. Tugwell kept his promise; several weeks later Moscoso began to receive a steady flow of written material.

In 1941, convinced that the U.S. entry into the war was inevitable, Tugwell volunteered to serve as governor of Puerto Rico. He believed that if Britain fell to the Nazis the Caribbean would become a decisive battleground, as Hitler would attempt to flank the United States all the way to the Panama

Canal. Yes, little Puerto Rico, now under Muñoz's liberal leadership, was a tempting laboratory to put into practice Tugwell's "radical" New Deal reforms, which in his eyes were being frustrated in Washington. But Tugwell's deeper motive for seeking the Puerto Rican governorship was patriotism. Since he could no longer be at Roosevelt's side (the conservatives in Congress having run him out of Washington), he wanted to serve his country and his president on this potentially decisive military outpost, contributing to the war against fascism.

Soon after becoming governor in September 1941, Tugwell returned to Ponce, this time driving through on the way to inspect a Puerto Rico Reconstruction Administration project in Guayama. A well-kept, neatly landscaped housing project caught his eye; he ordered the driver to stop the car. He was impressed by its cleanliness. At the entrance there was a plaque: it was a federally financed project built and maintained by the Ponce Housing Authority.

"So, Mr. George Reed is responsible for this," he commented, reading the name of the head of the Federal Housing Authority office in San Juan.

"Well, actually," someone commented, "it was done by a fellow from Ponce. His name is not there; he is a pharmacist by the name of Teodoro Moscoso."

Tugwell remembered the young man who seemed to know so much about Washington. Returning later that night to La Fortaleza, he listed among things to do the following day calling the Ponce pharmacist.

*   *   *

On a good day the seventy-mile drive from Ponce to San Juan took three and a half hours, unless the driver was forced to crawl at even a slower pace behind a sugarcane trailer. Moscoso left for his appointment with Governor Tugwell with time to spare. It was always a grueling drive. Although the paved, two-lane road was flat and straight from Ponce to Salinas, there were frequent exasperating stops. Each time one of the *públicos*—the private cars that drove people from town to town for a nickel or a dime—picked up or discharged a passenger, it meant another maddening stop for Moscoso.

The road to Salinas took him through sugarcane country; off in the distance he could see the faint outlines of the massive sugar mills, the black smoke from their high stacks announcing that the mills were grinding. In the municipalities of Juana Díaz and Santa Isabela the road cut through small communities of sugarcane workers, clusters of *bohíos* made out of wood and discarded metal.

After Salinas the road turned to the left and began climbing the winding, rugged road built by the Spaniards that cut through the three-thousand-foot-high central mountain range.

Even though Moscoso had made this trip often, he was still struck by the spectacular scenic beauty of the island's lush, green interior. But there was also, inescapably, the ugliness of poverty. Even up in these rugged mountains, where agriculture was impossible except for a few small coffee farms, there were clusters of shacks with scrawny, potbellied children, their skins yellowish from bilharzia and malnutrition.

Moscoso expected Tugwell to offer him the job of coordinating the federal housing programs in Puerto Rico. Would he have the courage to tell him that public housing was futile as long as these half-starved little children kept increasing in numbers? Yes, of course, it was necessary to rescue as many people as possible from the slums. But it was a losing battle. As had been the case in Ponce, for every family he relocated away from the slums several others moved in. If Tugwell gave him the opportunity, he would tell him that he wanted an assignment related to the causes, not the consequences, of poverty.

Muñoz, of course, was right; Puerto Rico needed fundamental social and economic reform. But it also needed economic development and a program to slow down the skyrocketing population growth. These goals, not public housing, Moscoso said to himself, were what really interested him. As he went down into the valley of Cayey and up again over the mountains to Caguas, he wondered if he would have the opportunity and the confidence to say all this to Tugwell.

But there was something else to think about. If Tugwell did offer him a job, where would he fit within the odd power tug between Tugwell, the governor, and Muñoz, the senate president and political leader? Moscoso's confidence in Muñoz remained unshaken, but like so many others, he had doubts about the amalgamation of politicians, professionals, writers, poets, and journalists who had joined Muñoz to form the Popular leadership.

In order to gain a degree of clarity, Moscoso divided the Popular Party leadership into three categories. There were the anti-American *independentistas* who believed that Muñoz's "no status" policy was only a temporary, tactical move to shore up his political power and that he would move from there to independence. The second group was made up of idealistic independentistas who recognized that there were major economic impediments to independence. They fully supported Muñoz's reform programs and believed that in the long run an economically developed Puerto Rico would opt for independence. The third group consisted of men and women whose primary interest was Muñoz's economic and social reform and who wanted to join a political movement dedicated to combating poverty and underdevelopment. A small minority within this group preferred autonomy or statehood over independence. Moscoso placed himself in the third category.

How would Tugwell, a man with such a strong personality and views, deal with the politically complex Popular party? Would he develop the same confidence in Muñoz that Moscoso felt? This, Moscoso thought, would depend also on Muñoz's success in neutralizing the more radical, pro-independence forces within his party.

After Caguas, Moscoso was now speeding on the road straight into San Juan. "I wondered," Moscoso recalled years later, "whether I was getting myself into a pickle."

As much as Moscoso had attempted to anticipate what the meeting would be like, what his options were, he was not prepared for what actually happened at La Fortaleza. The imposing structure over the massive walls of Old San Juan, the governor's palace, the seat of power through four centuries of Spanish governors-general and four decades of American governors, struck Moscoso as incongruously shabby. The place felt to him cold, unfriendly, even forbidding, as he climbed up the wide stairs to the governor's office. The walls were bare of decorations.

Had not anyone, the retired military officers and the civilians who were appointed governors, ever *cared* about La Fortaleza, he asked himself. Did he really want to work in this cold dungeon?

Tugwell was as friendly and striking in his good looks as when Moscoso first met him at the Ponce pharmacy. But Moscoso was quickly baffled. Yes, the governor wanted him to come to La Fortaleza as one of his assistants. But there was, Tugwell said, a problem: he could not pay him a salary. Nothing had been budgeted, and Tugwell believed that nothing would be. It was traditional, he explained, for the island's legislators to deny the "colonial governor" funds or personnel that would, in their eyes, increase his power over them and Puerto Rico. It had still not occurred to them, Tugwell added, that they were also denying the island any possibility of good, efficient government.

But there was another problem. It dawned on Moscoso that Tugwell was not clear on just what he was offering. What would be his duties and responsibilities? Tugwell answered that he was impressed with Moscoso's accomplishments in the Ponce housing program. His command of English and unusual knowledge of American economics and politics certainly qualified him to become a vital liaison between the appointed governor and Puerto

Rico: the legislators, the business community, the media, and, of course, Muñoz. Perhaps, Tugwell finally said, thinking out loud, the way to get around the salary problem was to name him assistant for housing, although his real duties would be broader. This would permit Tugwell to ask the federal housing authority that Moscoso work at La Fortaleza while still receiving his salary from the Ponce office. If the federal authority balked, Tugwell added, Moscoso would need to balance two part-time jobs, one in San Juan, one in Ponce.

Tugwell saw immediately that Moscoso was uncomfortable; this was not what the young man hoped for. Why don't we at least try it, the governor asked him, starting with four days a week at La Fortaleza? Before Moscoso could respond, Tugwell turned and walked out of the office into the narrow balcony overlooking Old San Juan. He remained there several minutes quietly contemplating the picturesque La Fortaleza street with the ornate, overhanging balconies and shops downstairs. Moscoso didn't know what to do, remain inside or join him outside. He heard the office door open; a photographer entered. Returning inside, Tugwell said, "Let's take a picture," and grabbed Moscoso's arm and positioned him near his side. The decision was made. The photograph and a press statement announcing Moscoso's appointment were sent to the media that afternoon.

Moscoso quickly discovered the best way to communicate Tugwell's thoughts to Muñoz. He would drop in unannounced at Muñoz's house in Isla Verde, where he would be invited to sit down, drink, and take part in the rambling *tertulias*, or friendly discussions, with Muñoz's political cronies, poet friends, and visiting journalists. Moscoso, of course, was interested to hear what Muñoz and the Popular leaders were thinking, their attitudes toward Tugwell, their plans and complaints. Moscoso knew that Muñoz also regarded him as a source of information about what was taking place at La Fortaleza. The camaraderie at these good-natured, free-wheeling discussions, which heavy drinking made easier, gave Moscoso exactly what he needed to serve as a bridge between the two strong-willed men.

"How would it be with Muñoz?" Tugwell asked himself repeatedly during this period. Uppermost in his mind was how Puerto Rico would react once the United States finally entered the war, which he considered inevitable, and the island found itself right in the middle of the conflict. Tugwell was aware that Spain's Generalísimo Francisco Franco had admirers among conservative, well-to-do Puerto Ricans. The more Tugwell got to know Muñoz, however, the more confident he felt about his loyalty. "I had this to count on," he wrote, "he (Muñoz) was with us on the issue of Democracy versus Fascism." Tugwell kept on his desk a copy of Muñoz's 1941 speech

Rexford Tugwell (left), one of President Franklin D. Roosevelt's brain trust advisers, served as Puerto Rico's last non-native governor from 1941 to 1946. He is pictured here with Teodoro Moscoso, whom he named as his assistant to serve as liaison with the insular Senate President, Luis Muñoz Marín, in enacting the first stage of Puerto Rico's democratic revolution. One of Tugwell's legislative innovations was the creation of the Industrial Development Company, Fomento.

on the Fourth of July—a holiday celebrated on the island with a strong dose of status politics. Tugwell disapproved of many of Muñoz's decisions and actions as the island's political boss, but rereading Muñoz's eloquent and emotional defense of democracy convinced him that "Muñoz and Muñoz's people are totally with us."[2]

The question, "How would it be with Muñoz?," however, went beyond Muñoz's loyalty, beyond his or Tugwell's personalities. As effectively as

Moscoso served as a conduit between them, Tugwell and Muñoz Marín remained inevitably on a collision course.

Tugwell was the first governor in four centuries of island history who intended to make fundamental reforms. Governor Theodore Roosevelt Jr. back in the late 1920s had attempted making changes, but Tugwell now set out to craft a public administration that did not exist anywhere else in Latin America: a government that embodied his doctrine of social and economic planning as the fourth power, with a strong executive and quality adminis-trators able to overcome the obstacles and corrosion of partisan politics. Perhaps Tugwell could do in Puerto Rico something more and realize the full potential of some of his socially advanced programs. He knew that Washington would be out of bounds for him and his theories, especially after Roosevelt—faced by the reality of war and the need to have Congress on his side—in Tugwell's opinion allowed "the economic interests" to re-take the temple of New Deal idealism.

Muñoz believed, though, that *his* was the mandate to govern. After the 1940 elections Muñoz spoke as if colonialism had in fact disappeared on November 5; what remained was its empty juridical shell. Muñoz expected Tugwell to understand and accept that real power was now in the hands of the people, which meant in Muñoz's hands. So, in effect, Tugwell was sub-ject not to the president and Congress that appointed him but to Muñoz. Once he accepted this, Tugwell—the authentic liberal dedicated to social justice—could be of great use to Puerto Rico. Muñoz understood and ac-cepted that in order to carry out a peaceful revolution he needed Tugwell's administrative talent and creativity. He was intrigued by Tugwell's ideas and theories on social and economic planning as tools to humanize capital-ist development.

Muñoz had no problem with Tugwell having the title of governor and living and working in La Fortaleza. Muñoz would leave to others the de-bate as to whether Puerto Rico was or was not a colony. What mattered was that Muñoz was now acting as if it no longer were.

Tugwell, the appointed governor, resented Muñoz's attitude toward him. Before seeking the governorship he had tried to understand the seemingly pitiful powerlessness of former Governor Guy Swope. It was the result of extremely clever and often vicious island politicians on the one hand and of well-intentioned but misguided American policy on the other. The United States had little idea about how to manage a colony. The colonies were not even recognized as such, and more often than not the men sent to represent the president turned out to be inept governors. But Tugwell came to Puerto Rico convinced that he could be the exception, that he could be an extraordinarily good governor and thus rescue America's honor on this little, miserable island. After all, his deepest motive for coming to Puerto Rico was patriotic. He wanted to serve his country and the people of this island, not to further American imperialism. He knew that he could always use this weapon in his tug-of-war with Muñoz. As important as the electoral mandate was to Muñoz, he certainly understood that it had to give way to Puerto Rico's role in the great world conflict between democracy and fascism. Muñoz, in turn, had his own weapon: how could Tugwell and America fight for the survival of democracy around the world while turning their backs on the democratic revolution that had taken place on November 5, 1940, under the American flag?

Moscoso knew that neither man would buckle under to the other. Tugwell was an enormously proud man, vain and arrogant according to some, a man who liked to shock and often succeeded.[3] His self-esteem would not allow him to be pushed around by Muñoz, as past weak American governors had been by island *políticos*.

On November 18, 1941, five weeks after his initial appointment, Tugwell named Moscoso coordinator for insular affairs. As the governor's only Puerto Rican, Spanish-speaking aide, this was his true role in La Fortaleza. But Moscoso felt that he needed a more precise job description. After all, wasn't Tugwell an expert in good management practices, and wasn't it a cardinal rule that one's responsibilities be as clearly defined as possible? It had become vividly evident to Moscoso that his role required him to cross political minefields, where any seemingly minor mistake could set off a political firestorm. Moscoso also knew that Tugwell followed a hands-off management style. He gave instructions and at times seemed unreasonably demanding, but he did not interfere directly in their execution; his subordinates were on their own. This suited Moscoso well; the more space the governor allowed him, the faster he could get things done. But now Moscoso had a new title and he decided to ask the governor in writing exactly what it entailed. Minutes after sending him the memorandum, Moscoso was summoned to his office.

The governor's office was impressive. Long and narrow, even after four decades of American rule the office retained an overbearing Spanish presence. It had served for centuries as "the throne room" where the long line of Spanish envoys, Tugwell wrote, had become "by transubstantiation, the person of the King." The dark authority of the Spanish Empire was there physically in this huge office. At the entrance there was a star engraved on the floor "for the first prostration on entering the Presence: and just in front of the desk I was to use, another star which indicated where the petitioner might come to rest." Behind the massive, dark desk there was the coat of arms, decreed to the island on November 8, 1511, by Queen Isabel and King Ferdinand. All this made Tugwell uncomfortable. He had originally decided that he would much prefer to live and work at the governor's summer home up in the mountains: "Jájome had appealed to my pessimistic mood. Up there I was like a Scotsman on a misty headland or a hermit on the shoulder of the Carpathians."4 But when his wife, Grace, and their child arrived from the U.S. mainland several days before his inauguration, she wondered if he had lost his senses. Did he really believe he could live the life of a hermit as governor of Puerto Rico, a winding two-hour mountain ride from San Juan? Without argument, he agreed to move into La Fortaleza. The old fortress, permeated by so much cold, dead history, Tugwell wrote, filled him with a "vague alarm."

This was precisely the emotion Moscoso felt as he walked over the stars engraved on the floor toward Tugwell, who was seated behind the desk. Motioning to him to sit down, Tugwell remained silent for several moments, his intelligent blue eyes staring at Moscoso as if he did not recognize him. "Ted," he said, "if I have to explain to you what the hell this job is all about, you can be of no use to me."

Another silence. Moscoso did not know what to say. Finally, Tugwell declared: "You better resign."

Then, Tugwell suddenly stood, threw open the doors to the balcony behind his desk, and looking up at the bright blue, late morning sky and the puffy clouds moving fast with the trade winds, he exclaimed, "My God, another beautiful day! Come over here. Take a look at all those birds."

Years later, recalling the incident that for a brief but terrible moment might have changed the course of his life, Moscoso commented that Tugwell simply ignored his own suggestion that he resign and never answered Moscoso's unfortunate memorandum: "That was the extent of the guidelines I got for my job."

As he walked out of the governor's office, a line from a Spanish poem came to his mind: *Caminante, no hay camino, el camino se hace al andar* (Traveler, there is no path: you make the path by walking). This line was to prove prophetic in Moscoso's public career.

Part

Two

The Fomentarian Revolution

There is a type of revolution which does not fit into any type of . . . category and which may be the most fundamental in the long run. I call it the 'Fomentarian Revolution' in honor of a remarkable institution in Puerto Rico which embodies it known as Fomento.

Kenneth E. Boulding, 1961

Chapter 3

The Idea of Fomento

The original idea to create Fomento, an agency dedicated exclusively to industrial promotion, came to Moscoso during a trip to Washington in early 1942. When he first mentioned to Tugwell the need to create an entity to push economic development, the governor suggested that Moscoso study the Haitian-American Development Society, which might serve as a model.[1] Moscoso quickly discarded it because it required a large and continuous input of government funds, which the insular government lacked. During trips to the mainland Moscoso visited libraries in Washington and New York, researching government-run development agencies in France, India, and Canada. One caught his attention: Chile's *Corporación de Fomento de la Producción*. He liked the word "fomento." Back on the island, he corresponded with the Chilean agency only to learn that the war had greatly curtailed its activities.

Moscoso persisted with his idea and put together a group of technicians whose task was to draft a proposal for Governor Tugwell. He began meeting with Tugwell's assistants, Fred Bartlett and Louis Sturcke, both of whom had worked with him in Washington and New York. Moscoso then invited his longtime friend, Esteban Bird, who worked for the Puerto Rico Reconstruction Administration and who in turn brought along Rafael Fernández García. Fernández, a Stanford University-educated chemist, was one of the authors of the Chardón Plan and had written the section on the need for new industries. They decided to meet regularly in the evenings at Bartlett's apartment in the Condado sector of San Juan.

Moscoso's idea of an agency dedicated to promoting industries was not new. As far back as 1899, progressive educator Henry Carroll had written: "The starting of new industries is an economical necessity and it should be the policy of the United States to encourage it. The prosperity of the island must be built on this basis."[2] Carroll compiled a long list of products that could be manufactured with local materials. He also listed the great obstacles: the lack of capital, technical know-how, and entrepreneurial initiative. Most readers of Carroll's study concluded that the island's industrialization was wishful thinking. Aside from the sugar industry's large grinding mills, nothing was done to industrialize Puerto Rico.

Three decades later, however, the Brookings Institution published a report declaring that "industrialization is regarded by many as the only solution for the pressing problems of underemployment and low wages."[3] The 1930 report went one step further than the Carroll study, pointing out that "markets of the Continental United States are the only potential takers of Island manufacturing large enough to encourage an immediate and extensive program of industrial development" (Clark, 463–64). The Brookings assessment, however, did not offer the means to achieve this, other than suggesting "honest advertising of industrial opportunities." Furthermore, the authors opposed giving local entrepreneurs any economic incentives: "the best business opinion on the mainland seems now to be against offering freedom from taxation, bounties, or similar encouragement to prospective manufacturing establishments on the ground that these favors do not promote the best possible localization of such enterprises" (Clark, 476).

The first industrial promotion agency was organized that same year, 1930, by Governor Theodore Roosevelt Jr.; the Bureau of Commerce and Industry was placed under the insular Department of Agriculture. The son of the famous American president had arrived on the island in 1928 "with great zeal and gusto."[4] He was determined to aggressively tackle the island's horrid economic ills. But when he left three years later, he was overcome by a sense of hopelessness. "By the time . . . . 1931, he had grown sick and tired of the politicians and the people themselves."[5] The incipient effort to create new industries had failed totally; the Bureau carried out ineffective "buy-at-home" campaigns, organized a data bank for potential investors, and conducted numerous feasibility studies. When it was finally dissolved in 1942 and absorbed by Moscoso's new agency, it had not promoted a single industry.

A decade afterward, at the brainstorming meetings at Bartlett's apartment, one of the participants, Rafael Fernández García, was the only person in Puerto Rico who had gone beyond generalizations and attempted to draw up a blueprint for industrialization. Moscoso had read carefully Fernández's section of the 1934 Chardón Plan. The chemist had made a careful appraisal of the realistic industrial opportunities on the island.

One of his recommendations had been realized already: a cement plant, built with U.S. funds, for which Puerto Rico had most of the raw materials. The idea was picked up by Interior Secretary Harold Ickes's Interdepartmental Committee on Puerto Rico. It was evident that once the United States became involved in the war and the island converted into a major military outpost, it would be extremely difficult to import the huge amounts of cement required to build the naval and air bases. Funds were assigned to the new Puerto Rico Reconstruction Administration to construct a cement plant with the capacity of one thousand barrels a day.[6] It was not without controversy: Ickes had to defend using American taxpayers' money to pay for non-American-made cement. In 1936 the massive plant was inaugurated in Cataño, on the outskirts of San Juan. It was the island's first non-agricultural heavy industry.

Fernández García was convinced that other heavy industries were viable. He also recommended in the Chardón Plan a glass bottle plant for the island's growing rum industry and a cardboard plant to supply the boxes for shipping the rum. But Fernández's ideas received little support from then-Governor Blanton Winship, who insisted that the island's only realistic potential was in tourism. In 1937 a bill had been introduced in the legislature to create the Insular Industrial Development Corporation. It died in committee. Two years later, the bill was reintroduced and approved, giving the agency ample power to provide loans and other incentives. Winship vetoed it, declaring that the legislature had failed to budget the meager $25,000 appropriated to the new agency.

That industrialization was impossible on this small island, a thousand miles from the U.S. mainland, was deeply ingrained in Puerto Rico's collective psyche. As late as 1950, economist Harvey Perloff wrote in *Puerto Rico's Economic Future,* "Agriculture is the backbone of Puerto Rico's economy and will undoubtedly continue to be the major key to the island's welfare for a long time to come."[7]

"Industrialization," he added, "must be conceived . . . as an extension of agricultural production, and the measure of its success will be to an important extent, in terms of 'value added' to the products raised in the farms in the island."[8]

*   *   *

Moscoso disagreed. Why should we limit ourselves, he asked, to operations related to the sugar and rum industries? Puerto Rico simply had to break its dependence on agriculture, he argued. This may have worked a century earlier, when the island's population was a half-million, but now it was over two million.

At the evening meetings at Bartlett's apartment, however, the debates could not ignore Tugwell's insistence that the new agency include agricultural development. The governor, as all the other economists who had studied the island, simply could not envision a local economy not dependent on the land. If this were true, Moscoso believed, then Puerto Rico was truly hopeless, because agriculture offered no hope of economic uplift.

It was simple arithmetic. Even a huge leap in agricultural production and related industries would still leave the island desperately poor, for there was not enough land to supply the employment needs of the growing population. If the island's per capita income of about $130 was tripled to $360 or $400, it still would not be nearly enough. Puerto Rico's only hope, Moscoso held, was a fundamental restructuring of its economic base, replacing agriculture with large-scale manufacturing. At the brainstorming session there was, as always, an edge of exasperation in his voice. How could anyone not see that while Puerto Rico's mostly poor land "was not growing," its population was, and explosively?

Adding to Moscoso's exasperation was the little support he received from his own party. The Popular leadership's approach to industrialization paralleled Tugwell's. There was nothing in the Populares' platform about industrialization. It was not part of Muñoz's rhetoric and clearly not part of his long-range vision of Puerto Rico. Muñoz understood vaguely that the island had to "create new wealth," that dividing what existed more evenly through radical land reform would leave the island's burgeoning population short. But Muñoz also accepted as self-evident that Puerto Rico somehow had to generate the new wealth from the land.

Muñoz had another problem with industrialization, of a philosophical nature. He shared the view that it was dehumanizing, prone to make robots out of people. Moscoso's vision of an industrialized Puerto Rico, of lines of industrial buildings and smoke-belching stacks, of thousands of Puerto Ricans glued to endless production lines, could not be further removed from his poet's vision of a *jíbaro* Puerto Rico. Muñoz's fundamental goal was to somehow lift the *jíbaro* from extreme poverty without damaging his values and culture. He envisioned a green and rural island.

Moscoso knew that Muñoz was largely uninterested in the fine points of economic theory; his driving concern was entirely social justice. Moscoso was also aware that Muñoz had read Aldous Huxley's warnings in *Brave New World,* the moving denunciation of the dehumanization of modern industrial society. It was easy to evoke in Muñoz visions of Charlie Chaplin's

Modern Times, nightmares of the *jíbaros* transformed into mindless cogs in production lines.

But Moscoso felt in his bones that in the conflict between Muñoz the poet and philosopher and Muñoz the practical, down-to-earth politician, in the end Muñoz the realist would win out. It was a gamble Moscoso would take again and again throughout his career, and it was a gamble he would take now.

One of Moscoso's advantages was that his bill to create an industrial development agency was one of many. In Muñoz's eyes, there were more important ones. Among them, Moscoso's bill would appear insignificant, as Muñoz and Tugwell pushed forward the creation of the several major government agencies. Moscoso's strategy was to make certain that nothing provoked Muñoz's opposition by overplaying the bill's importance.

The strategy was right; Muñoz quickly agreed to have the bill introduced in the senate. Moscoso recalled years later, "Muñoz was really going along with the bill. . . . I knew that he didn't see much potential in it. Like most of the politicians at the time, they really could not see much beyond the sugar industry as the big, fat cow that had to be milked as much as possible. You could readily get Muñoz's attention by talking about ways of doing this, and the many sins and greed of the sugar barons, and certainly his eyes would fill with excitement when he talked about his new Land Authority. But mention this new agency, and it would take some doing to get and keep him alert."[9]

Moscoso was confident that the bill would get through the legislature. But several days later Muñoz asked him to rush over to his senate office. The bill, he said, was in trouble. Several Popular senators had told him that they would join the Coalition and vote against it. The bill had caught the attention of the island's business leaders and their powerful associations: it was branded as another of Tugwell's attempts to "control the economy," and that once again it was Red Rex at work. They feared that the new agency would abuse its power of expropriation. It was the role of the private sector, not of the government, they argued, to industrialize Puerto Rico.

Muñoz informed Moscoso that the bill simply did not have the votes for approval. Once again, Moscoso saw how unimportant this was to the political leader; Muñoz was willing to let it die. What can we do to rescue it? Moscoso asked. Should he talk directly to the senators and prove to them how ridiculous their opposition was? The agency would promote, not replace, the private sector.

Moscoso then mentioned to Muñoz an idea that had been discussed briefly at La Fortaleza: to create a government development bank precisely to provide private investors with a new source of funds. Muñoz looked up; he had an idea. Why not, he asked, introduce another bill to create the development bank with a board composed mostly of prominent businesspeople, including those who expressed fear of the government's reforms? If Moscoso could get a leading banker to sit on the bank's board, then Muñoz would introduce the bill as a companion to the development agency bill.

At Muñoz's office at the time was one of Tugwell's protégés, James Curry, a young Washington lawyer and an expert on public corporation legislation. He had worked on the bill creating the new electric power authority, *Autoridad de Fuentes Fluviales,* approved a year earlier. Curry had also helped Moscoso and his group draft the development agency bill. Moscoso picked up a writing pad and asked him to draft a bill to create the Government Development Bank. A what? Curry asked. Just write a few lines, Moscoso answered, creating the bank, authorizing the governor to name a board of directors charged with establishing the bank's rules and regulations and naming its officers.

Moscoso knew exactly who the prominent businessman had to be whom he would ask to sit on the board: the island's leading banker and principal owner of the *Banco Popular de Puerto Rico,* Rafael Carrión. As Moscoso darted out of the office, Curry remained seated on the windowsill and began to draft the bill.

Carrión's office was several minutes away at the bank's ten-story tower in Old San Juan. A friend of the Moscoso family, the fifty-one-year-old Carrión was pleased to see the breathless young man who began immediately to explain his urgent request. As Moscoso talked, he could see out of the window the other building that dominated the city's skyline. There, in the penthouse, with certainly the most magnificent view of San Juan Bay, was the private dining room of Rexford Tugwell's nemesis, the newspaper magnate, publisher of *El Mundo,* Angel Ramos. What would Ramos say if Rafael Carrión joined the board of a Tugwell agency?

Carrión was totally apolitical and therefore had no motive for helping Tugwell and Muñoz. But Moscoso was persuasive. Carrión liked the young man and told him he would join the board. Moscoso rushed back to Muñoz's office with the good news. Curry's draft of the government bank bill was typed and officially introduced. The strategy worked. On May 11, 1942, Bill 188 creating the Puerto Rico Development Agency was approved. Two days later Bill 252, creating the Puerto Rico Government Development Bank was also approved. As Muñoz had anticipated, the bank bill dissipated the original objection to Moscoso's agency.

Moscoso's bill, however, was significantly amended on the senate floor. This time the critics came from the left. Now the fear was that Moscoso's agency would turn the island's economy over to a new kind of "absentee capitalists." The Popular Party, after all, had begun as a grassroots workers' movement against the American sugar corporations; would the party now bring to Puerto Rico outside industrial corporations to replace the sugar barons? Specific instructions to the new agency were written into the bill: it was ordered "to avoid the evils of absentee ownership of large scale capital." It authorized "preference and priority to resident persons in the granting of loans." Wherever possible, the agency was instructed to favor cooperative "or other nonprofit organizations to enterprises which give the greatest return of human welfare in Puerto Rico."[10]

This was not what Moscoso wanted. The purpose of the agency was not to assist nonprofit organizations but to promote highly profitable corporations that would create jobs. How can Puerto Rico be industrialized without large-scale absentee capital? "The wording of the act clearly expressed a preference," David Ross wrote, "and it was the preference of that faction which favored, if not independence, at least greater autonomy which viewed American capital, if not with loathing, at least with suspicion: and which was completely unimpressed with the conventional American doctrine of separation of business and state."[11] Moscoso knew that this reflected a narrow economic nationalism that would make life miserable for the new agency. Another disappointment for Moscoso was that the legislature appropriated only $500,000. But after the shock of Muñoz's initial declaration that the bill was dead, and having survived the Popular Party's ideological wringer, Moscoso was glad to get any bill approved.

On May 13, 1942, Governor Tugwell signed the measure into law. It was scarcely noted by the island's media. There was no ceremony or announcement at La Fortaleza. The leading newspaper, *El Mundo*, ran a thirteen-line story describing another law signed that day by Tugwell that provided relief to victims of fires and *público* car accidents. Tugwell later admitted that he "paid little attention" to this agency.[12] He did not even get around to naming the thirty-two-year-old Moscoso director of the agency until November 30, 1942, five and a half months later. "This is your idea," Tugwell said, "so you might as well head it."

Moscoso in fact had been working feverishly to launch the new agency. No one in Puerto Rico was aware of it—not even Tugwell or Muñoz—but the seed of Puerto Rico's "economic miracle" had been planted.

Chapter 4

Industrialize Puerto Rico?

Arthur D. Little Company Vice President Raymond Stevens's eyes widened. "Industrialize Puerto Rico? In wartime?"

"Yes," Moscoso answered.

Stevens was perplexed. The young Puerto Rican's visit and answer made no sense. At his office at the Massachusetts Institute of Technology in Cambridge, Stevens was vividly aware that industrialization meant only one thing in May 1942: living up to President Roosevelt's dramatic promise made in December 1940 to convert the entire nation into the "great arsenal of democracy." It did not mean building civilian factories in Puerto Rico.

The idea itself of "industrializing Puerto Rico"—even without a world war—rang fantastic and unreal in Stevens's ears. The Arthur D. Little Company, after all, had expertise on this matter. Little, the former head of the university's Industrial Chemistry Department, had been a pioneer in the design and operation of chemical-processing plants. The firm provided counseling and services to governments and private companies precisely on what kinds of industries were viable in given environments. Stevens knew very little about Puerto Rico, except that it was a small island. And "no one had ever brought about the industrialization of an overpopulated tropical agricultural island."[1]

Curious, Stevens asked about the island's new development company. Moscoso hesitated. There was, in fact, nothing to tell because the bill creating the agency had been approved only two weeks before. The agency did not exist, nor had Governor Tugwell named its board of directors. Stevens got up from his desk and began walking up and down the office. "Mr. Moscoso, can you tell me what exactly you want from us?"

"We know nothing about industrialization," Moscoso admitted. "Several years ago some very fine people prepared what was called the Chardón Plan that mentioned several specific industries that, at least in theory, can prosper in Puerto Rico. We need your help: tell us if this is correct, and then how to go about it."

To be frank, Moscoso continued, there was another reason. To get off the ground, the new agency had to overcome the initial incredulous reaction to the phrase "industrialize Puerto Rico." A firm like Arthur D. Little, with the institutional prestige of MIT, certainly would give the agency the credibility essential for the financing of its projects.

"Let's do this," Stevens concluded, "even though my boss is in Washington I'll make the decision to go ahead and do the study. Can you come up with $5,000?"

"Of course," Moscoso answered immediately. "The Government of Puerto Rico has a budget of $11 million."

Stevens was even more puzzled. "Who, what, will we be working for, since the agency still does not exist? Are you going to head it?" Moscoso nodded in agreement. "What's your background?" inquired Stevens. "Pharmacy," Moscoso replied.

Wartime industrialization of tropical Puerto Rico with a pharmacist in charge? Was this some kind of a joke?

Stevens soon learned that Moscoso was dead serious. On June 11, 1942, he received an official letter commissioning the Arthur D. Little study, with four specific objectives: to determine which manufacturing industries could operate profitably in Puerto Rico, particularly related to the war effort; to identify and suggest interested individuals capable of developing these industries; to analyze the available information needed to promote these industries; and to take the preliminary action to develop them.[2] Moscoso included a check for $5,000 supplied by the Agriculture Commission.

Arthur D. Little sent three professionals to the island who prepared a report that was more positive than Moscoso expected. Some of the industries proposed by the Chardón Plan were feasible, the report declared, as well as several additional ones. This was exactly what he needed to overcome the wall of negativism. Industrialize Puerto Rico? It was no longer an empty phrase, no longer a fantasy. The Arthur D. Little Company, no less, had said: "It can be done!"

Moscoso received the news at the small development agency office on the fifth floor of the Banco Popular building. The other member of his two-man team was equally elated: Rafael Fernández García, whose Chardón Plan laundry list of theoretically possible small industries was based on using local raw materials, such as molasses and bagasse. Fernández made clear that these were simply concepts, not concrete proposals: "We are not in a position to make very specific recommendations as to development of new industries, as this is a subject that has not been surveyed in Puerto Rico. ..."3 Many of the ideas raised obvious and difficult questions. The bottling of several hundred thousand boxes of orange juice to sell in the New York market using oranges that grow wild in the coffee plantations was mentioned as one possible new industry. But how could such a small quantity of juice be produced profitably and compete with the much bigger producers in the U.S. mainland? Fernández also mentioned the possibility of using blackstrap molasses to manufacture a motor fuel that would substitute imported gasoline. Again, this was a concept that required an enormous amount of research and study. At the end of the section, Fernández reiterated that these were merely suggestions "to be studied by qualified experts."

As much as Moscoso admired Fernández as a scientist and as a developmental planner, there were huge disagreements between them. For instance, Fernández believed that "it will be next to impossible" to develop any industry on the island without tariff protection from dumping and price-cutting by "the potent and highly organized continental American manufacturers." He recommended that the insular government be given the right to impose tariffs on all products from all countries, including the United States, in order to protect local industries. But Moscoso was dead set against this. In any case, Puerto Rico did not have the authority to impose its own tariffs, he argued. Fernández also recommended "the assessment of a high income tax, to be abated if invested in new industries on the basis of new job creation" (Chardón Report, 2). Moscoso opposed that idea as "too academic" and impractical.

Now, as they prepared to launch the new agency, they faced an ominous question: if everything else had ended in frustration and failure, why not this enterprise headed by an earnest but totally inexperienced duo? All they had to begin with was the Arthur D. Little report.

*   *   *

Ironically, the Moscoso-Fernández team, which was to prove crucial in the incubation of the Fomento program, was the result of an accident. In early 1942, Governor Tugwell asked Moscoso to meet Fernández to see if he would accept appointment as one of the three members of the new planning board. Tugwell envisioned a totally autonomous board that would guide both public and private development, anticipating and steering physical growth. The agency, Tugwell's famous "fourth power" of any government, would create a master plan for economic development. At least on paper this was "one of the most powerful planning agencies found in democratic government at the time."4

Fernández agreed to join the planning board, and soon after he and Board Chairman Rafael Picó were sent to New York by Tugwell to observe and study his old city planning agency. After returning, however, Fernández called Moscoso to inform him that he had a change of heart. As a scientist and researcher, Fernández said, he understood the vital importance of Tugwell's agency, but his stay in New York had convinced him that he was not really interested in planning nor in preparing more studies and reports on Puerto Rico's oppressive economic realities. He wanted to be part of the action in Moscoso's new development company. Moscoso jumped at the offer and quickly convinced Tugwell to bring Fernández García to La Fortaleza to help him in the organization of the new agency. Fernández García was given the title of technical director and became, after Moscoso, Fomento's first employee. When soon afterward Moscoso moved to a small office at the Banco Popular building, the Puerto Rico Development Company had a staff of two: a pharmacist and a chemist.

At the Ponce Housing Authority Moscoso had gained experience in dealing with the government bureaucracy in Puerto Rico and Washington and in negotiating with contractors. Fernández had a distinguished career as chairman of the chemistry department of the University of Puerto Rico and director of the agricultural experimental station. He also had considerable experience developing sugarcane operations in Puerto Rico and Venezuela and had traveled as far as Java to study sugar cultivation methods.

They sensed from the beginning how well they complemented one another. In this new venture Fernández gave Moscoso a sense of security. Twenty years Moscoso's senior, Fernández was precisely the mentor the University of Michigan graduate had looked for in Ponce when his father forced him to return to the island to run the family business. Fernández had interests far beyond the closed, insular world of Puerto Rico. A voracious reader of professional magazines and scientific books, he was also deeply interested in converting academic developmental issues into reality. Fernández's personal experience with the Chardón Plan was enormously interesting to Moscoso. Fernández, perhaps better than any other Puerto Rican, understood the anatomy of Puerto Rico's history of failure: the sense of hopelessness, the bedrock conviction that, regardless of effort, money, or talent, nothing in the end seemed to work.

Moscoso was particularly pleased to find that Fernández shared his view on the most fundamental obstacle to Puerto Rico's development. Fernández had written the first line of the Chardón Plan: "The economic problem of Puerto Rico, in so far as the bulk of its people is concerned, may be reduced to the simple term of progressive landlessness, chronic unemployment and implacable growth of the population." A footnote to that sentence reads: "Appendix A shows the appalling increase in population, with an increase in birth rate from 20.4 to 39.0 in 25 years and a decrease in death rate of 36.7 to 22.4" (Chardón Report, 1).

In fact, along with other prominent Puerto Ricans, mainly university Professors Rafael Cordero and Jorge Bermúdez, Fernández held it as gospel that the key to Puerto Rico's future was in controlling its skyrocketing population.

Moscoso was also aware that Fernández, himself apolitical, was nevertheless well connected to Muñoz and his Popular Party. His older brother, Benigno, had been the Liberal Party candidate for resident commissioner in the 1932 election and as insular attorney general had waged and won the legal battle to enforce the Five-Hundred Acre Law. There was no question now that he, Rafael, would help provide Moscoso the political influence the new agency needed in the coming months.

But it was, paradoxically, Fernández's reputation as one of the island's authorities on the sugar industry that made him invaluable to Moscoso. To industrialize Puerto Rico, the dependence on sugar had to be broken. As much as Fernández had defended the Chardón Plan's restructuring of the sugar industry and massive land reform, Fernández cold-bloodedly recognized that even assuming total success, the reform would scarcely make a dent in Puerto Rico's extreme poverty and unemployment: "even after this substantial achievement, the bulk of the Puerto Rican problem would remain before us" (Chardón Report, 4). Reading between the lines of the Chardón Plan, in fact, revived the old sense of hopelessness: under optimum success, the reform would have created over a period of years a total of 67,000 jobs: this is less than half the estimated 150,000 heads of households permanently unemployed. Better than anyone else in Puerto Rico, Fernández knew that the Chardón Plan—to which Muñoz and his generation of reformers and political leaders had pinned all their hopes in the 1930s—was not the answer to Puerto Rico's despair. He knew that as long as Puerto Rico saw its economic future in terms of agricultural development, the island was doomed to perpetual stagnation.

As 1942 came to a close, Moscoso and Fernández were determined to use their embryonic agency to take Puerto Rico on a totally different course. The choice lay between a return to hopelessness and the dream of industrialization based on the optimistic and highly hypothetical Arthur D. Little report.

Chapter 5

Despite the Odds

Moscoso decided to start big. Although the legislature had assigned his new agency a total budget of only $500,000, Moscoso convinced his board to approve the construction and operation of a $2.2 million glass container factory. On February 24, 1943, he made a detailed presentation of the magnificent plant: one hundred tons of glass would be produced every day by two fifty-ton furnaces. There would be six bottle-making machines, each making forty-eight units per minute, or 4.8 million cases a year. Physically the plant would be impressive: 123,000 square feet of floor placed on a sixteen-acre site.

Moscoso overwhelmed the board with more details than the members wanted: there would be six Hartford-Empire feeders connected to six Lynch-10 bottle-forming machines, three Hartford-Empire and three Simplex stackers. General Electric would supply and install the electrical equipment.

In spite of the severe restrictions imposed by World War II, Moscoso declared that the plant was scheduled to start production by the middle of 1944. There was little time to spare: the war had created a bonanza for Puerto Rican rum in the American market and the island could not produce enough to supply the enormous demand. Rum was the only spirit not affected by the restrictions on the use of grains in the production of alcoholic beverages, because, unlike other hard liquors, rum is made from molasses.

But there was still one more powerful argument, especially for the government. Since the 1900 Foraker Act, the U.S. Treasury had returned, or "rebated," to Puerto Rico all the federal excise taxes collected on the mainland on island rum and cigars. So, the wartime demand for Puerto Rican rum had become a windfall for the island treasury. Moscoso pointed out that just the increase in the rum tax rebates would cover several times the investment in the glass plant. It was precisely from the rum tax bonanza that he expected to get the huge appropriation. The legislature should understand his argument, he added, because by 1942 the rum excise tax represented one-half of the insular budget.

Six months after the organization of the development agency, the board gave Moscoso the green light. Three days later, the factory was incorporated as a subsidiary and given the authority to sell $2.5 million in stock.

Moscoso's goal was to attract private capital. He had to prove that his program was born of necessity, that his agency's goal was not to compete with private investors but to promote private enterprise. He would make available to them all the feasibility studies. The response from the island's business community however, was dismal. Moscoso was distraught because he believed that the capital he needed was available in Puerto Rico. Deposits in insular banks had grown from $37 million to $208 million in one decade. Yet, ten months later, less than 10 percent of the new glass factory's stock offering, or $178,000, had been sold. The business community was skeptical of Moscoso's venture into manufacturing. Tradition-bound island capitalists remained unwilling to invest in anything other than sugar. The hostility to Tugwell also played a part. The plant was seen as one of his "socialist schemes," bound to destroy the private sector. As much as Moscoso preached about the new partnership of government and private capital, he simply could not generate interest in his new venture.

There were also serious technical problems that Moscoso had underestimated. The most important one was the variety of sizes, shapes, and colors of bottles required for the rum industry. This drawback had been mentioned in an earlier study by a glass manufacturing firm, the Owens-Illinois Company. The recent Arthur D. Little report also stressed the problem and added two more: the cost of fuel and the effect of the factory's hellishly hot working environment on the productivity of the labor force, especially the mainland American technicians for whom the local climate was already warm enough. Arthur D. Little's endorsement was, indeed, tentative and conditional. The plant, the report said, "would seem feasible" provided that the standardization of sizes was enforced and that no local conditions complicated the picture.

By now, however, Moscoso and Fernández had generated their own rush of optimism and would not allow anything to dampen their enthusiasm. Along the margin of the report, especially the sections discussing the arguments against the plant, they scribbled numerous notes indicating that the report understated several key economic statistics and was much too pessimistic.[1]

There was another obstacle, even more immediate: getting authorization to build the factory from the War Production Board in Washington. Moscoso was faced with the monumental salesmanship task of convincing the WPB, whose conservative members were already hostile to Tugwell, that building a bottle plant for Puerto Rican rum deserved priority status in a nation totally mobilized for war. The board had extended to the island the prohibition against the construction of any building over the value of $500 unless a special permit was granted. Tugwell was furious. Paralyzing all public and private construction served no war-related purpose, as Puerto Rico did not possess any of the raw materials needed for war production. Regardless, the board repeatedly denied Tugwell's demands for an exception to Puerto Rico. Tugwell's outrage finally overcame him: he began to "stomp up and down my high-domed office and cursed the businessmen's red tape and inefficiency."[2] The governor reluctantly authorized Moscoso's and Fomento's newly hired attorney, Mariano Ramírez, to make the trip to Washington to try to convince the War Production Board to authorize the glass plant. However, Tugwell was sure that it would be a waste of time.

"They laughed," Mariano Ramírez recalled nearly a half-century later.[3] "Then, becoming quite serious, the WPB officials informed us flatly that there was absolutely no opportunity to get the permit." All the permits for the type of machinery needed for a bottling operation were already committed for the next three years, they declared.

But as they walked out of the office, Moscoso stopped and said: "I've got an idea; why not turn the tables?" Ramírez didn't understand. "Who in Washington most despises Tugwell?" Before Ramírez could answer, Moscoso said: "Of course, Mr. Republican, Senator Taft"—the man who led the battle against Tugwell's Senate confirmation as governor of Puerto Rico, referring to him as "one of the worst administrators who ever lived."[4]

"What is the point?" Ramírez asked. If there is anyone in Washington, Moscoso answered, who can get the "reactionaries" on the War Production Board to approve the permit, it's precisely Senator Taft. "So, let's go," Moscoso said. "Where?" the startled Ramírez asked. "To the Senate!"

*   *   *

Moscoso's decision to see Taft was not, however, a wild shot in the dark. A month earlier, in February 1943, he had been asked to assist the Ohio senator during his two-week stay in Puerto Rico. Taft was part of a committee sent to investigate Tugwell's administration in response to a new congressional campaign to get Red Rex removed, a campaign fueled by the island's conservative and business forces.

Tugwell asked Moscoso to testify before the committee chaired by Senator Dennis Chavez of New Mexico, who had family links to Puerto Rico's conservative business sector. Moscoso's task was to describe the new industrial development program in order to counter the anti-Tugwell presentations. Of course, Moscoso assured the senators, it's the private sector that will bring about the industrialization of Puerto Rico. His agency's goal was to make this happen. Taft listened intensely but with visible skepticism; then he turned to the likable young man who had been so diligent in attending to him and asked just how he was going to get investors to risk their money. "Senator," Moscoso answered, "I will do business with the devil himself if he comes and establishes a factory in Puerto Rico." Moscoso, Taft saw, was certainly no anti-business radical.

The U.S. Senate was in session when Moscoso and Ramírez arrived. Moscoso asked a page to take his business card to Taft, who recognized the name and came to meet him out in the hallway. "Senator, we need your help," Moscoso said. "Let me be very frank. We need your help at the War Production Board because we have been turned down and they are all, like yourself, Republicans. If you support us, they will listen."[5] Taft had no idea what Moscoso was talking about. Moscoso started again, describing the project to build the bottle plant. Taft interrupted and inquired about bringing a U.S. bottle manufacturer to the island. Moscoso pulled out of his pocket two letters, one from the president of Owens-Illinois and the other from the president of Anchor Hocking Company, the first- and second-largest glass manufacturers in the United States: both declined the invitation to come to Puerto Rico. They simply lacked the personnel due to the war effort. After glancing at the letters, Taft looked up and recalled what he had told Tugwell during his visit to the island: Puerto Rico must be seen as a "special case," in other words, what is unacceptable "socialism" in the American economy might be acceptable to get Puerto Rico's primitive economy going. If it would help, Taft said, he was willing to state his view in a letter. He asked Moscoso to call one of his assistants and help him draft the letter. Moscoso could pick it up after lunch.

Taft kept his word. That afternoon the senator's assistant delivered to Moscoso a copy of a letter endorsing the industrialization as "the only possibility of a decent standard of living" for these "people crowded into a small island." Taft emphasized, "I have never been very strong for government-supported industry, but the situation in Puerto Rico is such that I believe the government had a proper function in promoting the development of new industry."[6]

Ramírez, expecting Moscoso to rush to the War Production Board, heard him say instead: "Let's go to the White House." Why not, he asked, try to get a similar letter from President Roosevelt? The Board could not turn down Senator Taft *and* the president. Waiting outside the office of one of the president's assistants, they saw Admiral William Leahy, who replaced General Winthrop as Governor of Puerto Rico in 1939 and was not long afterward named U.S. ambassador to the Vichy government in France. After reading Taft's letter, Leahy commented: "Well, I cannot see the president doing anything less for Puerto Rico. Let me try: I'll take it to him." Soon, Leahy emerged with the news that the president would also endorse the project.

Moscoso and Ramírez then went to the Interior Department to show Secretary Harold Ickes the prized Taft letter. Ickes was stunned. He was on his way to a cabinet meeting with the president. "Give me a copy of Taft's letter," he said, "if you wait I may have a surprise for you." Moscoso and Ramírez went to visit the Under Secretary, Abe Fortas, who also expressed amazement. When Ickes returned, he told Moscoso and Fortas that the president had not only agreed to send a letter to the board but had asked if Taft had sent his letter by mail. Ickes didn't know but assumed he had. The president, Ickes said, gave instructions to have his own letter to War Production Board Chairman Donald Nelson delivered by special messenger within the next fifteen minutes. "I don't want Bob Taft to take the credit for helping these friends in Puerto Rico," Ickes quoted the president as saying.

The president's letter, in fact, did not go out until two weeks later. On March 31 Ickes sent a memo to Roosevelt describing the importance of the bottle plant to the island economy. The problem, Ickes said, was simply that there was no shipping space to get bottles to the island. Ickes attached copies of Taft's letter and a draft of his own letter supporting the project. On April 1, Moscoso received copies of Ickes's memo and the president's letter. With the three endorsements in hand—Taft's, Ickes's and Roosevelt's— Moscoso and Ramírez finally returned to the board. On April 10, 1943, the War Production Board approved the necessary priorities for the construction of the glass plant.

On this trip, Moscoso employed the modus operandi that he was to use often during the next two decades. He had made the decision to go to Taft without receiving authorization from or even informing Tugwell. As he was to do at several crossroads in his career, Moscoso was willing to take big risks without consulting his superiors. If it went well, the result itself would justify the risk, and if it didn't, he could always return to the family business.

Back in Puerto Rico Moscoso started to work at breakneck speed. His plans were already in place: before even leaving for Washington he had signed a contract for a glass plant design and for the preparation of a bid package with Frazier-Simplex, Inc., a Pennsylvania engineering firm recommended by Arthur D. Little. In May 1943, Robert Prann, the company with the lowest bid of $27,000, won the contract.

By now Fomento's attorney, Mariano Ramírez, was becoming increasingly concerned and nervous. Moscoso was making decisions approaching $5 million, yet not a single dollar had been appropriated by the legislature for his projects. These included a cardboard factory to supply boxes to the rum industry and a mill to manufacture wallboard using bagasse, a sugarcane by-product. But Moscoso was not worried. He was counting on the huge rum rebate windfall. He expected to get as much as $20 million in one year. And he knew he also had Tugwell's backing.

However, the appropriation had to be approved by Muñoz, who was president of the insular senate and head of a party with strong labor ties and an agenda based on social justice, not on industrialization. It was by no means a sure bet that Muñoz would agree to divert the rum taxes to building factories instead of investing them in direct, highly visible welfare programs. Ramírez convinced Moscoso that he simply had to face the issue.

Moscoso decided to ask the local banks for a $4 million loan. He first approached the Banco de Crédito y Ahorro Ponceño, where his friend, Esteban Bird, was vice president. After seeking legal counsel, the bank's board turned him down; the loan was "illegal," beyond the scope of the development agency's laws.[7] Word about Moscoso's loan request, however, soon reached the president of the Banco de Ponce, Pedro Juan Rosaly, who back in 1939 had asked the elder Moscoso to "lend" his son to the Ponce Housing Authority. Rosaly appeared at Moscoso's office: "They will never give you the money; bankers that seek lawyers' counsel never lend," he told Moscoso. "I'll give you the $4 million line of credit. The guarantee of the Government of Puerto Rico is good enough for me."

Construction of the glass plant began on May 12, 1943, and Moscoso informed his board that production would start within one year. But attempting to live up to his ambitious timetable, Moscoso was faced with one setback after another. The glass-making machinery failed to arrive; it had been stolen right from the assembly line before shipment to Puerto Rico. The glass plant's design was found to be critically defective. Moscoso kicked himself—of course, that was the reason why the bid had come in so low. This was a lesson he would not forget. The difficulties prevented the plant from opening until January 1945, too late to take advantage of the war-related demand for rum, the key to the plant's success. Once the plant opened, the A. D. Little caveats, which Moscoso and Fernández had chosen to ignore, became glaring impediments: manufacturing bottles in different sizes,

Moscoso was very proud of the early, Fomento-owned factories built to get
Operation Bootstrap started. Here he is in 1949 describing one of the machines in
the bottling plant built to support the island's big rum industry. The original
Fomento plants were all plagued with endless production and labor problems. In
1950, this and the other plants were sold to a local private industrialist, Ferré
Enterprises, taking Bootstrap into a new strategy based upon promoting private
investment.

shapes, and colors was next to impossible. There were off-size bottles that
had to be discarded and many breakages. Neither the American technicians
brought in to train the local workers nor the Puerto Rican labor force could
get the plant off the ground. More U.S. technicians were brought in, trigger-
ing a labor strike by the jittery local union, irate at "Moscoso's giving jobs
to outsiders." The machines ground to a stop; molten glass solidified. It
would eventually have to be hammered out.

Then the American technicians also went on strike; they had come lured
by Moscoso's claims that they would be working in "Puerto Rico, U.S.A."
But despite the presence of the American flag, they felt they were in a foreign country. They found little in San Juan that reminded them of the mainland. "It was terrible," recalled Ramírez. The American families had to be

housed in the Normandie Hotel, which was outfitted with a communal kitchen. "Some of the men," he added, "became so stressed that they fled from their screaming wives and took local mistresses."

Moscoso and his agency also had to survive the crucial elections of 1944. As the campaigns began in earnest, the Coalition—the strange union of the pro-business Republican Party and the pro-labor Socialist Party—escalated the attacks against Tugwell claiming that he favored Muñoz. Traditionally, the appointed American governors were expected to steer clear of local politics. But Tugwell indeed favored Muñoz, albeit with misgivings. In his memoirs published several years later, Tugwell confessed that he despised the Coalition leaders as self-serving hypocrites. He had, nevertheless, no partisan interests; he was mostly interested in the establishment of the first modern, efficient, essentially apolitical, government bureaucracy in Latin America. In fundamental agreement with Muñoz's peaceful revolution, Tugwell wanted to give him and Puerto Rico the administrative infrastructure needed to carry it out.

Moscoso's worries proved unnecessary. Muñoz and the Populares were able to declare victory with 65 percent of the vote. This assured the continued support of Fomento and its programs.

In the meantime, Moscoso and Fernández García continued to draft more plans for an industrialized Puerto Rico. Despite the failures in the glass factory, they went ahead with the cardboard mill proposal and added two factories to the list: clay products and shoes. They were in for more trouble.

As he had done with the glass factory, Moscoso convinced the board that the paperboard project was "a sure thing"—cardboard boxes were, after all, necessary to ship the rum bottles. The entire idea backfired; the second-hand machinery Moscoso bought was defective, and the plant opening was delayed until late 1947. Then the island merchants who had agreed to supply the plant with the waste paper needed to make cardboard decided to boycott the plant.

The shoe and ceramic factories were two more debacles. There was sufficient island-wide demand for shoes but in a variety of styles, sizes, and colors that the plant could not produce. There was also a postwar demand for ceramic fixtures to supply the homebuilding industry. But again, the agency's plant could only manufacture plain, white fixtures. Quality control became the biggest problem: the amount of breakages and seconds made the plant's losses escalate.

Four years after its ambitious launching, it was clear that Moscoso's program was at best a very costly learning process. Needing to create one hundred thousand jobs to keep up with the growing labor force, Moscoso had only created ten thousand at a cost of $21 million. But for Moscoso the idea of failure did not seem to exist. His answer to the growing chorus of critics was to push the programs even faster. He was now moving ahead with a $4.7 million textile plant and what was to become his most daring venture, a $7 million luxury hotel.

But Moscoso was not blind. He knew he had to come up with a new development strategy. The plants' string of losses could not go on, nor could the defeating confrontations with labor leaders, who insisted that the rum bonanza money be distributed among the workers instead of being invested in expansions and new plants. What he had suspected since the beginning was now self-evident: a labor-oriented government could not run the industrialization of Puerto Rico. There was an insurmountable conflict of interest. The private sector would have to do it. What he needed was an efficient industrial promotion program to attract private industrial capital, mostly from the United States. And to lure capital to a small, undeveloped tropical island, the Fomento trio—Moscoso, Fernández García, and Ramírez—had to use their imaginations as never before in order to come up with an industrial incentive powerful enough to produce the economic takeoff the island desperately needed.

Chapter 6

Muñoz's Conversion

The idea of offering tax exemptions to promote industry was hardly new. Since 1919 it had been tried in Puerto Rico but without success. The last attempt was in 1936 as part of the massive efforts to bring the New Deal to Puerto Rico; it was equally ineffective. This was in part because the exemptions, which were seen mostly as startup subsidies for fledgling industries, forgave only property and other minor taxes.

It was Rafael Fernández García, at one of the many brainstorming sessions at Moscoso's small Fomento office, who proposed the idea of exemption on all taxes on total profits for a fixed number of years. Moscoso snapped it up immediately. Since Puerto Rico had been exempted from U.S. taxes since 1900, local tax forgiveness would make it truly a 100 percent tax exemption.

As they kicked the idea around, Moscoso became increasingly attracted by the promotional value of offering this enormous incentive, regardless of whether an industry needed it. Moscoso and his team realized that it could be attacked as an appeal to greed because it would be most attractive to those industries making the highest profits. But they countered that the 100 percent exemption could also be considered a compensation for all the additional costs involved in establishing and running a plant on this small island. In Moscoso's mind it was self-evident: there were so many negatives to investing in Puerto Rico that only a big and powerful incentive could act as an equalizer.

Moscoso had been shocked by the intensity and emotion of Tugwell's opposition to a watered-down version of tax exemption first proposed in 1944. Tugwell vetoed the bill. Now, three years later, Moscoso was again unprepared for the magnitude of the crusade against his idea. Tugwell had left the island in 1946, but one of his favorite young Puerto Rican disciples, Cornell University economics graduate and statistician Sol Luis Descartes, took over the anti-tax-exemption campaign. Tall, handsome, and eloquent, Descartes resembled Tugwell not only in his good looks and patrician bearing but also in the tendency to impose his intellectual brilliance on others. Partly on Moscoso's recommendation, Tugwell had named him head of the new Office of Statistics. Now for the first time, the insular government had a source of reliable economic and social indicators, and this made Descartes particularly influential.

The arguments against tax exemptions used by professional economists and planners in the United States were well known to Descartes, and he used them with effect. He argued that it would undermine Puerto Rico's credibility and fundamental tax philosophy by violating two crucial tax principles: that taxes be fair and equitable and that they be governed by ability to pay. The economists did not refute Moscoso's contention that tax exemptions would probably lure new investment. But it was patently unfair to taxpayers—why give a new garment manufacturer employing fifty workers a government subsidy while denying it to an existing commercial establishment, say a retail store or a bank employing many times that number of workers? Additionally, Descartes and his group argued, tax exemption had the perverse effect of giving the biggest subsidies precisely to those corporations that least needed them. The higher the company's profitability, the bigger the tax break. It was the exact opposite of a sound tax policy based on the ability to pay.

But the most damaging argument against Moscoso's plan, Descartes believed, was that once the government began to parcel out tax exemptions to specific industrial sectors, it would inevitably find itself under irresistible pressure to extend the privilege to other sectors. The entire foundation of the tax system would be eroded. The government, by diminishing its tax base, would create a vicious circle: the more new industries, the greater the need for publicly funded infrastructure and services, yet the smaller the tax base. This circle became even more vicious because the few remaining taxpayers would have to carry a much higher burden to cover the needs of the exempted industries.

To his dismay, Moscoso saw several of his strongest supporters join Descartes' campaign against tax exemptions. Among them were close friends including Rafael de J. Cordero, the auditor of Puerto Rico; economics Professor Jorge Bermúdez; and the head of the planning board, Dr. Rafael Picó. Moscoso had to admit that in theory Descartes' arguments were powerful, even irrefutable. His defense was to draw the line between "theory" and "reality." Yes, the economists and tax experts were right in that his plan violated the principles of a sound and just tax system. But what good did it do Puerto Rico to follow a pure tax theory and to have a pristine taxation system on the books while lacking real-life industries and workers to pay the taxes? His critics, Moscoso argued, were using a rhetorical gimmick: they based their argument on the word "subsidy." Moscoso argued that it was a subsidy only if one assumed that the industry would come to Puerto Rico and operate without a tax exemption. But that was not the case. In Puerto Rico the government was giving nothing away because without exemption there was no industry. The anti-exemption argument, Moscoso insisted, had another fallacy. Once unemployed Puerto Ricans began to work, they would pay taxes. So tax exemption would in fact create a growing tax base where there was none.

As Moscoso carried out his campaign, he felt the pressure of the approaching deadline. He knew that unless he succeeded in obtaining the government's approval for a fundamentally new development strategy based on a sweeping tax exemption proposal, his program was speeding toward a crash. True, Puerto Rico had taken some impressive steps to combat poverty. The sheer physical impact of what he called "little Pittsburgh" across San Juan Bay — the factory buildings, the line of tall stacks, the congested traffic, the movement of goods, plus the noise — were all dramatic proof that Puerto Rico was being industrialized. *New York Herald-Tribune* reporter Emmet Crozier was taken to the top of the Banco Popular building in Old San Juan, from where he could see the factories; he described the "column of smoke as a symbol of [Puerto Rico's] economic revolution."[1] What was important, Moscoso stressed, was that "Fomento has become, more than anything else, a factory of hope."

But Moscoso knew that what was happening within those physically impressive industrial buildings contradicted his unbounded optimism. Even though he had proved to be a singularly effective communicator about the future of his program, he was deeply distressed about his inability to communicate with the workforce in the plants. The labor conflicts that had seriously damaged the economic viability of the glass plant and paralyzed both the cement and cardboard factories continued unabated. There seemed to be no way that he or his people could make the workers, particularly the union leaders, understand the nature of the industrialization program. Moscoso was now convinced that what was wrong beyond fixing was its very structure: workers for government-owned factories, under a government controlled by a pro-worker political party, would never accept his fundamental argument that these industrial plants belonged not to the workers who operated them but to all the people of Puerto Rico. Thus profits had to be reinvested to create more jobs, not merely to improve the salaries of the existing workers. There was a cruel paradox at the heart of the problem: once Moscoso created a job for a worker, that worker became, in effect, an obstacle to the creation of additional jobs.

This was, of course, a fundamentally political problem, and to solve it Moscoso had to turn to Muñoz. In the summer of 1945, after the glass plant strike was settled and the machinery was back to full operation, Moscoso decided to take Muñoz there. For Moscoso, the sheer size, speed, and power of machines frantically producing hundreds of bottles every few minutes was exhilarating. This was, indeed, a little Pittsburgh. However, Moscoso immediately saw that he had made a terrible mistake. As he led Muñoz toward the production lines, the inhuman roar and intolerable noise level made him visibly cringe in pain. Furious, Muñoz cried at the top of his lungs, "This is infernal!" and rushed out of the plant. This was not the way to sell El Vate—the Poet—on industrialization.

* * *

Back in 1944, Moscoso considered his failure to get Governor Tugwell to approve the tax exemption bill as a minor setback. But in his book on Puerto Rico's industrialization, *The Long Uphill Path,* David Ross wrote: "It is certainly not clear that Moscoso realized the importance of what he was trying to do when he lobbied his first tax exemption law through the legislature in 1944; if he had, the logic of his position would have required him to tender his resignation when the act was vetoed by Governor Tugwell" (95).

In 1947, though, Moscoso was aware of the magnitude of his proposal; tax exemption had become in his and his colleagues' thinking the essential tool of the new industrialization strategy. Now, certainly, a defeat in getting Muñoz and the Populares to approve his new proposal would provoke his resignation.

The 1947 proposal also carried extraordinary political and personal consequences for Muñoz. The bill's timing coincided with his growing doubts about the best way to resolve the island's political status. His decision about a tax exemption proposal benefiting U.S. investors—the key part of a radically new direction in his party's program—was to become pivotal in his own ideological transition. Moscoso's drive forced Muñoz to face and resolve what was now an inescapable dilemma: the type of economic development that Moscoso and his people wanted was incompatible with an independent Republic of Puerto Rico. Contrary to what Muñoz had written and declared hundreds of times since his earliest newspaper articles, the peaceful revolution Puerto Ricans desperately needed to climb out of extreme poverty simply could not take place if Puerto Rico broke its special political and economic relationship to the United States. It had become evident that no agricultural reform could lift the island's two million people from their misery; new wealth had to be created. It was also evident that the original mandate given to Moscoso's agency—to establish factories with public funds and somehow convince local entrepreneurs to launch new industrial ventures—could never keep up with the rapidly expanding labor force.

An unlikely event made Muñoz finally end his emotionally wrenching status conflict. Senator Millard Tydings, who strongly favored independence for Puerto Rico, asked the U.S. Tariff Commission to prepare a study on the trade consequences of separation. Written mostly by economist Ben Dorfman in a cold, no-nonsense, bureaucratic style, the report had the effect on Muñoz of reading a death certificate for a beloved person who one knew, intellectually, had been terminally ill. Years later, Moscoso recalled that he saw Muñoz cry only twice, at the funeral of the venerated Antonio Lucchetti, the father of Puerto Rico's electric power system, and while leaving a long private meeting with Ben Dorfman.

With surgical precision, one by one, Dorfman cut through all the fundamental assumptions of the political status debate that had consumed Puerto Rico for the past half-century.

Although the original purpose of the study was to analyze the effects of independence, statehood, and "dominion" status on Puerto Rico's trade with the United States, the report tackled the totality of the island's economic situation. Dorfman's report emerged as a chilling message to both Puerto Rican leaders and members of Congress. Its cold message was that all of Muñoz's and Tugwell's reforms notwithstanding, even with all the enthusiasm and hopes that they had ignited in the Puerto Rican people, the island's economic realities remained unchanged. They were as implacable as ever. The report, wrote historian Arturo Morales Carrión, was "essentially a no-exit document."[2] Had Dorfman revived the old specter of hopelessness?

Dorfman's basic conclusion was that because the source of Puerto Rico's desperate situation was not political but economic, no change in the political status—the island's political relation to the United States—in itself would result in economic improvement.[3] On the contrary, as the vast majority of Puerto Ricans lived barely above subsistence level, they depended on the flow of U.S. special funds to the island not given to any independent nation. As statehood was out of the question for this poverty-stricken island, what should Puerto Rico do? Dorfman, Morales Carrión added, "with careful, persuasive logic . . . tried to justify the status quo."[4] Any change in the existing Puerto Rico-United States relationship could result in tragic consequences. But the status quo was what all island politicians denounced as colonialism. Dorfman was not attempting to justify the island's current status; instead his brutally direct description of the basic economic issues demolished the underlying assumptions of the island's ideological conflict—that at the root of Puerto Rico's economic and social misery was a colonial political status. In the process, he demolished the last glimmer of hope alive within Muñoz that somehow a way could be found to lead Puerto Rico to political independence with what he termed "economic conditions of life."

Throughout the report Dorfman made blunt, direct statements about the island's grim realities that had been overlooked in the past mostly because they were so obvious. Dorfman began by declaring that Puerto Rico, even with optimum utilization of its land, could not feed itself; aside from areas in China, Egypt, and India, there was no other place in the world with a worse ratio of people to arable land. With a population growing at about 45,000 a year, regardless of its future status the island's survival depended on "continued aid from the outside." As deplorable as the existing living conditions were, Dorfman continued, maintaining even that level of subsistence "rests in large measure on the unique fiscal and trade relations which exist between the island and continental United States." The total accumulated amount of U.S. financial aid to the island up to June 30, 1945, had been $580 million; in addition there was $82.6 million in low-interest loans plus $167 million in military expenditures in the two years after the start of the war.

Free trade, he continued, had benefited the island economy, whereas "the United States has lost more than it has gained." The backbone of the economy, the sugar industry, was totally dependent not only on free access to the U.S. market and an artificially inflated, protected price but also on large-scale federal subsidies to the farmers and producers.

The argument often used to explain American colonialism, that free trade benefited American business because it made Puerto Ricans captives of high-priced American products, Dorfman declared incorrect as proven by a comprehensive review of American imports to the island. American products were in fact cheaper than those of European and other exporters. This explained why many neighboring independent countries such as the Dominican Republic also purchased the same American goods.

Dorfman turned to another favorite accusation, that free trade benefited mostly the absentee American sugar corporations. Total dividends paid to nonresident investors in the industry were $6.6 million in 1942 and 1943. This, Dorfman argued, could be compared to just one item in the flow of

U.S. funds to Puerto Rico: the rebate of U.S. excise taxes on Puerto Rican products. In the same two-year period, due to the rum windfall, the rebate had totaled much more than the dividends.

Dorfman then took on the arguments used to favor statehood. That the United States would greatly increase the flow of federal funds to the island to bring its economy up to national standards, Dorfman declared, was a misconception; there was no direct relation between a state's per capita income and the disbursements of federal funds. Since Puerto Rico would then pay all federal income and excise taxes and lose the excise tax rebates, statehood could result in a net loss in federal funds. In addition, many federal programs required state participation beyond the capacity of a new state government whose own income would then be greatly reduced.

Another frequently used argument was that the benefit to the United States from military bases on the island more than made up for the economic aid given to Puerto Rico. If the United States had never taken the island, Dorfman wrote, it would have had no difficulty establishing military bases in other Caribbean areas at a moderate cost; the bases at Guantanamo Bay in Cuba and elsewhere in the Caribbean paid minimal rentals.

Dorfman then directed his analysis to the most popular and seemingly irrefutable argument in favor of statehood: that the island's welfare could be defended by having two senators and six representatives. Many of the vital trade decisions, including setting the sugar quota, he pointed out, are not made by members of Congress but delegated to the executive. In the real world of Washington politics, Dorfman added, statehood could result in less, not more, influence: "As a state Puerto Rico might well find it more difficult than at present to obtain economic concessions not enjoyed by any other state" (22). The island's lone resident commissioner, a nonvoting member of Congress, he wrote, "does receive from various federal agencies and officials and appointees of the federal government considerable support for measures which are in the island's interest. If Puerto Rico were to become a State, support of such character would no doubt be greatly reduced" (22).

In discussing independence, Dorfman also sent a pointed warning to Tydings. Like others in Washington, including President Roosevelt and Interior Secretary Ickes, Tydings seemed to take particular satisfaction in challenging those Puerto Ricans who endlessly denounced colonialism. Beware, Dorfman warned, for whereas independence would certainly benefit the United States economically, its impact on the Puerto Rican people would be so devastating, surely causing starvation and other calamities and most likely serious political instability, that it would likely force the United States to take absolute control of the island. Certainly the United States would suffer a serious decline in "world prestige" as global opinion became aware of the terrible consequences.

Dorfman gave scant attention to the dominion alternative, in large measure because it was not clear just what it meant or how it would fit into the American constitutional system. As described in a Muñoz-sponsored bill, dominion was similar to independence except that Puerto Ricans, as U.S. citizens, would continue to enjoy free movement to the mainland. But Dorfman found little positive about this alternative, declaring that while less damaging than any variation of independence, it "would not likely offer the island any better opportunity for solving its basic economic ills" than the existing status.

Dorfman was still not finished. Turning to the island's private sector for solutions would be just as futile. Taking aim at the local chamber of commerce's much-heralded "Businessmen's Ten Year Plan," Dorfman argued that its essential ingredient was based on a wrong premise—that by increasing U.S. tariff protection for island products, Puerto Rico's standard of living would rise. Increasing tariffs might well keep low-wage competitors out of the American market, but there was no reason to believe that this in itself would increase the demand for island products. It was more likely that other mainland producers would enter the market. The businesspeople's plan and the insular government's strategy, Dorfman continued, rested on Puerto Rico's ability to industrialize. Both were assuming that there would be no change in the existing economic relations with the United States; indeed, the Puerto Rico Development Company's program depended totally on continued free access to the American market for island rum, plus the continued rebate.

Even Moscoso and his agency did not escape the chill of Dorfman's brutally cold analysis. The optimism and the enthusiasm in Moscoso and his people, Dorfman pointed out, were not enough. He took a careful, detailed look at the numerous projects and bluntly noted that whereas the political leaders intensely debated the future of Puerto Rico's economic and political relation to the United States, the island's industrialization program was based entirely on the existing relation. The factories were all related to the mainland sale of island rum. In any case, Dorfman added, "There is little prospect . . . that the present industrialization program will reduce the number of unemployed below the present level" (28). Dorfman concluded this section quoting the latest Development Company annual report, which directly admitted that the program simply could not keep up with the island's population growth.

Finally, Dorfman went after Moscoso's unshakable tenet that the most fundamental long-range solution was to lower the island's birth rate dramatically through widespread birth control programs. Too late, Dorfman answered: Puerto Rico's overpopulation was already so far advanced and poverty so dismal that it would take decades for such programs to have a significant economic effect.

Dorfman's pessimism was unrelenting. "Puerto Rico's resources and productive capacity," he stated, "afforded no great promise of ever being able to satisfactorily support a population of over two million that is increasing at a rate of well over one hundred per day" (31). Dorfman seriously suggested that perhaps the island would experience some improvement if it reduced the number of people on the island—by one-half! But he was not by any means convinced that even this would work, adding immediately that this "would not of itself assure a solution to the island's major economic problems, but would merely make a solution possible." Little would be gained if steps were not taken to ensure that the one million remaining Puerto Ricans did not rapidly become two million again.

This was as close as Dorfman came to offering a hint toward a solution: a massive exodus of Puerto Ricans from the island, equally massive programs on the island to vastly improve education, health, sanitation, and housing, plus "carefully selected industrialization." Dorfman added that islanders are legally able to move to the mainland. Obviously, he added, "as an independent country, they would not be free to do so."

Muñoz could have dismissed the Dorfman's doomsday vision of Puerto Rico as exaggerated, even bizarre. He did not.

Morales Carrión recorded that the Dorfman report "profoundly influenced Muñoz and the status controversy."[5] It jolted Muñoz; for the first time he admitted that he had been deluding himself. While he had always insisted that to him the economic life-and-death realities had priority in his thinking and motivation, he had been avoiding them. Explaining his ideological conversion years later, he said, "Rationalization works where understanding is the servant instead of the master of emotions . . . we were victims of wishful thinking in believing that separate independence would be feasible if the economic conditions in the Tydings bill" could be worked out.[6]

Dorfman's devastating analyses confirmed what Muñoz had been suspecting for years but had not dared to admit to himself and his followers. He confirmed what others had been telling Muñoz all along—Rexford Tugwell, his aide Frederick Bartlett, economist Rafael J. de Cordero, Sol Luis Descartes, Jorge Bermúdez, Esteban Bird, geographer Rafael Picó, and Teodoro Moscoso himself. Independence as well as statehood was simply economically impossible for Puerto Rico. The existing political and economic relationship of Puerto Rico to the United States—what all island political leaders across the entire ideological spectrum denounced as colonialism—was in fact the life-or-death relationship that sustained the survival of two million Puerto Ricans.

Muñoz, however, would not accept that Puerto Rico was totally trapped. There had to be an exit. The Dorfman jolt finally produced the decisive battle in his internal "civil war." He could no longer doubt that trying to find a formula of independence with the economic conditions of life was futile. It was now a question of timing to abandon publicly his independence ideal.

*   *   *

In April 1946, Congress began to consider legislation to grant the Philippines independence. Muñoz traveled to Washington and attended the hearings. He took copies of the testimonies and all the available documentation back to the hotel every night, carefully reading the provisions on free trade. Dorfman had explained to him in great detail the crucial negotiations to ease the Philippines out of its free-trade arrangement with the United States. Once again, Muñoz was faced with the economic realities involved in making the island independent. He finally made his decision. The Philippines hearings, he wrote years later, "convinced me that Puerto Rico would never obtain the right to choose separate independence in a plebiscite except under economic conditions which would be disastrous to the welfare of the people of Puerto Rico and which would destroy any hope of continuing to improve the standard of living. The most important factor that led me to this conviction was the most-favored-nation clause in trade treaties between the United States and many other countries."[7] The United States could not extend to Puerto Rico trade concessions without extending them to all other countries with most-favored-nation treaties. Thus full free trade was as much out of the question for an independent Puerto Rico as it was for an independent Philippines.

Muñoz returned to Puerto Rico finally determined to make a politically momentous announcement. The public hearings on the Philippines, he declared, "had convinced me that it is impossible, totally impossible, irrefutably impossible" for Puerto Rico to become independent.

In late June 1946, Muñoz published two additional articles in *El Mundo* under the title "New Roads toward Old Objectives." It is time, he wrote, to stop wasting Puerto Rico's and his own time searching for a status formula that simply did not exist. Since both statehood and independence were economically destructive, it was time to use "creative statesmanship" to "create" a new political status. "We must change the political situation without destroying the economic conditions that are absolutely necessary for the survival of the people—and to the political status itself since no political status can survive if the economy within which it functions is destroyed."[8]

Now Muñoz made a pivotal declaration. There was for Puerto Rico, he said, one exit: industrialization. And for the first time, Muñoz linked it directly and irrevocably to the political status issue. Puerto Rico, he wrote, must "increase, rapidly and efficiently, the volume of wealth that is produced. It must be increased principally through industrialization, at four speeds. Fast enough to substantially abolish the existing unemployment. Faster still to keep it at that level in spite of the fifty five thousand additional inhabitants every year in Puerto Rico. Faster still so that the moment will arrive when this will be done without the artificial aids from the United States government. And with still greater speed so that the minimum family income—at least for the vast majority of the families—will reach around $700 to $800 annual income, which is the economic level when, according to the experience of developed nations, the birth rate would decrease and the population stabilize."[9]

Muñoz crossed a frontier in his thinking. Free trade was essential for Puerto Rico not only to sustain the existing economic structure, dependent on agriculture, but also because otherwise it would close off the island's only hope of economic improvement—industrialization:

> To bring about this industrialization, Puerto Rico needs to have free access to the United States market, the biggest and most prosperous market in the world, that is, at the same time, protected against Puerto Rico's competitors. Without that free access to that protected market, Puerto Rico—a land without much prime material—cannot live, much less accumulate through its exports, the capital needed for the intense industrialization it inexorably needs . . . . Puerto Rico needed a great local, protected market, the great local protected market of the United States with its 140 million prosperous consumers. It cannot do it on the basis of the minuscule local market of two million poor consumers.

Muñoz was finally a convert to Moscoso and his program. Industrialization, the idea that Muñoz's party as well as Tugwell had underplayed just two years earlier, was now the engine driving Muñoz's peaceful revolution. It was, for Muñoz, a remarkable transition and leap of faith. Teodoro Moscoso and Fomento were now the core, the controlling factor in Puerto Rico's attempt to erase four centuries of poverty.

*   *   *

Free trade with the United States, as essential as it was, would not in itself bring industry to Puerto Rico. The island needed a powerful magnet; in Moscoso's mind it could only be full tax exemption.

Moscoso believed that he had won that battle. He had convinced Muñoz, and the legislature had approved an industrial tax exemption bill in May 1947. But the bill was seriously flawed and had to be amended. This gave the opponents an unexpected opportunity to conduct a renewed assault on Moscoso's plan. Muñoz finally decided that he must put an end to the heated debate; he called Moscoso and the opponents, led by Sol Luis Descartes, to his home in Trujillo Alto to go over, once again, all the arguments in favor and against and to arrive at a final determination. Descartes had brought in from the mainland a tax expert, Milton Taylor, a scholarly but determined foe of tax exemption, who insisted not only that Moscoso's plan was destructive of many fundamental tax principles but also that it simply would not work: "Several empirical studies have concluded that tax subsides have been notably insignificant on the mainland United States as an incentive on the location of industry in particular areas, on the grounds that relative tax burdens are a minor location consideration. . . . The conclusion must therefore be drawn that heavy taxation has not acted as a check upon industrial development in periods of prosperity, nor has a light tax burden acted as a stimulus to industry in depression years."[10]

Late at night, a weary Muñoz, swamped with arguments against the plan, interrupted the conversation and made his decision: Moscoso's tax exemption bill would *not* be approved.

Moscoso didn't sleep that night. As he lay awake, he kept asking himself the same question endlessly: What do we have to lose? He turned and looked at the clock—five o'clock in the morning. He jumped out of bed and into his clothing and drove back out to Trujillo Alto. A groggy Muñoz appeared in his robe: "What's happened?" Moscoso asked Muñoz to sit down. Moscoso stared at Muñoz for several seconds: "Muñoz, we have nothing now. If we do nothing, we will continue with nothing. If we try, and it fails, we will still have nothing. But if we succeed?" Another long pause: "Muñoz, what do we have to lose?" Muñoz stood up to escape from Moscoso's intensity. "Let me try it," Moscoso pleaded. "If Sol Luis is right, and I fail, what do we lose? But if I'm right, and it succeeds . . ." Muñoz walked around silently. Finally he said, "All right. Let's do it."

On May 13, 1948, the legislature approved Act No. 184 granting full tax exemption—income, property, excise, and municipal taxes—to new industries for a period of ten years, with an additional three years of partial exemption. The law would expire on June 30, 1962. Any new industry was eligible that would manufacture a product not being produced on the island before January 2, 1947, plus forty-two specific industries then in existence. Responsibility for administering the law was placed on the executive council; a Special Secretary for Industrial Tax Exemption was responsible for bringing petitions before the council for discussion and approval. The council was composed of the governor and all members of the cabinet; clearly the intention was to get the entire administration engaged in the tax exemption process. (In 1950, the cumbersome system was changed: an Office of Industrial Tax Exemption was created to process all petitions, distributing them to the treasury, labor, and justice departments for their review and approval. The petitions would then be submitted for the governor's signature.)

On November 2, 1948, Muñoz and the Populares again swept the elections. Muñoz became Puerto Rico's first elected governor, with 61 percent of the vote. (Jesús T. Piñero, who preceded Muñoz, was the first Puerto Rican appointed to the governorship.) The Republican-Socialist Coalition got 29 percent, and the new Independence Party led by former Muñoz followers received 10 percent. Of the fifty-eight members of the legislature, all but three were Populares. Muñoz became the 118th governor of Puerto Rico—beginning with Juan Ponce de León—98 of them Spanish, 18 American, and 1 Puerto Rican. The overwhelming victory, of course, confirmed that Muñoz had become the most popular political leader in island history: for Muñoz, it confirmed something much more important. The Independentistas had made the 1948 elections a sort of status plebiscite. Muñoz's decision to renounce independence as strongly as he did statehood was now dramatically vindicated. Muñoz was right, the overwhelming majority of Puerto Ricans favored one form or another of "permanent union" with the United States.

The convergence of these two events—the approval of Moscoso's tax exemption law as the centerpiece of a new economic development strategy and the election to the governorship of a Muñoz liberated from the futility of unreal political status formulas—produced the turning point in Puerto Rican history. Moscoso's industrialization would have been impossible if Puerto Rico had taken a different road toward a different political status. In turn, Puerto Rico's decision to overcome juridical colonialism by becoming part of the United States as a commonwealth in 1952 was a direct result of the success of Moscoso's industrialization. The commonwealth formula retained the elements essential for Operation Bootstrap: Puerto Ricans re-

Teodoro Moscoso reading a short speech at the inauguration of a new manufacturing plant in the mid-1950s, when Operation Bootstrap, after a decade of trial and error, was beginning to take off.

tained American citizenship and thus free trade into the United States, while also retaining "fiscal autonomy," that is, exemption from all federal taxes.

From 1943 to 1948, Moscoso's agency had promoted a total of thirteen plants, most of these in anticipation of his promised tax exemption law. The total number of manufacturing plants in operation in 1948 was 24. The following year it doubled to 50 and the next to 80. By 1955, there were over 300 factories. Four years later, there were 530 in operation and another 91 being established.[11]

For the first time in its history, Puerto Rico was finally in full-fledged economic takeoff.

Chapter 7

From Public to Private Ownership

As a teenager in Ponce, Moscoso admired Luis A. Ferré. Moscoso's senior by six years, the MIT graduate worked in the Ferré family business, the Puerto Rico Iron Works, a huge repair shop for sugar-manufacturing machines. Ferré was cultured, a fine piano player, an excellent fencer, and he had a life-long passion for partisan politics. He had run and lost in 1940 as a candidate for mayor of Ponce under the pro-statehood banner.

Now, in 1948, Moscoso was furious with Ferré. His colleagues at the development company were at a loss to fathom Moscoso's uncharacteristic emotional outbursts. His anger certainly had nothing to do with Ferré's increasing political activity; he was running for resident commissioner in Washington. Moscoso's behavior stemmed from his belief that if anyone could and should understand what he was trying to do about Puerto Rico's economic condition, it was Ferré. He was by 1948 one of the island's leading industrialists, whose family enterprises were expanding throughout Puerto Rico, the Caribbean, and Florida. He knew how difficult it was to create jobs for poor Puerto Ricans.

During his campaign against Muñoz and the Populares, Ferré had occasionally criticized Moscoso and his program. But six weeks prior to the 1948 elections, Ferré made an attack that Moscoso took personally. Ferré accused Moscoso and his agency of having neglected the island's troubled needle industry. Moscoso shot back in a long statement published in *El Mundo* on September 21, 1948, that this attack was not only "inadmissible" but also "unforgivable." If Ferré was so interested in the needle industry, why didn't he invest in it instead of establishing a new cement plant to compete against the government plant? Worse still, Moscoso pointed out, Ferré sat on the local board of directors of Textron, a large American company brought to the island by Fomento precisely to give the needle industry a giant shot in the arm. Ferré, Moscoso declared with unusual sharp-

61

ness, was making serious, gratuitous accusations that he knew from direct experience were false.

*   *   *

Meanwhile, Moscoso's public relations machine was producing impressive results. The approval of the initial tax exemption bill in 1947 appeared in the *Wall Street Journal* with a headline reading: "Taxpayers' Paradise, Puerto Rico Aspires to Role: New Industries Get 7 Year Tax Holiday." *The New York Times* ran the banner: "New Business Tax Holiday Starts in Puerto Rico." *Barron's* wrote: "Puerto Rico Spreads Bounty for Industry," and the *New York Journal of Commerce* stated: "Puerto Rico Woos Industry with Tax Aid."

Fomento's publicity apparatus was also working well locally. The press lined up behind the new program. Moscoso persuaded *El Mundo* to print the prediction that in 1948 Fomento would bring private investments totaling $30 million to the island with a payroll of $4 million, a forecast that appeared on the newspaper's front page of December 24, 1947. On December 15, *El Mundo* had reported on a Moscoso speech announcing that Textron planned to set up fourteen textile plants throughout the island. And this, he added, was the beginning "of a great movement of the American textile industry to Puerto Rico." When a spokesman for the insular engineer's association called on the planning board to completely liquidate the Puerto Rico Development Company and allow the private sector to industrialize the island, Moscoso responded that his government program was "doing the most to lift Puerto Rico's standard of living." The new tax exemption law and the stepped-up construction of industrial buildings (eighteen were going up at the moment and eight more were on the way) would bring a big flow of private capital to the island. He also flatly declared in the December 23 issue of *El Mundo* that the development company had "discarded" all previous plans to build and run its own factories. And on January 12, 1948, Moscoso and the new developmental policy even received strong editorial support from *El Mundo*.

Moscoso kept Muñoz informed on the number of investors who had applied for a government-built factory building. Back in mid-1947, less than three months after the initial tax exemption bill was passed, Moscoso wrote to Muñoz that sixteen applications had been approved and that "many continental firms are actively considering extending their operations to Puerto Rico." Just one of these, Cargill, Inc., among the largest grain operators in the world, was "proposing to establish a flour mill, soap factory, edible oil plant and a cattle and poultry feed plant."[1]

In addition to tax exemption, the new developmental policy called for the politically difficult decision to sell or close the money-losing government factories. The glass plant's losses had leaped from $162,870 in fiscal year 1947 to $518,949 in fiscal 1948. The losses in the cardboard plant were up from $52,586 to $299,844 in the same time period. Moscoso knew that he had to shut down these two unproductive plants. Should the shoe and ceramic plants also go down, it would mean throwing nine hundred employees out of work.

The cardboard factory became the first to be threatened with closure, mostly because of its soured relations with a box manufacturer, the Puerto Rico Container Corporation, which was part of newspaper magnate Angel Ramos's holdings. In 1947, claiming poor cardboard quality and reduced postwar demand for boxes, Ramos stopped doing business with the government factory. Moscoso decided that he had to either add a box division to "his" factory or purchase Ramos's operation. The development agency's board authorized $300,000 for the purchase. Ramos, however, wanted $2 million and refused to budge, unmoved by Moscoso's many lower-priced counteroffers. As a result, the government's cardboard plant began to cut down production, and it shut down entirely in early 1949.

The sale of the other government-owned factories—cement, glass, and clay—became a big gamble. In order to give his program a push forward, Moscoso announced a $200 million loan request from the National Industrial Recovery Administration. By mid-1948, Moscoso's honeymoon with the insular media already was waning. Ramos's *El Mundo* objected to the loan with an outraged editorial. The newspaper reiterated that it was convinced that industrialization was the island's only "salvation." But it went on to revive the familiar attack that all the government plants were losing money and had not created the expected jobs, and that the cement plant was profitable only because it charged an "excessively high price" for its product. *El Mundo* added a new twist, as well, in its March 27, 1948, edition. Previously Moscoso was described as Tugwell's "co-conspirator" in making the island a "socialist laboratory." Now, in a 180-degree turn, the newspaper accused Moscoso of being excessively generous in favoring "outside" capitalists while discriminating against local investors. Instead of playing "Santa Claus" to the outside investors, *El Mundo* asked, why not stem the outflow of Puerto Rican capital, estimated at $30 million in the preceding years?

To Moscoso's consternation, this new line of criticism was picked up by Luis Ferré, who owned the small, regional *El Día* newspaper of Ponce that he used as a sounding board in his political campaigns. He now added an element that once again infuriated Moscoso. Ferré called on the Puerto Rico Development Company to eliminate its factories by simply putting them on the block, selling them at public auction for whatever sum anyone was willing to pay. Moscoso answered sarcastically that he was "surprised" that the owner of the only private cement plant on the island would recommend that the government virtually give away its own profitable cement plant. To do so, Moscoso said, would be to act as if the government plants had to be desperately sold at a price far below their true market value. This was not the case, he said: on the contrary, the reason for offering to sell the plants was to reinvest the money in another form of industrialization. Moscoso ended his sharp statement by recognizing that Ferré's proposal was motivated by his own interest in the cement business. The government, Moscoso said, will protect the public's interest by not creating a monopoly in the production and sale of cement.[2]

Two years later, almost to the date, Moscoso would have to eat those words.

In order to sell the government plants to the private sector, Moscoso first had to convince Muñoz and to assure him that the initial investment would be recovered. This was an even greater challenge than the battle for the tax exemption bill. Now he was asking Muñoz and the Populares, on the eve of an election, to publicly abandon their socialist roots and to change the essential ideological underpinning of an administration that gained power as the defender of the workers, the unions, and the small farmers. Muñoz, who liberated Puerto Rico from the absentee sugar corporations, was not about to allow Moscoso to deliver the island to another form of absentee capitalism.

Muñoz had emerged from his first ideological conversion—his stunning decision to reject independence for Puerto Rico. Already accused by the new Independence Party of betraying political freedom for Puerto Rico, he would now be accused of betraying social justice.

Moscoso, however, was having no success finding buyers for the government plants. The approaches made to glass, paper, and other industries in the United States had not elicited any interest. In late 1949, though, he was introduced to a young American businessman of Rumanian origin who had a reputation for transforming failed paper factories into profitable businesses. It soon became evident to Moscoso and his staff that Karl F. Landegger and his lawyer believed that they could acquire the closed paper plant for a fraction of its original cost. Since Moscoso had insisted publicly, and personally to Muñoz, that he would settle for nothing less than the original government investment, Landegger's probes were not taken seriously. But instead of withdrawing as expected, Landegger surprised Moscoso by returning with a new offer: he was willing to purchase all four government plants.

This was the first bid received by the government. Moscoso asked the company's attorney, Mariano Ramírez, and a young former cement salesman, Guillermo Rodríguez, whom Moscoso had made president of all five subsidiaries, to enter into serious negotiations. They were further encouraged when Landegger accepted the non-negotiable price of $10 million. This price permitted Moscoso and Muñoz to assure the public that the government had recovered its entire original investment. Landegger responded that he was willing to give $2 million as a down payment but wanted to pay the balance, interest free, over a ten-year period.

Years later Ramírez recalled: "I thought, at the time, that we would close the deal, but we had a hell of a time with Landegger's lawyer. He was not the right man to make a difficult, complex deal: he was what some of us in the legal profession call a semicolon lawyer. He drove us crazy with his commas and semicolons."

While Ramírez and Guillermo Rodríguez were struggling with Landegger, they were again surprised by a new offer from a most unlikely source. Moscoso had suspected that Luis Ferré's annoying attacks during the 1948 campaign had been a not-too-well disguised attempt, although Ferré had publicly denied it,[3] to see if the family could appropriate the profitable cement plant, thus giving Ferré Enterprises a monopoly on this key industry. Now Moscoso was visited by Luis Ferré's older brother, José, who immediately informed him that he had directly asked Muñoz to suspend Moscoso's negotiations with Landegger—Ferré Enterprises, he had told the governor, was interested in buying all four plants.

"Joe" Ferré was different in many ways from his brother, Luis. Of the four brothers, Joe was the only one who had not become an engineer. He had a degree in business administration from Boston College and had done graduate work at the University of Miami. While the family was politically conservative—Luis had emerged as the island's top Republican, pro-statehood leader—Joe described himself as a Popular, a liberal who supported Muñoz's reformist policies. Joe had the reputation of being the family's hard-nosed "promoter." Like Moscoso, he was aggressive, always looking for new opportunities and willing to take risks. This was in contrast to Luis, who was the family's cautious, surefooted administrator. Once Joe returned from a hunting expedition with a new acquisition, it was Luis's responsibility to make Joe's new venture profitable. But Luis had an additional important role. He was the growing Ferré empire's public relations man and had the ability to generate goodwill for himself and his enterprises.

There was another reason why Moscoso considered Joe Ferré's offer. Although Joe was clearly not cut in the same mold as Puerto Rico's typical businessman, particularly those from tradition-bound Ponce, it was satisfying to have, finally, a Puerto Rican businessman willing to make a major investment in these plants. It had been eight years since Moscoso's futile effort to get even a modicum of local participation.

"It was Joe's idea totally to buy all the factories," the Ferré family attorney, José Trías Monge, recalled years later. "Luis went along and, later, he was quite proud of the purchase. Why did Joe want three operations that had experienced considerable losses as well as labor and production problems? In part because Joe was enterprising. I can say that Joe offered to buy the four plants without ever once visiting them, before or after the deal was made. Secondly, Joe was an admirer of Muñoz and supported his reforms. But mostly, I believe, because Joe had faith in what Moscoso and Fomento were doing. He made a bet on Puerto Rico's future: I think he foresaw that Puerto Rico, under Muñoz and Moscoso, was on the verge of a takeoff."[4]

Joe advised Moscoso that negotiations for the sale would be under a rigid deadline. He said his brother, Luis, was vacationing in Europe and would return to Puerto Rico in eight days. The only hope of making a deal, Joe said, would be if they agreed to negotiate around the clock so as to reach an agreement before Luis's return to the island.

Fomento's attorney, Mariano Ramírez, recalled that Joe seemed extremely concerned about his brother. Luis, Joe insisted, had an "engineer's mentality" and would look for and find a thousand reasons to pick apart any agreement. Ramírez and Moscoso found it difficult to believe that Joe had any intention of making a $10 million-plus deal behind his brother's back. This seemed like another clever Ferré family negotiating tactic. Joe's message was: If you really want to unload these factories, I'm foolish enough to take them off your hands. So you better work something out with me before my sensible brother stops me.

Moscoso assigned Guillermo Rodríguez, whom he considered Joe Ferré's peer in *malicia*—the ability to see through someone else's deceptions and traps—to conduct the negotiations along with Mariano Ramírez. For added insurance, Moscoso brought in several consultants from Wall Street.

Moscoso knew, however, that he was taking a risk. His mind was now racing with the pros and cons. No doubt Joe was serious about buying the plants and knew that Moscoso could not go below the $10 million bottom price. But having to close the deal before Luis returned was indeed a transparent negotiating scheme. The tactic applied as much pressure on Moscoso and his team as on the Ferrés. Furthermore, it removed the possible friction between Luis and Moscoso after the angry statements they exchanged during the 1948 campaign.

But how would Muñoz react? Obviously, it was a wiser political decision to sell the plants to a Puerto Rican family than to a mainland businessman like Landegger. But the Ferrés were precisely the symbol of the Republican, economically elitist families who had controlled this island before the Muñoz revolution. Wouldn't this be seen as irrefutable proof that Muñoz, the once-undisputed champion of social justice, had now sold his soul to precisely the same economic class that had oppressed and exploited poor Puerto Ricans for so long? But then, couldn't this be interpreted also as proof of Muñoz's deep-seated trust in democracy and the capitalist system, to the point of turning his main political opponent into the most powerful industrialist in Puerto Rico?

Amid the doubts, only one thing was clear. Joe Ferré's offer to rush the deal was political dynamite. Adding to the potential backlash was the fact that on July 3, 1948, Moscoso had assured the people of Puerto Rico that he would not permit a monopoly in the production and sale of cement. How was he to persuade Muñoz and the Popular Party to approve such a flagrant turnaround?

Having made his decision to go along with Joe Ferré's insistence on an eight-day deadline, Moscoso instructed Guillermo Rodríguez and Mariano Ramírez to reserve several adjoining suites in San Juan's big, new, government-owned tourist hotel, the Caribe Hilton. They would all negotiate around the clock.

Three days into the negotiations, the Fomento team began to believe that they were on the road to a sale. The deal was enormously complex and many of the technical difficulties were set aside to be resolved later. Ramírez was now convinced that Joe really meant to push through a deal before his brother arrived. Trías Monge, the Ferrés' attorney, a soft-spoken graduate of Harvard Law School with a post-graduate degree from Yale Law School, was also considered one of Muñoz's legal "whiz kids." His presence reinforced the message that Joe communicated at the beginning: while they were, of course, negotiating on behalf of the Ferré interests, they were politically and ideologically on Muñoz's and Moscoso's side. The Fomento team witnessed the emergence of a sale favorable to the government. Ferré Enterprises would pay a total of $10.5 million for the four subsidiaries, a $2 million down payment, and from $3\frac{1}{2}$ to 4 percent interest on the balance. It was worth about $3 million more to the government than the Landegger offer.

But Moscoso had made a decision that he withheld from his negotiator, Mariano Ramírez. He decided to sign the agreement without prior approval from Muñoz. Joe Ferré added still another political element to the signing. Brother Luis was finally back in Puerto Rico; in order to ensure Luis's approval, Joe said, "Let's give him all the credit having *him* sign the agreement." Ramírez was not as confident as Moscoso that Muñoz would go along. He and Guillermo Rodríguez were stunned to learn that Moscoso had indeed signed the contract without Muñoz's knowledge.

"When Muñoz was informed that I had signed the contract for the sale of these plants," Moscoso recalled later, "he became very angry at me. He felt that he should have signed it himself, or at least participated somehow. I felt that I had enough clearance from him, from the legislature, from everybody, to go ahead. I also knew that Muñoz had nothing to contribute to the evaluation of the plants, whether they should be ten or eleven million."[5]

Muñoz's immediate reaction was to advise them, as well as Joe Ferré, that the contract was not valid. When Luis returned from Europe, he found a telegram from the governor at his home in Ponce. The sale, Muñoz informed him, would not go through until he, Muñoz, had additional time to study and approve it. Now it was Ferré who was furious; he threatened to sue the government for breach of contract. This reaction confirmed in Ramírez's mind that the story of Joe negotiating behind Luis's back was a clever ploy— it was obvious that Luis wanted to consummate the deal as much as Joe did. After a seemingly heated argument between the brothers, Joe prevailed: they answered Muñoz's telegram accepting the postponement of the agreement, giving the governor all the time he needed to approve or reject it. Joe insisted that they specifically add that while he and Luis believed it was a good contract for all the parties, if Muñoz rejected it, they would accept the decision. Joe's tactic worked. Moscoso and Ramírez were able to overcome Muñoz's objection to giving the Ferrés the cement monopoly by informing the governor that both sides had agreed to freeze the price of cement by placing it under government control. Muñoz gave his approval within the week.

So many technical details had been deferred in the rush to conclude the agreement "before Luis returns" that it took both teams of lawyers another six months to work them all out. The Ferrés took possession of the plants soon after Muñoz's approval, but it was not until April 1951 that the final transfer of title was completed.[6]

Chapter 8

From Operation Bootstrap
to Operation Serenity

"In the last few years we have abandoned what we might call 'Operation Lament' and are now in the midst of 'Operation Bootstrap,'" Muñoz proudly told a congressional committee in July 1949, seven months after being sworn in as governor. "We are trying to lift ourselves by our own bootstraps."[1]

Muñoz had given Moscoso a name for Fomento's program: a slogan that communicated exactly the message both wanted to convey to Congress and the American people. In 1938, when Muñoz began to organize the Popular Party, it had adopted as its unofficial anthem "Lamento Borincano" (*Borinquen* is the indigenous name of Puerto Rico), a sad ballad by composer Rafael Hernández that captured the resignation and hopelessness of the *jíbaro*. Now Puerto Rico, no longer paralyzed by hopelessness, was making a superhuman effort to help itself.

The end of Operation Lament meant that Muñoz and the Puerto Ricans could no longer blame U.S. colonialism or neglect for the island's ills. For what was taking place on the island during this period was not only a remarkable economic transformation but also a profound political transformation that altered the relationship between the United States and Puerto Rico. The elections of 1948, when Puerto Ricans elected their governor for the first time, ended the unworkable political arrangement that had defeated all attempts to govern the island with rational effectiveness. As Tugwell himself so often decried, the appointed governor, supposedly the representative of American sovereignty over Puerto Rico, was effectively stripped of power by the Puerto Rican legislature and the self-destructive nature of local politics. If Puerto Rico had indeed been a colony during the first half-century of American rule, it had been an absurd colony; the rule of the appointed governors was undermined not only by Puerto Rican politics but also by Washington's own administrative inefficiency and even by Congress. The U.S. Constitution gave Congress power over Puerto Rico as an "unincorporated territory." This, of course, made the island juridically a colony. But that power was so fragmented by the system created by Congress that exercising it, as Tugwell discovered to his dismay, was virtually impossible.

Now, for the first time, power was consolidated. Luis Muñoz Marín controlled the executive and legislative branches and presided over the party that had won all but three legislative seats and all but one of the municipal governments.

But what to do with this power? Muñoz and his party leaders, with a few exceptions, knew virtually nothing about public administration. During the five difficult years with Tugwell, Muñoz had depended entirely on him, a nationally recognized expert on government administration who was committed to the proposition that government has the duty to shape human conduct as well as society.

The more Tugwell was attacked by the island's business establishment and by conservative members of Congress, the more Muñoz and the Populares tended to support him. But at the same time, nothing angered Muñoz more than Tugwell's insistence that Muñoz promoted, or at best tolerated, outrageous political patronage. It was easy, Muñoz wrote decades later in his *Memorias,* for Tugwell to ignore Puerto Rico's political realities. In order to carry out the peaceful revolution, Muñoz had to dedicate great personal effort to win over his party leaders. Muñoz insisted that no one, not even Tugwell, despised political cronyism, nepotism, and patronage as much as he did.

Years later, in the early 1970s, Muñoz wrote with unusual emotion: "It caused me profound irritation that Tugwell thought that he believed in good government and that I did not: that I was committed to patronage. That offended me."[2] Following Tugwell's departure and the presidential appointment of one of Muñoz's most loyal followers as governor, Jesús T. Piñero, the situation became even more difficult and sensitive for Muñoz. Many expected Piñero to continue to be loyal and subservient to Muñoz, who was considered the de facto governor. In his *Memorias,* Muñoz admitted that he was unaware of how awkward and annoying the situation had become for Piñero.

In 1948, after he himself was elected governor, Muñoz felt he had to prove to Tugwell how mistaken he had been. Muñoz was determined to answer the insulting question that ran through Tugwell's long, sad, pessimistic account of his governorship, *The Stricken Land:* Just what kind of leader was Muñoz? A charismatic but ultimately typical Latin American political boss striving for power for power's sake, or a rare leader determined to use political power to forge an efficient, scientific, modern governmental machine?

Unlike Tugwell, who believed in a decentralized government administration, Muñoz wanted close control of the executive branch. What he found when he took over the administration in 1949 was a confused conglomeration of agencies and programs, many of which duplicated each other. There were no clear lines of jurisdiction or accountability. No one could tell him with exactitude how many agencies existed. A survey performed by the University of Puerto Rico School of Public Administration concluded that there were "around 100." Twenty new agencies had been created during the Tugwell era. Muñoz asked the young, talented director of the Budget Bureau, Roberto de Jesús, one of Tugwell's protégés, to make sense of the clutter. "I know of many cases where the public corporations made very important decisions without the governor's knowledge, much less that of the Legislative Assembly," de Jesús wrote later. "As a result, the government often appeared to follow a contradictory policy."3 In theory, fifty-seven agencies reported directly to the governor, while in practice very few did. It was not possible to determine to whom, if anyone, the other eleven agencies reported.

Muñoz decided to carry out a broad reorganization. He appointed a "little Hoover Commission" headed by Washington attorney James Rowe, who had served in the 1947 federal government reorganization directed by former President Herbert Hoover. Also on the commission was Louis Brownlaw, who was part of a 1936 reform carried out by President Roosevelt and who had gained the reputation of being "the dean of public administration who had done the most to upgrade the quality of government."4 Several island legislators and administrators were also named. The committee's task was to eliminate, consolidate, and restructure as many agencies as possible, grouping them together in a rational hierarchy. The goal was to give the new governor what he wanted: total administrative control.

The commission worked quickly; in five months it submitted to Muñoz a radically different administrative organization. The number of agencies was reduced to twenty-three. Many of the boards of directors of the public corporations were eliminated, giving the governor a direct line of authority over these agencies. In its simplicity and logic, the reorganization was praised by professionals as a model of efficient and action-oriented public administration. "The Puerto Rican executive branch might be said to be the professional organizer's dream come true. Since nowhere on the mainland have the goals of the reorganization movement been realized so completely as in the island Commonwealth," wrote Henry Wells.[5]

The biggest winner was Teodoro Moscoso. A new agency, the Economic Development Administration, was created. Moscoso was given authority not only over industrialization but also over the overall economic development of the island. The original Puerto Rico Industrial Development Company was retained as a public corporation to act mostly as the EDA's real estate arm. Its board was eliminated and its functions absorbed by Moscoso, as EDA administrator. Placed under his jurisdiction were Puerto Rico's air and sea transportation facilities, including, against his will, San Juan's bus system. He also was given the responsibility for tourism development, and several offices dealing with economic statistics were consolidated under his command.

With all this additional power in his hands—a good part of which he in fact had exercised all along without officially having it—the freewheeling Moscoso was now expected to conform to the reorganization's fundamental goal. He was to "join the team" under the governor's authority as an integral part of the administration. Instead of reporting to a friendly, admiring board that rarely failed to endorse his actions, Moscoso was to report directly to the governor. It was one thing for Moscoso to take matters of unusual importance, such as the tax exemption bill, to Muñoz; it was another to find himself under the governor's continuous surveillance. Moscoso had never considered himself a politician and had always acted as if his agency was not really part of the government bureaucracy. He remained well aware, however, that Muñoz's chief of staff, Roberto Sánchez Vilella (Moscoso's brother-in-law), often complained about Moscoso's excessive freedom and about his frequent "recklessness."

As Moscoso's authority and recognition grew in Puerto Rico, so did mistrust and even fear of the profound changes being brought about by industrialization. Moscoso's enormous drive was seen by some within the government as threatening. He was so single-minded in his effort to industrialize Puerto Rico that he appeared blind to the social, political, and cultural consequences. Moscoso's ability to get things done, coupled with his desire to always "think big" regardless of the effects on such a small island, had to be harnessed. This was Governor Muñoz's task, now made easier by Moscoso's membership in his cabinet and by the Economic Development Administration's accountability to the budget and personnel offices, which were given jurisdiction over it.

As Sánchez Vilella put it, the need to "put the brakes on Moscoso" was clearly demonstrated by the Textron promotion. Moscoso had heralded the Textron venture as precisely the type of "bellwether" project that Fomento needed to give a degree of credibility to its new promotional campaigns to attract investment. And as Ross wrote in *The Long Uphill Path*, "The name of Textron did shed its magic on Puerto Rico's selling effort when it was most needed." Textron directors even talked of making a gigantic investment in a string of textile plants throughout the island.

But the more Moscoso trumpeted this breakthrough project, the more critics attacked it. First there was the allegation that, once again and in order to attract the firm, Moscoso had gone too far and given too much away. The investment required of Textron was "relatively small and the terms of the lease and purchase mortgage were generous to an extent not subsequently repeated."[6] The negative publicity prompted attacks against the island from the New England region for using unfair tactics to attract "runaway" industries. Textron became a symbol of the textile industries' flight to the south—it had closed six plants in the North, throwing 3,500 employees out of work. A furious Republican senator from New Hampshire, Charles Tobey, bitterly attacked the island: "The United States has been acting as a wet nurse for Puerto Rico for years. It is robbing United States workers of their livelihood by subsidizing companies like Textron in the territory by granting Federal tax exemption. We are killing off things here to build in Puerto Rico."[7]

This forced Muñoz to carry out a defensive campaign to assure the insular and mainland public that Moscoso's program excluded runaway industries: they would not be granted tax exemption. In his first message to the legislature as governor in 1949, Muñoz declared, "In regard to investments that come from the United States, we should make the following very clear: It is not the philosophy of the government that I head to seek to close factories in the North to have them open in Puerto Rico. Puerto Rico is part of the United States economy and to close factories there hurts us here, just as to impede that they open here, hurts there."[8]

Several months later, testifying before a congressional committee, Muñoz reiterated his policy: "I want to say that our executive council, which is the organism entrusted by the law to grant or withhold tax exemption, will not grant it to any industry where it knows that it is going to close a factory in any state or territory of the Union in order to open it in Puerto Rico."[9]

During the years that followed, the Textron promotion continued to haunt Moscoso. Although he had anticipated six or more Textron mills by 1951, the management became so bitter over the company's experiences in Puerto Rico that there were only two plants running. What began as a war of words between Textron's management and Moscoso's agency now appeared ominous: "In 1951 the Textron management in Ponce prepared a twelve-point indictment of Puerto Rico as a location for a textile plant, based on a comparison with their experience in Southeastern United States."[10] Moscoso's mainland promoters reported that Textron was carrying out a concerted campaign against investing in Puerto Rico. One Fomento executive advised Moscoso, "Almost every day I get reports from my men in New England telling of one manufacturer or another who has heard very bad things about production conditions in Puerto Rico. As a rule these rumors originated with Textron."[11] By the middle of the decade, Textron had sold its two plants and left the island. The high-visibility industrial promotion that Moscoso hoped would give credibility to his program instead became a nightmare of broken promises and bitterness.

*   *   *

While the Textron battle was being waged, Muñoz had to combat another negative campaign resulting from Moscoso's program: the image that Puerto Rico had become a haven for sweatshops taking advantage of the island's cheap labor. Through the course of Operation Bootstrap, Muñoz, the old socialist, would find it necessary to court organized labor in the United States, justifying Puerto Rico's industrial incentives, particularly the island's crucial exemption from federal minimum wage laws. At the end of his inaugural address on January 2, 1949, directing his remarks to the more than fifty U.S. industrialists and bankers whom Moscoso had brought to Puerto Rico plus scores of mainland reporters, Muñoz declared: "I want to state here as emphatically as possible, that among the incentives that we give to new investment for industrial development—the exploitation of labor, what in English is called 'sweatshop labor'—is not one of them."

But there were still deeper misgivings about Moscoso's program. By 1950 Puerto Rico was beginning to realize Tugwell's dream of economic and social planning. Tugwell's pride, the Puerto Rico Planning Board headed by Dr. Rafael Picó, organized an Economic Division to prepare long-range projections, mainly a ten-year plan. Moscoso considered this a major victory for his program. For the first time Muñoz and the legislature were presented with a picture of what was required from both the government and the private sector to achieve the administration's social and economic goals. An analysis of the previous ten years dramatized how crucial Moscoso's agency had become and brought into focus the need to give Fomento more funding if it was to meet its job-creating goals. But at the same time, the work done at the planning board revealed the magnitude of the forces being unleashed by Muñoz's peaceful revolution and by Moscoso's ability to drum up enthusiasm for Operation Bootstrap. The hope of industrialization had ignited a full-fledged "revolution of rising expectations" throughout Puerto Rico, setting into motion a massive migration from the country to the cities and grotesquely inflating the horrid slums that had appalled the Roosevelt New Dealers fifteen years earlier; the migration grew so huge that it spilled over the Atlantic to the slums of New York City.

The most consistent accusation against Moscoso was precisely his lack of long-range planning. Treasury Secretary Sol Luis Descartes, who led and lost the battle against Moscoso's tax exemption law, wrote in June 1950, "I am one who believes that in many instances the Company [Fomento] has acted too hastily. Long-term views have not received enough consideration ... Many mistakes have been made, but also a lot of good has been done."[12] Descartes, as well as Muñoz's chief of staff, Sánchez Vilella, were increasingly alarmed that while Moscoso had created "a pushing agency whose vigorous and bold actions have been a good stimulant in insular business and public life," he had become an increasingly dangerous loose cannon in the turmoil of Muñoz's peaceful revolution. In a seven-point list of the criticism generally made of Moscoso's program, in addition to the often-stated failures of the initial government-owned factories, Descartes included "quick turn-abouts in policies that reveal the lack of long-term, well-studied objectives." Moscoso was so focused on catching each prospective investor that he seemed to have no strategy. It was all, the critics argued, improvisation to make the catch.

Another frequent criticism of Moscoso was his "tendency to act on his own," losing the broad perspective of the island's program and its close tie to other public policies. It seemed to Descartes and others in the Muñoz administration that Moscoso believed that industrialization was the alpha and omega of government of Puerto Rico, whereas in fact Moscoso's program was creating a number of very significant social problems that had to be addressed. Moscoso insisted that Puerto Rico needed to place its limited resources more on fundamental development and on infrastructure and less on social, remedial, and welfare programs. But the migration of hundreds of thousands of Puerto Ricans to urban areas was making those welfare programs even more crucial. Moscoso's lack of planning, the critics continued, was aggravating the problem by allowing excessive concentration of new industries in the already-exploding San Juan area. Moscoso argued that it was hard enough to get an American executive to establish a plant and move his family to San Juan, let alone to an isolated rural area up in the central mountain range.

Puerto Rico's political leader, Luis Muñoz Marín, gave Moscoso and Operation Bootstrap his full support. But Muñoz was also deeply concerned about the effect of rapid industrialization on Puerto Rico's culture. By the end of the 1950s, Muñoz talked often about Operation Serenity, his goal to preserve the island's cultural values. Here he is seen lecturing an attentive Moscoso in 1959.

The most serious source of opposition to Moscoso, though, was difficult to define and express but deep and growing.

The old Puerto Rico was being destroyed; poverty and injustice were disappearing, but so were the *jíbaro* civilization that Muñoz had glorified often and the *jíbaro* values, the essential decency, tolerance, and generosity that had made life bearable for centuries. Muñoz's followers understood the idea of industrialization: the desirability of replacing inhuman, backbreaking, agricultural labor under the torrid sun with well-paid factory jobs. But the effect of what Moscoso was doing seemed to negate everything that Muñoz and the Populares stood for. As the critics pointed out from the very beginning, Fomento seemed to be a program of benefits, concessions, and privileges for the rich, the capitalists, the outside economic interests.

Responding to this, Moscoso wrote in 1953: "Government officials and policy makers, who are familiar with the traditions of their own area but unfamiliar with the traditions and conditions in advanced nations, often regard the steps necessary for industrial development as favors extended to a special class of persons. Thus necessary measures frequently become politically unpopular, and this opposition tends to slow the elaborations of a comprehensive and effective industrialization policy."[13] No, Moscoso insisted once again: he was not offering privileges but equalizers to overcome the many disadvantages of operating in Puerto Rico.

The solution to this philosophical and ideological conflict within the Popular Party, Muñoz concluded, was not only to keep Moscoso and his program under harness but also to give Bootstrap a clearly humanistic face.

"Being determined to produce, we must ask ourselves: Production for what?" Muñoz asked in his 1949 legislative message. "Production to serve what class of life? Economic productivity merely to produce, without an objective of life to guide it, can only lead in this modern world to greed for property and a twisting of the spirit . . . People do not exist for industrialization. Industrialization exists for the people."[14]

Puerto Rico was now seeing, in counterpoint to the economic takeoff of Operation Bootstrap, the beginning of a new movement that would become a major force in the 1970s and 1980s. This was, in Muñoz's thinking, the foundation of what he called in a series of lectures at Harvard University in the mid-1950s "Operation Serenity." It was not, he assured a skeptical Moscoso, antidevelopment. Instead it was an attempt to make the enormous economic and social force unleashed by Operation Bootstrap into a wise and intelligent agent, a servant and not a blind, mindless master of Puerto Rico's political and economic transformation.

Part

Three

How to Perform a Miracle

Puerto Rico . . . is the most hopeful example in the Americas
of how to develop an underdeveloped community in the
clean atmosphere of freedom.

Britannica Yearbook, 1962

Chapter 9

Industrial Promotion and Economic Research

Moscoso saw the new Economic Development Administration as a "giant conveyer belt" crossing the Atlantic from the U.S. east coast to Puerto Rico. The small "freight-forwarding" office he opened in New York in 1945 had become by 1955 the big, plush headquarters for Fomento's Continental Operations Branch, buzzing with young American and Puerto Rican marketing and public relations professionals.

The mission was to place as many prospects as possible on the conveyer belt to the island. Regional offices were set up in Miami, Chicago, and Los Angeles. The Continental Operations Branch was organized into three functions: industrial promotion, public relations, and advertising. In addition its goal was to increase the sale of Puerto Rican rums in the United States, a key source of tax rebate funds for the island. Marketing experts were hired to carry out the advertising and to direct the economists' preliminary screening of "leads." Moscoso was not overly concerned about whether those expressing a desire to visit the island were true potential investors or businessmen looking for a free Caribbean junket. His instructions were to throw out the widest net to catch the largest number of prospects possible. By mid-decade, the Continental Operations Branch had a staff of more than one hundred men and women in New York alone.

The heart of the mainland operation was Moscoso's carefully selected corps of salesmen, called "Industrial Representatives" or IRs, who were mostly young Puerto Ricans with educational and practical experience in business and attracted to public service. Moscoso knew from personal experience the obstacles these bright, eager IRs would face as they attempted to gain entry into the offices of investors and executives in order to "sell" Puerto Rico.

* * *

It was a quintessential New Englander by the name of Reid Weedon who along with Moscoso paved the way for the IRs. Back in 1945, long before the official reorientation from public to private industrialization, Moscoso began to dedicate a large part of his time to visiting potential manufacturing investors in the United States. To overcome his biggest problem, the absence of credibility, Moscoso asked the Arthur D. Little consultants, many of whom were MIT professors, to arrange the visits and to select one of their top professionals to accompany him. The assignment was given to Weedon, an articulate Bostonian who joined the firm in 1946. He was exactly the person Moscoso wanted by his side when visiting businessmen who confused Puerto Rico with the steaming tropical jungles of the Philippines or Central America.

"I wore out a lot of shoe leather for Puerto Rico tailspinning back and forth across this country and particularly up and down the streets of New York City, beating on doors to try to get people to understand that Puerto Rico was a part of the United States and a reasonable place to do business in," Weedon recalled decades later.[1]

Moscoso and Weedon were in fact pioneers in the art of industrial promotion. The first lesson emerged in 1947 after the insular legislature approved the first tax exemption law. The law was a worthless promotional tool unless it was backed by a high degree of trust in the government of Puerto Rico. According to Weedon, "It was crucial to assure the potential investors that if they met the standards of the law, they would get the exemption. Otherwise they were not willing to take the time to visit the island." The law was amended in 1948 specifically to provide for that assurance.

Weedon and Moscoso also discovered that they had a much higher probability of getting a favorable initial response from a firm run by a single, strong leader. Presentations made to committees often failed. Committees require consensus in order to make a difficult decision; once one person expressed opposition, Weedon said, that was always "the kiss of death for the project." There were simply too many reasons not to take the risk and also serious doubts about Puerto Rico's tax exemption program. Some said that it would not work, while others believed that the U.S. government would strike it down. On the other hand, when an interview went well with a strong leader, a confident entrepreneur, and when the "chemistry" with Moscoso was right, often there were openings and at least a willingness to consider Puerto Rico.

The Arthur D. Little experts advised Moscoso that he should make a special effort with Sylvania, the electronics manufacturer. After considerable effort, they got him an appointment with the president, Donald Mitchell. The goal was to convince Mitchell to visit the island. When Moscoso and Weedon walked into his office they were surprised and delighted to see that one of the paintings on the wall was of San Juan's massive eighteenth-century fortress, El Morro. They made reference to the "beautiful painting": Moscoso and Weedon grasped at this straw. "It was a very good opening," Weedon recalled. "He liked the painting so much that it provided us with a little light." The meeting went well, and Mitchell decided to follow up with subsequent explorations by his top management. In the end, however, Sylvania informed them it had decided against operating in Puerto Rico. It was not until a decade later, when Moscoso and his salesmen demonstrated to the company that several of its competitors already were taking advantage of the island's tax incentives, that Sylvania finally established a plant on the island.

Weedon became the prototype of Moscoso's future industrial representatives, making the contacts and accompanying the prospects on their visits to the island. One big plywood manufacturer, he recalled, seemed especially interested but insisted that to do business in any "Latin American" country required frequent bribes to government officials. Weedon attempted unsuccessfully to convince him that Puerto Rico was different. The man brought with him a thick wad of hundred-dollar bills for the expected payoffs. He returned to the mainland with all his bills. The islanders' honesty, though, proved not to be enough of an incentive; the investor decided not to locate in Puerto Rico.

Most of these early promotional efforts suffered the same fate. But Weedon never saw Moscoso's upbeat drive slow down: "He was a man with an idea a minute, some of them sensible, some of them not." Arthur D. Little had decided that one of its principal services to Moscoso—who by the end of the 1940s was the firm's largest client—was precisely to act as a brake on his more outlandish ideas and initiatives. "It was good," Weedon said, "that he had a lot of crazy ideas. . . . It stimulated us to keep on our toes and to keep looking at things we otherwise wouldn't have looked at."

One day Moscoso mentioned to Weedon the possibility of promoting a plant to manufacture buttons from freshwater clam shells. A quick investigation showed that this was a particularly labor-intensive activity. This was one idea that flourished: "It was the first time that an entire industry came to Puerto Rico," Weedon quipped.

Now, in the early 1950s, Moscoso asked Weedon and the Arthur D. Little staff to train the young men being hired as industrial representatives for the new Economic Development Administration. They were a key part of the large-scale operation that Moscoso was putting together, which proved to be a forerunner in the art of industrial promotion. There were several state governments, mostly in the South, that had established industrial development offices backed by advertising in specialized publications and direct mailings. But Moscoso organized a nationwide program that ranged from door-to-door selling to national advertising, sophisticated marketing, and aggressive public relations.

The Fomento process began with a media advertising and public relations campaign carefully designed to communicate a single idea: that Puerto Rico was the *only* part of the United States where industry can operate with 100 percent tax exemption from both local and federal taxes. The experience of brothers James and Gus Smith was a good example of the power of that idea.[2] Owners and operators of a nylon hosiery plant in Paducah, Kentucky, they had never heard of Puerto Rico. In late April 1949, they and another partner were returning by train to Kentucky after attending a trade show in Atlanta. Excited about the new machinery and materials they had seen and feeling good about their business, they talked loosely about expanding. Gradually they convinced themselves that they should really do it; the conversation turned to the location for a new plant. Tired, they were about to break up when there was a knock on the compartment door by a man selling newspapers and magazines. Gus Smith bought a copy of *Time*. On the cover was the newly elected governor of Puerto Rico, Luis Muñoz Marín, who was waging in an unlikely island in the Caribbean something he called the "Battle for Production." One of the Smiths leaned back and read the cover story. Suddenly he cried out: "I know where we will set up our new factory!"

"Where?" the startled brother asked.

"Puerto Rico! Listen to this." Smith proceeded to read the description of Fomento's tax incentives. The story mentioned that Puerto Rico had a resident commissioner in Washington. Why not, Smith asked, go on to Washington and visit the man? Gus gathered his things and the next day was in Dr. Antonio Fernós Isern's office. The following year, the brothers inaugurated their new plant, Señorita Hosiery Mills, in the small town of Gurabo.

Moscoso's IRs were armed with information and material on Puerto Rico — its "pro-business" government, the security of being part of the United States and under the jurisdiction of U.S. federal courts, plus the host of incentives, from prefabricated plant buildings at low rents to training of personnel to direct start-up subsidies. But what should have been obvious from the start now became glaringly evident to Moscoso and Weedon: the key to selling Puerto Rico did not depend on how much the island wanted or needed the new industry but on proving to the prospect that he and his company *needed* Puerto Rico to significantly improve earnings and meet the competition. Clearly, this kind of presentation required the IRs to be experts on both the companies they were targeting and Fomento's program. The industrial representatives were in fact the army of Operation Bootstrap.

One veteran IR recalled decades later:

> Even in the golden years of Fomento and Puerto Rico, it was never easy. We would always, of course, mention our government's commitment to reducing our very high unemployment. We described both our progress and our great problems because it was important, from the very first moment, to convince them the government was really pro-business and that the people themselves really welcomed them and their operation. But we were not appealing to their social conscience: our poverty and our unemployment were our problems. We were appealing to their bottom line. My goal was very precise: to somehow get that Chief Financial Officer, seated behind the desk, after looking at the tax advantages, to begin to ask himself, "Can I afford not to go to Puerto Rico? Will I miss the train if I decide not to go?"
>
> Tax exemption was the incentive that got their attention. There was no doubt about that. It's what got us through the door in the first place. That's why most of the time we were invited to see the financial officers. But we also learned not to come up front with our tax exemption package. Our message was not "Come to Puerto Rico to avoid taxes." It was "Come to Puerto Rico because it's a good business decision, because it makes business sense." Then, we would bring in the great benefit of tax exemption as the clincher. Of course, by the early 1960s, when we had many Fortune 500 companies in Puerto Rico, we then had the success stories, hopefully of competitors. That, needless to say, was a powerful tool. But by then we, in Fomento, were competing with many other industrial representatives from many state and regional governments, many representing foreign countries, all doing the same thing we were doing. Now we were after larger corporations and we had to deal with large management committees. Our success now depended on relentless follow-up. The Moscoso spirit of never giving up. So, to repeat, it was never easy.[3]

By 1957, of the total of 636 professionals and staff in the Economic Development Administration, 108 worked in the Continental Operations Branch. Of these, 53 were part of the industrial development section—28 industrial representatives and 25 support personnel. This was the U.S. end of Moscoso's giant conveyer belt. At the other end were the counterparts in Puerto Rico, the industrial development branch with a total staff of 111 persons, 16 of them "promoters."

Through the years, the Fomento people debated internally where and when a new industrial promotion took place—in the initial contacts made by the mainland operation, culminating in a visit to the island, or in the subsequent negotiations with the prospect that took place in Puerto Rico. The debate created within the organization a competitive spirit between the mainland and island-based IRs. Pushed relentlessly by Moscoso to increase the annual promotions and plant openings, the competition generated conflicts between what evolved, against Moscoso's intentions, into two distinct selling operations. The mainland IRs insisted that once an industrialist came to the island, the battle had been virtually won, so that Puerto Rico's was mostly a "mopping up" action. The island promoters replied that while the mainland IRs could give effective, compelling presentations of the wonders of the island, it was the local promoters who presented the investors with the real Puerto Rico. It was one thing to fill a CEO's head with beautiful photographs of island beaches and with statistical projections of huge profits; it was another to convince the management to make the final decision once the visiting investors saw for themselves the drawbacks and obstacles that also exist on the island.

*   *   *

Fomento soon learned how important it was to add the human touch to its clockwork organization. The combination was meant to answer favorably questions sure to trouble most visitors: Do I like this place, Puerto Rico? Do I like these people, Puerto Ricans? The answers to the questions began from the moment the Fomento promoter greeted the visitor at the airport.

"I believe that investors saw a special quality in everyone in Fomento with whom they came in contact," recalled Amadeo Francis, the St. Croix native who joined Fomento in 1955 as an industrial economist and was made director of the mainland operation two decades later.

> Yes, Moscoso drove us very hard: he was very demanding and impatient, but this had the effect of imbuing us with his boundless energy. It also had an inspirational impact on those of us who worked for him. Everyone at the agency wore the Fomento pin on the lapel or the dress; it was a true badge of distinction. It meant that you were someone special. We were the elite in the government, where all of us young

people wanted to be, where the action was. I cannot overstate what it meant to me, to all of us, the pride of being part of Fomento. We were not bureaucrats. Moscoso never allowed us to forget that there was nothing more important than what we were doing—we were creating jobs for unemployed Puerto Ricans. All of this was transmitted to the visitors.[4]

Francis could never forget Arturo Torres Braschi, who took his job "literally personally," Francis said. "When he went to meet a prospect at the airport, if he knew that the wife came along, he would take his own wife with a bouquet of flowers. The visitor was not met by a cold, official, government employee, by a bureaucrat, but by a friend and his wife. . . . Torres knew how to make him feel not just wanted, but good."

Francis pointed out, "It is important to remember what Puerto Rico was like in the mid-1950s. We wanted to take factories out to Mayagüez, about eighty miles from San Juan. But to make a telephone call from San Juan to Mayagüez, our third largest city, we had to make a reservation with the operator in the morning hopefully to get the call through in the afternoon."

*   *   *

Moscoso himself added to the problems of the San Juan operation with his famous excesses in selling Puerto Rico. Foremost was the endlessly repeated reference to the island as "Puerto Rico, U.S.A." Politically, it was true: Puerto Rico was under the American flag. As far as the prospects were concerned, it was vital to know that their investments and rights would be as protected by the laws and courts of the United States as anywhere on the mainland. But as soon as an American stepped off the airplane at the old naval base airstrip at Isla Grande after an eight-hour trip from New York City, he realized, often to his surprise, that he had entered a culturally foreign land.

At the same time, it was precisely Moscoso's ability to communicate with American businessmen that became Fomento's top asset. Within the Puerto Rican government Moscoso was called "the chart man." Unlike other members of the Muñoz cabinet, articulate men able to communicate their ideas with eloquence and emotion, Moscoso was one government official who gave extraordinary importance to big and colorful charts. To other cabinet members, it seemed he needed the visual aids due to his shortcomings as a speaker. He talked much too fast, tossed out too many figures and statistics, and quoted too many expert opinions. On the other hand, Moscoso's passion for high-powered visual aids served to reassure potential investors and to add to his air of professionalism. His concrete, to-the-point style was reassuringly free of Latin American-type posturing. As Weedon had learned years earlier, Moscoso had the ability to create bridges of credibility so sturdy that they withstood the unrestrained enthusiasm that often led to unchecked exaggerations.

* * *

By the mid-1950s, however, Moscoso and Fomento began to fall victim to their own success. It was now inaccurately assumed in Puerto Rico that Moscoso, the "super-salesman," had only to target a certain industry or a certain kind of industry and Fomento would surely bring it to the island. He was chastised for concentrating excessively on light industries; true, they created many jobs with relatively little investment, but on the other hand, these were volatile, insecure projects that seemed to leave as easily as they came. Moscoso, critics said, should concentrate more on bringing capital-intensive and thus more secure industries. The old argument that there was too little long-range strategic planning in Fomento was revived. After all, in his Operation Serenity, wasn't Muñoz talking about giving direction and purpose to the island's industrialization?

The fact was that Moscoso brought to the island whatever he could get. If he was a super-salesman, he was certainly not a magician. Getting *any* factory, light or heavy, integrated or not, was an achievement. But Moscoso could not continue to ignore the critics. He set out to bring to Fomento the best economists he could attract from both the mainland and the island and to organize the Office of Economic Research to provide strategic planning. One of its main goals was to give Fomento the economic data and statistics needed to go after the big game: America's "blue-chip" industries.

* * *

Walter K. Joelson knew that Puerto Rico was somewhere in the Caribbean, but he knew little else about the island. Born in Germany, he earned a Ph.D. in economics in Switzerland then in February 1948 immigrated to the United States to look for work. He quickly found employment in economic forecasting. However, within a year he felt bored and decided to find "more exciting work." He had befriended the Director of the Research Institute of America, Leo Cherne, who one day casually asked him, "Would you be interested in going to Puerto Rico?" His first reaction was that if Cherne were somehow involved with this island, there must be something exciting going on down there. Three days later, at the Fomento office in New York at 4 West Fifty-Eighth Street, Joelson met Moscoso.

"What struck me about him," Joelson recalled four decades later, "was a sort of electric quality about him: he generated enormous enthusiasm."[5] Moscoso invited him to join his new economic research team. Two days later, Joelson received a call from the Arthur D. Little Company's Dr. Gerald Tallman, who later was involved in founding MIT's Alfred P. Sloan School of Management. Tallman identified himself as a Moscoso advisor. He talked at length about the plans to greatly expand the scope of the Fomento program. Joelson realized that Tallman was also probing him: Moscoso was clearly double-checking his immediate, almost instinctive, job offer. Joelson knew that he passed Tallman's interview when, within a few days, he received a telephone call from San Juan asking how soon he could come down. It was late January 1949 and he could not leave until early June, but he agreed to study as much as possible about Puerto Rico. "The more I read, the more I asked myself, 'My gosh, what am I getting into?'" Joelson recalled.

Upon arriving in San Juan, he was pleasantly surprised by the quality of the other economists who had also been attracted to Puerto Rico. He found Harvard's Dr. Wassily Leontief and several colleagues performing pioneer work on input-output analysis. The Russian-born Leontief, who was to be honored in 1973 with the Nobel prize in economics, had been teaching economics at Harvard since 1931. In 1948 he was named director of the Harvard Economic Research Project on the Structure of the United States Economy.

At the University of Puerto Rico, Joelson also found Dr. Simon Ruttenberg, a labor economist from the University of Chicago who had been recruited to head the Social Science Research Center. Also from the University of Chicago was Dr. Harvey Perloff, who took a leave of absence as director of the university's Program of Education and Research in Planning to head the island planning board's new Economic Division. This was the agency that produced Puerto Rico's first ten-year economic development plan that proved vital to Moscoso's program.

Joelson met another Harvard economics professor, a tall, thin man who during the war served as deputy administrator of the U.S. Office of Price Administration and after the war headed the U.S. Strategic Bombing Survey. Dr. J. Kenneth Galbraith had been brought down along with other economists to conduct a study of the highly inefficient and costly food distribution system.

"All of a sudden," Joelson recalled, "I was fascinated to find myself hobnobbing with people whom I might never have come in contact with in the mainland United States. I, a relative newcomer to the Western Hemisphere, all of a sudden met people like Leontieff and Galbraith—and a man who had become very important in Puerto Rico, the head economist of the United States Trade Commission, a fellow named Ben Dorfman."

Instead of the lazy, sleepy tropical island he expected, Joelson found himself in an environment that another prominent American economist, Stuart Chase, compared to the effervescence in Washington in the early days of the New Deal. In a report published by the National Planning Association, Chase wrote: "When President Roosevelt was leading the crusade against unemployment and depression, young men çame to help him from all the universities, and idealism ran high. San Juan in 1951 reminded me in some ways of Washington in 1935."[6]

"Looking back at that era," Joelson recalled, "there were several things that were clearly important. Number one, the quality of the people . . . honesty in government, clean government was what jumped into your face." The people he saw in Fomento and the other insular agencies were not "a provincial clique that belonged to a party, had worked for the party, political war horses that were therefore rewarded with . . . government jobs."

But as impressed as Joelson was with the quality of the professionals, Puerto Ricans as well as "outsiders" like himself, he could not for a moment minimize the sheer magnitude of the task they had set for themselves. It made him seriously wonder if it would succeed. It all began with the island's population explosion, the bedrock problem identified by all visiting economists. Now Joelson was facing an equally difficult question. While the quality of the Puerto Rican leadership was unquestionable, what about the quality of the Puerto Rican workers? Would the productivity be so low as to wipe out the incentives that Fomento and his people were offering the potential investors? Joelson convinced his new boss, Santiago Díaz Pacheco, head of economic research, to allow him to visit every new factory systematically and spend long hours with the plant managers, reviewing carefully their successes and failures. Now Joelson confronted the magnitude of the down-to-earth realities of industrializing an undeveloped country. He observed the vast differences between the "wonderful numbers" of operating in the island—lower wages, tax breaks, the many other economic incentives offered by Fomento—and the real-life costs. "What made it difficult to run a factory was that when you needed, let's say, a machine tool engineer because your machine broke down, you couldn't find him. When you needed certain core services that every factory needs, they were not available in Puerto Rico. The customs of workers were quite different from the United States. Many more holidays. The women had a lot of children and that caused problems."

Joelson began to advise potential investors to avoid the mistake of sending to the island second-rate managers and equipment; rather, he argued, in order to take full advantage of the unique cost-saving conditions, they should send the very best people and the latest technology. Minimizing costs in anticipation of failure in Puerto Rico's exotic environment was in fact, he insisted, a leading cause of failure. "The quality of management, of supervision, of people who can deal with workers of a different culture, the quality of the people that built and planned the layout of the factories was all absolutely critical," Joelson recalled. On the other hand, he added, there were also companies that came to Puerto Rico with the mistaken attitude of "This is the way we do it in Fort Wayne, Indiana, and we're not going to do it one whit different in Cayey or Caguas." Joelson learned another lesson that he had to keep to himself because it ran contrary to Moscoso's style and philosophy. The future of Fomento, he believed, depended on its ability "to figure out what made sense" on the island—to identify and sell to that very thin slice of American manufacturing industries that possessed the right qualifications for success under Puerto Rico's unique conditions. And this in turn required Fomento's industrial representatives, beginning with Moscoso himself, to be absolutely objective in telling potential investors whether they should or *should not* consider operating on the island.

In 1952, Joelson was transferred to the New York office, where he took a huge gamble. He advised one interested company *not* to come to Puerto Rico. It happened to be the blue-chip firm Moscoso most coveted, indeed the firm Moscoso believed would give Operation Bootstrap the thrust needed to go after the other blue chips: General Electric.

When Joelson arrived in New York, he found that the Fomento staff had reached the conclusion that it was hopeless to continue knocking on General Electric's doors. "But Ted was not easy to dislodge from a certain plan or a certain idea, no matter how discouraging things were," Joelson said. "He went back over and over and over again. And it was this tenacity, in my opinion, that perhaps more than anything else was absolutely critical in trying to solve, or partly solve, the seemingly unsolvable economic problem that Puerto Rico represented."7

In one of his frequent trips to New York, Moscoso asked Joelson to take one more crack at General Electric. Joelson nodded and said he would try, but he had no idea of how to go about it. Then he had a stroke of "pure luck." While chatting with the secretary of Jack Snyder, the head of the Fomento mainland operation, she commented that she had run across the name of one GE executive who was described as "entrepreneurially oriented." She had written down his name: John Lockton. Joelson called his office, discovered that he was one of the company's treasurers, and was surprised when he came to the phone. Lockton listened for several minutes as Joelson went through his "story line" very quickly, then interrupted him: "I have an idea. I'll have someone call you back." Several days later, he received a call from Arthur Vinson, a vice president for manufacturing services, who said that he was interested in learning about Puerto Rico.

Joelson discovered one major reason why Fomento's efforts in the past had failed: the initial Fomento contacts had been channeled automatically to the international General Electric company, which was an export operation. Fomento's people would attempt to explain that they were not interested in buying anything from GE but in getting GE plants down to the island. The international operation had no interest in manufacturing in Puerto Rico. The Fomento initiatives invariably hit a solid wall. Now Joelson saw that Lockton had directed him to exactly the person Fomento needed to reach.

Vinson's responsibility was to improve GE's manufacturing cost competitiveness. Over lunch, Joelson was encouraged by Vinson's growing interest in Puerto Rico's economic incentives, beginning with tax exemption. Finally, Vinson invited him to make a presentation to a group of about fifteen manufacturing managers who were meeting in New York. Consulting first with Snyder, then with Moscoso, they agreed to do something different. This was clearly the opportunity Fomento had been looking for; Vinson was sympathetic, and now it was up to Fomento to make the sale. But instead of attempting to overwhelm the GE managers with a high-powered presentation led by Moscoso himself, with his battery of experts and charts, they agreed that Joelson should go alone. After the meeting he called an anxious Moscoso. How did it go? Joelson had absolutely no idea.

Several days later, however, Vinson called: "Walter, I have good news. One of the manufacturing guys is running an operation that is not doing well and he would like to go to Puerto Rico and consider making the product there." What product? Household clocks, Vinson answered. An appointment was made for Joelson to visit the troubled plant in Bridgeport, Connecticut. At the factory, Joelson found himself acting more as an in-house troubleshooter than a Fomento promoter. The more he observed the operation and the more he looked into the production costs and other financial data, the more evident it seemed to him that this project would not prosper in Puerto Rico. He called Vinson: "Art, I don't think it makes sense to make these clocks and timers there. I'm sorry." Vinson was incredulous. "Art could not believe that there was this outfit [Fomento] that has tried for years to get them to come to Puerto Rico, this guy was willing to come, and we tell him it's not a good idea," Joelson recalled. Moscoso was also incredulous when he heard Joelson's report; for once he was at a loss for words. But Joelson sensed Moscoso's thoughts: "How could you do this to me? Have we now lost GE forever?"

Joelson, in fact, won GE. Impressed by his and thus Fomento's integrity, Vinson kept thinking about Puerto Rico. He called Joelson again: Would he visit another plant in Plainville, Connecticut, that produced circuit breakers? Unlike the heavy wood clocks, the circuit breakers could be made totally on the island with minimal shipping costs. Most importantly, however, was Puerto Rico's large labor supply. The Plainville plant, already functioning at full capacity, was unable to expand to meet the expected increase in demand due to a labor shortage in the area. Vinson wanted Joelson to tell him if Puerto Rico offered "cost leadership" to this particular product. "I guess I asked the [Plainville plant] general manager about twenty questions," Joelson recalled, "on wages, man-hours per product, where the product will be sold, and on and on—then I took out a pen, we had no calculators in those days, made a few calculations and said: 'Mr. Gifford, I would judge that if you made these products in Puerto Rico that your costs would be about $675,000 less a year than what it costs you here—and that does not take into account tax exemption.'" Moscoso, finally, was about to get his first blue-chip plant.

*   *   *

Jerry Maldonado was assigned the General Electric promotion in Puerto Rico, the single most important catch in Fomento's history. He had joined Fomento in 1952, at a salary of $250 a month, just after graduating from the University of Alabama with a degree in industrial engineering.

From the beginning it was evident to Maldonado and Fomento that this was indeed a different level of promotion, the big leagues. Teams of GE managers and engineers flew in on company aircraft. "I met them at the airport and, days or weeks later, took them back to the airport," recalled Maldonado. "In between I did everything but sleep in the same room with them. We saw plant sites, we visited government agencies; whatever information they wanted, whomever they wanted to see, from the governor on down, I got it for them."[8] He was also impressed by how rapidly they made decisions. They knew exactly what they wanted. Their marketing studies and cost analyses had established the criteria that had to be met in order to proceed with the plant: the product required a high labor content but at the same time needed to be sufficiently standardized for relatively unskilled labor; the product had to be small in weight and bulk in order to reduce transportation costs; production volume should be high; and the machinery should require minimal skilled maintenance. Reasonable proximity of source of materials and markets also had to be assured with total transportation costs not exceeding 10 percent of shop costs. Special packaging required for marine shipment should not exceed 5 percent of manufacturing cost.[9]

On July 22, 1955, GE determined that the profitable manufacture of the circuit breakers was indeed possible in Puerto Rico. Less than two weeks later, on August 1, preliminary work on the project began. A team of five engineers and five clerks was organized to coordinate the planning, scheduling, procurement, methods selection, and preparation of the plant and utility layouts. A run-down, 88,000-square-foot industrial building, used and abandoned by a failed textile operation, was selected. The Fomento-owned building located in Palmer, twenty miles east of San Juan at the base of the road that climbs to El Yunque rain forest, was leased by the GE Realty Corporation. Organizational charts and job descriptions for all the positions were prepared. On December 1, all this material was submitted to the GE board of directors. On December 15, GE's board gave the green light to the Puerto Rico project.

Jerry Maldonado was offered the job of plant manager. "I accepted because it was a very big challenge. On one side there was this enormous, big, efficient, high-powered company with all these American executives and professionals coming down in company airplanes. On the other side were the sugarcane workers who we were going to recruit and somehow train to this work that required absolute precision. This was a test for Fomento, for Puerto Rico. Would these sugarcane workers be as productive as GE, Fomento, as all Puerto Rico needed them to be?"

While the plant building and surrounding areas were being extensively reconditioned, Maldonado had no place to conduct his interviews. He decided to use a 30-square-foot discarded safe that had been dragged out of the building. Inside he placed a small table and chair, and hundreds of men and women lined up outside for the interviews. With the exception of local GE President J. M. Whittenton and Assistant Treasurer W. R. Woodstock, everyone else was to be local. Some of the applicants were high school graduates; all the supervisors needed college degrees. "But what most pleased and impressed us, once the factory started, were precisely those men and women who had done nothing in their lives but work in sugarcane fields," Maldonado said. "It was a matter of motivation. They wanted to work. They wanted *very much* to work, and this made all the difference in the world."

The plant began production in mid-1956 with 190 full-time workers. The normal ten-week training period was accomplished in six weeks. The supervisors were trained in mainland factories. Most of the paperwork was translated into Spanish. New concepts in productivity improvement were designed and introduced into the operation. A new system of plastic parts molding was installed. The major overhaul of the plant site required building new power distribution and lighting systems; a humidity-controlled laboratory was also built. All the machinery was shipped in from the United States. "Yet," Maldonado recalled, "we were informed that we had set a record in establishing a new plant. Soon we were operating the plant twenty-four hours a day, seven days a week; we were up to 400 workers in four shifts. By the time I left the firm in the early 1960s, there were a thousand workers in the plant."

On May 8, 1956, Governor Muñoz Marín attended the plant's inauguration. To add drama and another newsworthy touch to the event, Moscoso had seen to it that this would be the four-hundredth Operation Bootstrap plant established on the island. He could not help but recall, still with a shudder, the terrible mistake he made a decade earlier when he took Muñoz to Fomento's new bottling plant and the political leader angrily broke away to escape the infernal noise of machinery and glass inside the factory.

Now Muñoz was taken into the brightly painted building with the surrounding land beautifully landscaped. There he saw the former farm workers on their stools along the production line, welding and assembling the breakers—the women operating the high-precision calibration machines, the men in the impressively modern, fully-equipped tool room. Everything needed to make the circuit breakers, Muñoz was informed by the GE officials, was done under that roof, from molding all the plastic and metal parts to the final precision testing. Also on hand for the ceremony were several young professionals and exchange students from India and several South American countries, visiting Puerto Rico under the U.S. Point Four program. Muñoz spoke enthusiastically to more than eight hundred guests at the event and afterward amiably posed with many of them and the employees who approached him.

"General Electric had great success in Puerto Rico," said Ignacio Rivera, GE's general manager for the Caribbean region in the late 1970s and early 1980s, who had previously worked for the U.S. Central Intelligence Agency after graduating from the University of Maryland.[10] "General Electric's great interest in Puerto Rico is easy to explain," Rivera added. "The island offered many of the advantages of the Third World, such as an abundant, relatively low-cost and eager-to-work labor force, but none of the disadvantages. Puerto Rico offered absolute political stability and a government that welcomed industrial investment with open arms. This was very important;

Americans felt accepted and wanted in Puerto Rico. Also important for GE was the availability of high-quality electric power and an ample water supply. All the elements were there. But what impressed the top people in GE, something I often heard, was the talent and training level of the Puerto Rican workforce, something that is very rare to find around the world. The Puerto Rican plants, mostly producing circuit breakers, fuses, and wall switches, were the most productive in all of General Electric."

* * *

The organization of the new Economic Development Administration in 1950 gave Moscoso the opportunity to expand greatly his own economic think tank. The statistical divisions of the Budget Bureau and the Department of Agriculture and Commerce were transferred to Fomento. He brought in Dr. Richard F. Behrendt from the International Development Bank and Colgate University. The Office of Economic Research filled the need for credible studies on the real costs of operating in Puerto Rico, particularly of energy and transportation, and most important, the analysis of real labor costs and worker productivity. This was part of the vital package of information requested by serious industrial prospects.

The Economic Research data also served to clarify the reasons for factory closings. Moscoso and the Fomento people heard the cries of local political leaders and legislators each time there were reports of a factory in difficulty. There were also rumblings from factory owners and operators that Fomento's interest in them and their problems seemed to diminish markedly after the plants were inaugurated. By 1955, the OER had been expanded to more than fifty professionals and staff members under the direction of Hubert Barton, one of Moscoso's closest collaborators, who became his alter ego.

"It is a mistake to believe that Fomento was a one-man operation," said Rafael Fábregas, Fomento's head of finance during the 1950s.[11] "Moscoso generated an endless flow of ideas for new projects, initiatives, programs. They were not the usual ideas that would occur to the rest of us. Many, perhaps most, of the ideas were novel, some outrageous. But he had all of us around him to pick up on these ideas and determine which would and which would not work. It was true team effort. We were all part of it. But the one person Moscoso most relied on—the one whose reaction he most respected— was Hu Barton."

Barton arrived in Puerto Rico in 1951 under a cloud of suspicion. He had been summarily fired from the U.S. State Department in 1947 the same day that his deputy, Carl Marzani, was indicted for having lied about membership in the American Communist Party. Barton went to Washington in 1934 as one of the young idealists eager to be part of Roosevelt's New Deal. A magna cum laude graduate from Maine's Bowdoin College with a master's degree in economics from Amherst College, he was hired by the Federal Research Board, where he performed analyses and studies on productivity, manpower, and labor relations. At the outbreak of World War II, Colonel William "Wild Bill" Donovan recruited him for the Office of Strategic Services. Barton was put in charge of a large staff of artists, architects, and film technicians whose mission was to prepare visual presentations for both internal and public purposes. After the war, Barton's division prepared the visual evidence against the accused at the Nuremberg trials and the San Francisco United Nations Conference. When the OSS was disbanded and many of its staff moved to the CIA, Barton was transferred to the State Department. He took with him his deputy, Marzani, a Williams College graduate and former fellow at Oxford University whom he had recruited back in 1942. According to Marzani, when Barton hired him he was aware of accusations of Communist sympathies made by Marzani's former Williams College professors. But Marzani gave Barton his word that he was no longer a member of any Communist organization. Years later, he speculated that Donovan knew of his past Communist associations, as this explained why the Office of Strategic Services deliberately circumvented FBI clearance; Marzani added that "it didn't hurt that Donavan despised J. Edgar Hoover." When Marzani became one of the targets of Senator Joseph McCarthy's investigation of Communist infiltration in the State Department, Barton came to his defense.

Barton was dismissed "for the good of the Service" the same day that Marzini was formally indicted. There were no charges against Barton for violating security laws; instead he was cited for "administrative irregularities." In Barton's mind there was no doubt about the true reason for his abrupt dismissal: the State Department knew that Barton intended to testify in Marzani's favor. Although there was nothing official questioning his loyalty and although he had never been associated with a Communist group, Barton was certain that he was blacklisted as a fellow traveler.

Unable to make a living in Washington, Barton and his family moved to Puerto Rico in 1951 to work with the Puerto Rico Planning Board economist, Alvin Mayne. Barton was to remain on the island for the rest of his life. Through the years, he and members of his family continued to be occasionally visited by FBI agents who questioned them about former government officials with Communist connections. Shortly before he joined Fomento in 1954, FBI agents had informed Governor Muñoz that Barton had been linked with the Alger Hiss case. In fact, Barton's only contact with

Hiss was a chance meeting during the preparation for the UN conference in San Francisco. The most "radical" thing he had done in his college days was to vote for Norman Thomas of the Socialist Party. For Muñoz, Moscoso, and others in Puerto Rico, the lingering cloud of suspicion as to Barton's loyalties had a touch of the bizarre. Since joining Fomento as Operation Bootstrap's chief economist and one of Fomento's most effective boosters, Barton was seen as being as conservative and pro-business as Moscoso himself.

Unconcerned about Barton's controversial background, Moscoso named him director of Fomento's Office of Economic Research in 1954. Trim, athletic, with a boyish crew cut, an avid scuba diver and naturalist, Barton shared Moscoso's dynamic single-mindedness. Barton had to temper the natural inclination of professional economists to see the dark side, particularly when viewing Puerto Rico's economic realities, with Moscoso's relentless optimism. This was all the more challenging to Barton because he had focused much of his interest and expertise in measuring the structure and full extent of Puerto Rico's fundamental and difficult problem—its real, not statistical, unemployment. Puerto Rico's low labor participation rate, explained in part by the mushrooming young population growth, revealed that statistical unemployment fell far short of the real situation because a large number of Puerto Ricans simply withdrew from the labor market by not actively looking for work. Once they withdrew, they were no longer counted among the unemployed.

"Barton was a unique personality in the atmosphere that Moscoso had created in Fomento," Amadeo Francis, who worked for Barton in the mid-1950s, recalled years later. "Whereas Moscoso was always rushing here and there, always with documents and reports under his arm, always behind his schedule, running to get something done or get to some meeting, Barton was incredibly deliberate, as in slow motion. Whenever he had to write something it became a ritual: his secretary would place the exact same number of pencils and pads on his desk and close his office door. Every word, and of course, every number, seemed to Barton to be a matter of life or death. At times I saw how he wrote and erased a word again and again until it was exactly right."

It was in Fomento's fight to preserve tax exemption that Barton's figures proved most helpful.

The tax exemption period authorized in the 1948 law expired in 1962. In the late-1950s Muñoz and the Populares had to decide whether to extend the tax exemption program. Treasury Secretary Sol Luis Descartes and his own team of anti-exemption economists had never accepted defeat. Now they began a new assault. Back in 1947 and 1948 Moscoso had clamored for tax exemption as a temporary tool to get Bootstrap going. Indeed, the law itself referred to the incentive as temporary. But Descartes knew that Moscoso was now after more than an extension of the law. Just as they had warned Muñoz, Descartes argued, once a government falls into the trap of this kind of incentive, it simply cannot escape. Moscoso was now demanding a fixed ten-year period of full tax exemption for all qualifying industries, regardless of when they applied for the incentive. Under the existing law, the length of the exemption period depended on the years remaining before the law's expiration. Descartes believed that Moscoso had made his program and Puerto Rico's economic future totally dependent on this bad policy. Now he was convinced that Moscoso was determined to make the tax exemption program permanent.

In 1948 Moscoso had successfully used his personal power of persuasion with Muñoz. Anticipating an even fiercer attack, Moscoso now turned to Barton and his think tank. This was Amadeo Francis's first assignment when he joined Fomento in 1955: to provide Barton and Moscoso with the statistical ammunition needed for the coming grand battle over tax exemption. In their view, the cold numbers should have decided the issue once and for all. The impact of the 1948 tax exemption law was indisputable. The number of factories promoted by Fomento jumped from ten in fiscal 1948 to thirty-one the following year. By mid-1955 Fomento was rushing toward its four-hundredth plant.

The Barton operation churned out a flow of data that left no doubt that it was precisely tax exemption that provided the lift for the island's remarkable economic takeoff: net income from manufacturing had reached $122.5 million in fiscal 1953, an increase of nearly 100 percent in the previous decade. Per capita income had increased from $122 in fiscal 1940 to $433 in 1953. Manufacturing employment had almost doubled to 59,700; of those jobs, 70 percent were in Fomento-promoted plants. Barton's office made the "conservative" estimate that Operation Bootstrap had already directly and indirectly created 50,000 new jobs.

But Descartes countered with a scholarly work by his own economist, Dr. Milton Taylor, who painstakingly attempted to refute Moscoso's and Barton's campaign.

The Descartes-Taylor team aimed their attack, however, not just at the specific, technical issue of tax exemption but also at Fomento and Operation Bootstrap. The euphoria that Moscoso, Barton, and the Fomento publicity machine had created to make Puerto Rico believe that Bootstrap would solve the island's economic problems was not only false, they declared, but

TRIO KNITTING CORP.
otra
FABRICA
del programa de
FOMENTO

To overcome the centuries-old sense of hopelessness and futility, Moscoso plastered big Fomento signs with a worker pushing the Fomento wheel throughout the island. By the late 1950s, these signs were seen as synonymous with progress: they were displayed with pride by both factory owners and local political leaders.

also a dangerous self-delusion. While there was no question that the island was undergoing a period of economic recovery and that the principal factor was industrialization, Taylor argued that it was simply not true that it was due to tax exemption. Instead, the cause was a fortuitous combination of factors; the two most important ones were Puerto Rico's abundant cheap labor in a period of labor shortage on the mainland and its security as part of the U.S. monetary and legal systems.

The opponents attacked what they considered the insidious effect of Moscoso's and Barton's barrage of glowing statistics. These were seen as creating a dangerous mirage that, in turn, was allowing overly optimistic island leaders to ignore Puerto Rico's problems.

No one disputed that Moscoso was a master salesman able to sell the advantages of Fomento's program not only to outside investors but also to Muñoz and the Puerto Rican people. He installed huge billboards in front of all the factories in operation announcing, "Another Fomento plant." The Fomento logo became the symbol of progress in all the island towns.

But Descartes, Taylor, and other economists believed that all this was really a cosmetic face-lift and not the fundamental economic restructuring that Puerto Rico needed. Taylor wrote: "[M]ore realistically, the new industrial plants should perhaps be compared to the old-fashioned false shirt-front, or a good layer of makeup on a rather plain feminine face."[12] Behind Moscoso's public relations and hype, Puerto Rico's reality was still ugly: 70 percent of all island families had annual incomes of less than $500. Yes, the numbers of new factories were exciting and impressive, but Taylor was quick to point out that it was only toward the mid-1950s that a handful of stable industries had been brought to the island: two oil refineries plus several plants built by well-known firms such as Sylvania, U.S. Rubber, and Mead Corporation.

For the most part, according to Descartes's troops, tax exemption's main success was getting the attention of "hobo industries." Most of them "were small and labor-oriented and, at best, represented entrepreneurial mediocrity. At worst, they were a motley group of entrepreneurial migrants, some of which were frankly attracted by low-cost labor and a tax holiday" (Taylor, 13).

In the end, however, Moscoso, Barton, Francis, and the other Fomentarians—Sam Van Hyning, Al Mayne, Morris Moses, Robert Fullmer, Alex Firfer, Larry Berlin—survived the new assault on their program. On December 15, 1953, Governor Muñoz Marín approved an extension for another ten-year period.

*   *   *

Moscoso learned still another lesson: he could win battles, some of them crucial, but the war against Operation Bootstrap was permanent. In 1956, while Moscoso and Fomento were excitedly preparing to inaugurate the first General Electric plant, he received another troubling request from Muñoz. The political leader, Moscoso saw, had entered another anxiety bout over Fomento. The governor suggested that Moscoso begin to seriously consider the effects of dropping tax exemption. He should include in his projections for 1964 to 1974 an analysis of what would occur without the incentive.

Moscoso asked one of the Office of Economic Research economists, David Ross, who had come over from the University of Puerto Rico, to prepare the report. Ross did not foresee an immediate exodus of the existing industries. Those that were not profitable would have nothing to gain by relocating to the mainland because they would not, in any event, pay any taxes. Those that were highly profitable would probably remain because their earnings would still be higher on the island than on the mainland. The huge effect, Ross predicted, would be in the promotion of new industry. Ross made the "very conservative estimate" of a 50 percent decline in new plant promotion, resulting in the loss of 108,000 new jobs, which in turn would mean a loss of $1 billion in Puerto Rico's net national income.

The grim predictions in the Ross study impressed Muñoz but not such critics of Moscoso and tax exemption as Dr. Milton Taylor. Taylor's *Industrial Tax Exemption in Puerto Rico,* published in 1957, began by expressing amazement that the island had followed a development strategy based on tax forgiveness in view of "the reputation of tax exemption as a perverse, inequitable, and even unethical devise" (4). The Fomento critics were implacable.

*　　*　　*

Moscoso was unrelenting in attempting to clear Hubert Barton's name in Washington. In April 1961, after leaving Fomento to accept the post of U.S. Ambassador to Venezuela, Moscoso asked Barton to join him in Caracas. Barton turned down the offer believing that his appointment would be rejected for security reasons and that it would hurt Moscoso's new career. When in November 1961 President Kennedy named Moscoso coordinator of the Alliance for Progress, he again tried to hire Barton. Moscoso finally discovered indirectly that Barton was off the blacklist. Barton's wife, Marie, was investigated for a federal post in the Atomic Energy Commission program in Puerto Rico that required security clearance. When she received her clearance, the Bartons felt confident that, at long last, the cloud of suspicion over him had dissipated, that in their lives the McCarthy Era had finally come to an end. Moscoso was now free to recruit his services in the Alliance for Progress.

Chapter 10

How to Change an Abysmal Image

The Manhattan girl, homesick for her native Puerto Rico, cries out plaintively, "Puerto Rico, you lovely island."

Anita objects: "Puerto Rico, you ugly island . . . . I left the tropical diseases . . . , always the hurricanes blowing and the population growing and the babies crying and the bullets flying."

Homesick girl: "Hundreds of flowers in full bloom." Anita: "Hundreds of babies in each room."

Homesick girl: "I'd like a few weeks in San Juan."

Anita: "If there's a road you can drive on."

Homesick girl: "I'll bring a TV to San Juan."

Anita: "If there's a current to turn on."

The hit musical *West Side Story* opened on Broadway on September 26, 1957. Three decades later, during a televised recording of his extraordinarily successful work, composer Leonard Bernstein lowered his head for several moments after the "I Want to Live in America" scene ended, and while the singers, musicians, and technical personnel stood by anxiously, he murmured in obvious satisfaction, "This is my favorite."

For generations of Puerto Ricans these lyrics were both insulting and untrue. Of course, Puerto Rico was economically backward and teeming with people. But no Puerto Rican had ever heard another refer to their homeland as "you ugly island." Indeed, islanders who migrated to New York and other American cities nurtured a romanticized vision of the island paradise they left behind.

Moscoso asked Fomento's public relations man, Scott Runkle, to try to get these lines eliminated or changed. The producers, Runkle quickly discovered, would not hear of it. For the millions of people throughout the world who listened to the musical—translated into their native languages, from Malay to German to Japanese—or who saw the 1962 movie that won ten Oscars including best film of the year, this was the indelible image of that small island in the Caribbean called Puerto Rico. An ugly island of crying babies and flying bullets, a primitive jungle without roads or electricity or even "anything to keep clean." Little wonder Anita preferred the New York slum.

The abysmal image of Puerto Rico in *West Side Story* highlighted another major obstacle facing Moscoso and Fomento. Clearly this was not the glowing place in the Caribbean pictured in Moscoso's promotional advertisements as Puerto Rico, U.S.A., not the place for Americans to invest their money or send executives and their families to live. And certainly these warring, knife-wielding Puerto Rican gangs were unlike the legions of supposedly disciplined workers desperate to find jobs.

To be sure, extreme poverty in Puerto Rico was all too real and ugly. Before New York's Spanish Harlem, there was San Juan's El Fanguito— "the Little Mudhole"—the sea of wood, cardboard, and tin shacks extending two miles along the Martín Peña canal, "the disgrace to the American flag" that President Roosevelt had ordered Rexford Tugwell to eliminate.

Fomento needed to dispel the dismal image that posed such an enormous threat to Bootstrap. It was, of course, not just *West Side Story*. The magnitude of the task was well illustrated in a *Life* magazine story back in 1943: "There are few places in the world," *Life* reported, "with slimier slums and more acute poverty."[1] Typically, the magazine laid the blame on U.S. neglect: a "shocking disgrace to the United States . . . the cesspool of Puerto Rico has been festering in our backyard for over forty years." The headline captured Puerto Rico's centuries of hopelessness: "Puerto Rico: Senate Investigating Committee Finds It an Unsolvable Problem." The large photos above and on the following six pages told the grim story; they were mostly of El Fanguito—mud, pigs, children with garbage all around, two men carrying baby bodies in tiny coffins to burial. The story was critical of Governor Tugwell, suggesting that he had done little but create a futile bureaucracy (a 20 percent increase in insular government jobs in just one year) and depicting him as defeated. "Even the idealistic Tugwell is beginning to admit that Puerto Rico and some of his reforms are incompatible. Even the best economic theory needs an economic base to make it work and Puerto Rico has none."

The problem in attempting to counter the *West Side Story* stereotype was also the attitude and prejudices that resulted from the massive migration of poor Puerto Ricans, most from the island's rural areas, to New York and other East Coast cities.

By the mid-1950s, the migration rate had surpassed fifty thousand a year.

The number of islanders on the mainland grew by nearly six hundred thousand in this decade. The real-life Puerto Ricans invading the streets and subways of New York were seen as foreign, backward, messy, loud, and undisciplined. Whereas in the past Puerto Rico's plight evoked a sense of pity and, in some, a sense of guilt, now the massive migration triggered revulsion.

How could this awful image be turned around?

A golden opportunity had presented itself back in early 1949 when newly elected Governor Muñoz Marín asked Moscoso and his agency to organize his inauguration. Moscoso jumped at the chance to insert into the gala affair a strong Fomento flavor and to convert it into a positive media event. Moscoso and his people made the most of it. The U.S. media coverage of the January 2, 1949, event targeted not only the swearing-in of an elected governor for the first time in nearly five centuries and the outpouring of emotion of the "greatest crowd in the history of this Caribbean island" but also the launching of an ambitious industrialization program. What made it all news was that it was so unexpected. The *New York Times* ran the story on its front page and carried additional stories for three consecutive days. One described the impressive list of more than fifty top American business leaders in attendance, including presidents of several major banks and brokerage houses; David Rockefeller led a delegation from the Chase National Bank, Beardsley Ruml led another from Macy's. Moscoso organized a six-day program of recreational affairs, picnics, and beach parties that were in fact Fomento promotional events. A third story described the inauguration of a new $10 million, 11,000-kilowatt hydroelectric plant. This was no typical Caribbean fiesta.

For Moscoso and his communications people it was a resounding public relations coup. They had convinced the major U.S. print media that there was another Puerto Rico, starkly different from the dirty, lazy, squalid island of old. Puerto Rico was now alive, bursting with growth and optimism. A *New York Times* story on January 4, 1949, captured the mood: "Puerto Rico dedicated its great Caonillas Dam today as the major link in a power system being developed as the hub of a movement to change the island from an agricultural to an industrial economy."

Moscoso's biggest public relations triumph, however, was the January 24, 1949, issue of *Life*. The magazine came out with a nine-page spread: "A New Puerto Rico Shows Off." Its enthusiastic report clearly revealed the Fomento spin. "Hardheaded businessmen, skillfully entertained and indoctrinated at the inaugural parties saw what Governor Muñoz was talking about when he said that the island is now a good place for investment and industry. They also saw Puerto Rico's seamy side, which other visitors have seen, deplored and despaired for half a century. It still looked bad. But Governor Muñoz said there was a good time coming and most were inclined to believe him."

Life's sparkling story was a milestone for Muñoz and Moscoso, especially after the horrendously negative report published by the magazine six years earlier. Referring to its previous story, *Life* reported: "The Island begins to find answers for its old 'unsolvable problem.'" Instead of El Fanguito, there were photos of seemingly endless rows of new private housing, new industrial plants, three hundred workers being trained at the university to operate modern machine tools, and Muñoz talking intensely to bankers and businessmen.

The story described Muñoz's own transformation from a "Greenwich Village poet" to a capital investment promoter for his island. "During the round of parties before and after his inauguration, Muñoz busily talked with every well-known visitor who might put in a plug for Puerto Rico or make an investment there." Those Moscoso-generated stories had the effect of creating a new image for Muñoz, who now basked in all this favorable publicity as the man producing Puerto Rico's economic miracle. *Time* magazine, in a subsequent cover story, dubbed him the Bard of Bootstrap. Moscoso, of course, knew that he, not Muñoz, was the engine that drove Bootstrap. But the national projection of Muñoz as the force behind the economic changes served Moscoso's and Fomento's purposes by turning both Muñoz and his enormous political power into the virtual captive of this very image. In advertising terminology, it "positioned" Muñoz in U.S. and eventually world public opinion as pro-business and pro-industry.

Public relations, media relations, image-building now moved to the heart of the Fomento program.

*   *   *

The public relations firm that helped Moscoso achieve the 1949 publicity coup had been hired in early 1948. The Hamilton Wright organization, which *El Mundo* owner Angel Ramos recommended to Moscoso, was hired for three years at a cost of $375,000. Muñoz expressed the concern that while he understood Moscoso's desire to have Puerto Rico painted as a paradise in order to attract investors and visitors, "we must take care that this does not lead to the belief that we do not need any help."[2] The media campaign, Muñoz told the public relations men, should candidly describe the many difficult problems on the island, but it should project also the image of a people who had been aroused from centuries of listlessness and hopelessness and now were working feverishly to overcome their problems within a democratic system. "The help we need," Muñoz added, "should not be portrayed as that of a beggar, but that of a virile people in difficult circumstances—help earned by anyone that courageously faces his problems." Knowing Moscoso's tendency to exaggerate, Muñoz gave him clear guidelines: improve our image, but don't get carried away.

Hamilton Wright gave Muñoz and Moscoso a detailed media plan that included not just newspaper and magazine stories but at least five news stories in cinema newsreels plus several feature stories on the island. Wright went further: he guaranteed that his agency would generate newspaper and magazine news stories worth more than seven times the annual cost of the contract, that is, worth over $875,000 in advertising. He backed his guarantee, declaring that if the agency fell short, Puerto Rico could withhold a corresponding percent of the fee. Wright also agreed to establish a news bureau in Fomento that would generate the flow of stories to American media and tend to visiting journalists.

*   *   *

Several years later, in 1955, Moscoso made what turned out to be another crucial decision. He hired a Scotsman, David Ogilvy, founder of one of Madison Avenue's top advertising firms. It did not take Ogilvy long to discover that more than a well-planned media campaign was needed to counter the island's still negative image. What was needed, Ogilvy quickly concluded, was a communications miracle.

Ogilvy and Moscoso were similar in various ways. They were cultured and creative yet result-oriented. Both measured success in terms of what worked. And both were, in their individual ways, elitists, determined to travel first-class through life. The son of a classics scholar and a broker, Ogilvy dropped out of Oxford University to work as a chef in a French restaurant and later as a stove salesman. Like Moscoso, he had difficulty discovering his vocation. He was in his thirties when he joined a British advertising agency and was sent for training to the United States, where he became a fierce advocate of scientific research. During World War II, Ogilvy worked for British Intelligence under the famous William Stephenson, code-named "Intrepid." In 1949, at the age of 38, Ogilvy founded his own advertising agency on Madison Avenue. He did so, he wrote in 1983, because he didn't think that an established agency such as Young and Rubicam would hire him. "How many advertising agencies would hire a 38-year-old man whose curriculum vitae read: Unemployed farmer, former cook and university drop-out?" he wrote.[3] He quickly gained a reputation for outstanding, creative copy. During the following three decades the Ogilvy agency become one of the four largest in the world. In his memoirs Ogilvy noted that the agency had no fewer than 249 vice presidents, 67 senior vice presidents, 8 executive vice presidents, 3 presidents, and 2 chairmen, working in 140 offices in 40 countries. Ogilvy also confessed that nothing had given him more personal satisfaction than working with Moscoso to change Puerto Rico's image.

"The first time I saw Ogilvy," Moscoso recalled, "he made a very negative impression on me."[4] It was in 1951, when the agency was a small, "creative Madison Avenue boutique." Ogilvy struck Moscoso as arrogant, a stereotypical British snob. "I thought we had a good story to tell. We were not there begging him to do something for nothing." Moscoso, in fact, was offering a million-dollar budget to initiate a Puerto Rico rum advertising campaign throughout the United States. Yet Ogilvy seemed uninterested. Reid Weedon of Arthur D. Little, who organized the rum project and suggested to Moscoso that he visit several agencies before assigning the account, accompanied Moscoso. He recalled years later that Ogilvy, puffing on his pipe, turned his back on Moscoso, swinging around in his swivel chair to stare out of the window. Moscoso continued talking to Ogilvy's back for several seconds, then quickly got up to leave. "I thought that he was incredibly rude," Moscoso recalled years later. Now he snapped at Weedon as they walked out of the office. "We're not going to hire him." The campaign was given to McCann Erickson. Weedon called Ogilvy a few days later and mentioned the incident; Ogilvy said that he was surprised to hear that he had irritated and offended Moscoso. But Ogilvy made clear that he was not at all distressed at having lost this potential client.[5]

In his memoirs, Ogilvy attributed his career success in large part to his determined drive to come up with "the big idea"—a decisive advertising concept that would last for years or even decades—of course keeping the big clients happy. He could make another claim: "There are better copywriters than I am, and scores of better administrators, but I doubt if many people have matched my record as a new business collector." Ogilvy set out to secure contracts with the giant advertisers—General Foods, Lever Brother, Bristol Myers, Campbell Soups—and he won them all. In time, he wrote, he added others to his "hit" list: American Express, Sears Roebuck, Merrill Lynch, and IBM. When he turned his back on Moscoso in 1951, little, impoverished Puerto Rico was not on that list.

Moscoso returned four years later, however. Always meticulous in his choice of clothing, he had noticed in several national magazines the striking ads for Hathaway, the Waterville, Maine, shirt manufacturer, that featured an elegant male model with an eye patch. "This was clearly the work of a media genius," Moscoso said, "and I made a note to find out who was behind it."[6] When he learned that it was Ogilvy, Moscoso decided to ignore the unfortunate incident and visit him again, this time with his hard-nosed deputy, Guillermo Rodríguez. "I believe that this time I was able to communicate something different to Ogilvy," Moscoso said. "I told him that he would have the personal satisfaction, not of knowing that Hathaway sold one million more shirts because of your ad. No! You are going to get the satisfaction of knowing that one hundred fifty thousand kids in Puerto Rico were going to be able to go to school because your ad sold so much rum, bringing so much in rebates to the Puerto Rican Treasury to be used for the public schools. That, I think, finally captivated him."

Ogilvy invited Moscoso to his home in Connecticut; he had an idea he wanted to discuss in an informal atmosphere. "I told Moscoso that this—substituting a lovely image of Puerto Rico for the squalid image which now exists in most mainlanders' minds—was of prime importance to his industrial development, rum industry, tourism and to its political evolution." He said, "First we must decide what we want Puerto Rico to be in the future. An old Spanish colony, asleep in the sun? A bridge between the United States and Latin America? An industrial beehive? An island in renaissance?

"I argued," Ogilvy went on, "that it was of overriding importance to *correct* this image and Moscoso agreed. The campaign I created had that basic purpose, even when it was camouflaged as advertising for tourism and rum. As far as I know, it is the only case of advertising being used to change the image of a country." They talked deep into the night. Ogilvy's wife would interrupt them to serve what they considered good daiquiris. At one point, Moscoso pulled out his small pad and made a note, commenting: "I will send you a box of *good* limes." Ten days later, Ogilvy recalled, "they arrived in an old shoe box."

The first ad that Ogilvy wrote for Puerto Rico's industrial promotion in 1955, Ogilvy recalled, "was wholly without creativity—nothing but words. Nobody has ever congratulated me on it. But judged by results, it was the best advertisement I have ever written. Fourteen thousand people cut, filled out and mailed the coupon included in the ad: they all wanted more information about doing business in Puerto Rico."

Each effective ad, according to Ogilvy, must have a "hero." The hero in this ad was the famous Bearsley Ruml assuring American business that there were very big profits to be made in Puerto Rico. "Now Puerto Rico Offers 100% Tax Exemption to New Industries" was the full-page headline in big, bold letters. In the center of the text appeared a chart describing the actual effect of tax exemption: a net profit of $485,500 after federal taxes becomes $1 million in Puerto Rico—a gain of 106 percent. At the other end, a net profit of $17,500 in the United States becomes $25,000 in Puerto Rico, a gain of 43 percent. In addition, the ad continued, the industrialist would live in an island "paradise . . . the swimming, sailing and fishing, are out of this world, and your wife will rejoice to hear that domestic help is abundant."

Besides the bottom-line hard sell, Ogilvy injected into the ad what became his own, personal missionary zeal: "You will also find it immensely stimulating to be a part of Operation Bootstrap: to share in the upsurge of one of the fastest growing communities in the Western Hemisphere. This is, perhaps, Puerto Rico's finest hour. And the United States manufacturers who decide to become a part of it will not go unrewarded, financially or spiritually."

The evening at his home in Connecticut convinced Ogilvy that there was a chemistry between Moscoso and himself, which was absolutely essential for a successful communications program. Years later he wrote in *Confessions of an Advertising Man* that publicity that leads to "fame and fortune have resulted from the partnership of two men—a sure-footed copywriter and an inspiring client." Ogilvy was certain that they formed that partnership. His secret was being able to really appreciate just what the client wanted, at times better than the client himself. Moscoso was a man of action; he wanted no-nonsense ads that went straight to the investors' guts. Ogilvy gave Moscoso exactly what he wanted, but he needed to go beyond. He asked Moscoso key questions: What is Puerto Rico? What is its personality? What is its essence? Is Puerto Rico no more than a backward country in the throes of its industrial revolution? Ogilvy was not satisfied with the enormous challenge of selling Puerto Rico as a profitable industrial site; he wanted to discover, depict, and sell Puerto Rico's "soul." He latched on to the word "renaissance." What was happening on the island, his ads implied, went much deeper than building roads and clearing the slums: it was the reawakening of an old and rich culture.

*   *   *

The person who could embody Ogilvy's concept of a Puerto Rican renaissance had already arrived on the island. For Ogilvy and Moscoso it was an extraordinary stroke of good luck. Pablo Casals, the internationally known cellist, composer, and conductor, the admired symbol of the resistance to Generalissimo Francisco Franco's dictatorship in his native Spain, had decided to reside in Puerto Rico. In late 1955, the seventy-nine-year-old Casals visited Puerto Rico for the first time. He was curious and nostalgic about the stories his mother, Pilar Defilló, had told him about the sleepy island in the tropics where she had been born and reared. A few weeks later Moscoso received a call from Governor Muñoz. Would he and Gloria come over for dinner at La Fortaleza? Muñoz had invited three or four other couples to spend the evening with the legendary Casals and Marta Montañez, his Puerto Rican student.

That evening Casals informed Muñoz of his decision to establish his residence in San Juan. His visit to the island, arriving from France on the ocean liner SS *Flandres* on December 11, 1955, was a major news event. His mother had left Mayagüez and Puerto Rico at the age of eighteen and moved with her family to Vendrell, a small town near Barcelona, never to return again. There she married a musician and gave birth to eleven children, five of whom died young. Pau Casals (Pablo's Catalan name) had idolized his mother, who died in 1931 at the age of seventy-seven.

But there was another reason for Casals's first visit. He had fallen in love with the beautiful nineteen-year-old student, Marta Montañez, a brilliant Puerto Rican cellist who bore a resemblance to his mother. He had met her at the music festival in Prades, France; four years later she returned as one of his select students. He was stunned to learn that Marta's mother had been born in the same house as his mother, in the city of Mayagüez on the island's west coast. An unusually well-organized young woman, fluent in French and English as well as in Spanish, Marta became Casals's constant companion.

It was, for Casals, a glorious visit filled with official ceremonies, including a special session of the island legislature and a gala banquet at the splendid Hall of Mirrors in the restored, beautiful, and imposing La Fortaleza. As detailed in H. L. Kirk's biography, Casals was surprised and delighted to find on this small island so much interest in classical music and so many fine musicians. The emotional highlight was the visit to his mother's Mayagüez birthplace: 21 Mendez Vigo Street. Accompanied only by "Martita" and Muñoz's wife, Inés, Casals had planned to walk silently through the house and play several lullabies his mother had sung to him. But the big crowd outside pushed its way into the house. Casals went out onto the balcony and played for the adoring public.

At the Muñoz dinner in his honor at La Fortaleza, Moscoso was astounded by Casals's physical and mental vigor. Over good Spanish sherry, the cellist talked enthusiastically about his many projects for the future. Unlike Moscoso, Muñoz had little knowledge of classical music or taste for it. But toward the end of the evening he cautiously began probing Casals. Would it be possible, he asked, to organize in Puerto Rico something similar to his world-famous Prades festival in southwestern France? After such a warm, satisfying evening, with Martita sitting at his side and obviously delighted with everything he had seen and heard in his new home, Puerto Rico, how could Casals say no?

There was, however, a serious problem Muñoz and Moscoso had to address. In early 1947 Casals had vowed never to perform in a public concert in his homeland or in any country that recognized the Franco regime. Casals had witnessed firsthand the bloodletting during the Spanish Civil War and had been forced to escape across the border to France. This decision was vindicated when a Spanish army general close to Franco declared publicly that if Casals returned, he would cut off both his arms.

But did Casals break his solemn vow when he organized and performed in the annual Bach festival in Prades? After all, France had recognized the Spanish regime. Casals attempted to describe to Muñoz how he arrived at the difficult decision. A young, exceptionally gifted American violinist and concertmaster with the Frankfurt Symphony, Alexander "Sacha" Schneider, approached him with a proposal: in view of the two-hundredth anniversary of Bach's birth, why not have a festival in his honor to be held at the small Prades cathedral in the summer of 1949? Schneider argued imaginatively that Casals would not really violate his vow as it would be a "private performance," like playing at home before friends, in homage to Bach.

Casals relented, and the Prades Music Festival was born. Schneider's private performance in fact was magnified into a major international musical event. It was, after all, the return of Casals. Such was the commotion as world-renowned musicians, some of whom had not heard Casals perform since early in the century, descended on this small town, that "Prades became convinced that it had become the musical capital of the world."[7]

During the dinner at La Fortaleza, Muñoz and Moscoso set out to convince Casals to do for his new home, Puerto Rico, what he had done for Prades. But the Schneider argument was not applicable; no stretch of the imagination could make a Casals festival in Puerto Rico, performed before big audiences and televised throughout the island, a private performance. How could they get around this, as Puerto Rico was part of the United States, a nation that had diplomatic relations with Franco's Spain?

Muñoz and Moscoso had to use their own imagination. They informed Casals that the island had a unique political status under the American flag. It was a commonwealth of the United States, an exclusive political and economic relationship created in 1952 that allowed the island a high degree of autonomy. Puerto Ricans were American citizens, but they did not participate in the formulation or approval of U.S. foreign affairs. The island did not vote in presidential elections and did not have voting congressional representation. Therefore, Puerto Rico could be seen as outside the U.S. recognition of the Franco regime.

"We had been imbibing that good Spanish sherry and wine deep into the night by now," Moscoso recalled.[8] "Don Pablo and Martita rose. He said nothing. But looking directly at Muñoz, he reached out and shook his hand." Moscoso felt that Casals would do it; there would be a Casals festival in Puerto Rico.

As Muñoz and Doña Inés escorted Casals and Martita to their car, Muñoz asked Moscoso and Gloria to remain a moment. Casals, it was evident, had started to think about his new festival. He mentioned that he would ask Alexander Schneider to come soon to Puerto Rico to organize the event, as he had the Prades festival. Moscoso recalled that after the car departed, "Muñoz winked at me. It meant two things. First, he had accomplished his mission. Second, 'Moscoso, you take care of it in Fomento.'"

Early the next morning Ogilvy's phone rang in his Connecticut home. Moscoso could barely wait to tell him about Casals's decision. It was only a few months before that Ogilvy described how Rudolf Bing organized the Edinburgh Music Festival, radically changing the city's image. Edinburgh, he told Moscoso, was transformed into a "country of pilgrimage for civilized people from every nation in Europe." Now, elated with Moscoso's news, Ogilvy recalled the conversation during which Moscoso opened his small black notebook to write himself a memo about the Edinburgh festival. How, he asked Moscoso, did you do it? Ogilvy was convinced that Moscoso could do anything once he set his mind to it and once he jotted it down in his small pad—be it a box of excellent limes for daiquiris or a major international musical event with perhaps the world's greatest living musician.

In April 1956, Ogilvy had written to Moscoso that the "Commonwealth image campaign" had to persuade American public opinion "that Puerto Rico has history, dignity and tradition." Pablo Casals was the embodiment of all three.

*   *   *

Fully financed by the Puerto Rican government and entirely organized by Moscoso and his staff to the last detail—ticket sales, publicity, accommodations for musicians—the Casals festival became much more ambitious than the Prades festival. Incongruous as it seemed, Moscoso decided to place it within the Puerto Rico Industrial Development Company (PRIDCO), whose primary mission was to prebuild factory plants. The rationale was mainly based on the public corporation's greater financial flexibility that the parent agency, the Economic Development Administration, could not match. Moscoso knew that this would be a costly venture. But his decision also had to do with PRIDCO Director Carlos Passalacqua, not only a good administrator and engineer but also an ardent music lover with a lifelong passion for the violin. "I knew that he loved good music," Moscoso later commented. "But I did not know that he loved it as much as he did; in any case, he was so happy when I told him that he began to clap his hands in joy." Passalacqua would be in charge of the production. Casals and Martita, with Alexander Schneider's tireless help, would make all the artistic decisions.

This was for Moscoso another pioneering adventure: no one in Puerto Rico had any idea of how to structure and run an international music festival. Muñoz and Moscoso asked Abe Fortas, now Puerto Rico's principal lawyer in Washington and also a talented violinist, to join the festival's board along with several prominent Puerto Ricans. Fortas happily accepted. Five years later, Fortas was to play a key role in the organization of the famous Casals concert at the White House following a dinner in honor of Muñoz—the glittering cultural event that gave rise to John F. Kennedy's Camelot legend.

But in 1956, it was up to Moscoso to ensure that the festival actually happened. Passalacqua, soft-spoken, methodical, and well-organized, proved to be a perfect complement to the energetic, exuberant Schneider, and the ambitious enterprise moved forward. Moscoso and Passalacqua quickly discovered the remarkable efficiency of Casals's worldwide network of loyal former students and admirers who had become renowned artists. A quality international festival takes several years to organize; the great soloists are often fully booked years in advance. Moscoso and Puerto Rico were unrealistically impatient—they asked Schneider to hold the first festival in December 1956 to celebrate Casals's eightieth birthday. Schneider already had in mind many of the musicians invited to form part of the festival orchestra. It was to be an outstanding one with many of the musicians themselves soloists and several of them concertmasters in major orchestras. Schneider explained that musicians of this quality could only be available in the summer, certainly not at the height of the concert season. The opening concert of the first Casals Music Festival was set for April 22, 1957.

The other event taking place—one that no one knew just how to handle—was the relationship between the eighty-year-old Casals with the twenty-year-old Martita Montañez. It was evident to Schneider and the group of artists that formed Casals's "family"—Rudolph Serkin, Mieczyslaw Horszowsky, and the young American pianist from New York, Eugene

Istomin—that Casals "was happier than he had ever been."9 Tropical Puerto Rico allowed Casals to take long walks along the Ocean Park and Isla Verde beaches every morning before it became too hot. This together with the excitement of creating a major festival had helped to revitalize him. But those close to him knew that his happiness and youthful vigor were the result of his deepening love for the young Puerto Rican.

Finally, the time arrived for the gala inaugural concert. All twelve concerts had been sold out since December. When Casals arrived at the University of Puerto Rico Theater for the rehearsal, the hall was full. After running through a Mozart symphony, Casals began Schubert's *Unfinished Symphony* when suddenly he put down the baton and staggered from the podium. He was suffering a serious heart attack. Carlos Passalacqua's brother, a prominent heart specialist who had been tending to Casals, was called. Governor Muñoz, meanwhile, called Dr. Paul Dudley White, who had treated President Eisenhower after his heart attack. White immediately agreed to fly to Puerto Rico. Casals never lost consciousness: "Through everything," H. L. Kirk wrote, "Casals continued to communicate in four languages, speaking Catalan to Martita and his sister-in-law María, French with Schneider, Spanish with the Puerto Ricans, and English with Dr. White" (495).

The decision was made to continue with the festival. Schneider conducted from his seat as concertmaster with Casals's empty chair in place up on the podium. Moscoso and Ogilvy placed full two-page ads in the national media featuring a moving, dramatic photograph capturing the musicians on their feet before the empty podium while a recording of the old Catalan ballad, "Song of the Bird," performed by Casals, was played. Ogilvy's photographer, Elliot Erwitt, captured the deep emotion. It was a classic Ogilvy ad. The headline was "Tribute to the man who wasn't there—a poignant moment at last year's Festival Casals in Puerto Rico." Casals, however, would return: "Who can doubt that this year's festival will be even more brilliant than the last. The great man himself will be there."

Casals and Martita were married on August 3, 1957. She had been at his bedside continuously during his illness and convalescence. It was not just whether Casals would recover but whether he would regain the strength to play again. To no one's surprise, he credited his total recovery to her presence and absolute confidence. Their decision to marry stunned everyone, but they "were undeterred by shock and early opposition on the part of both families." Years later, Casals joked with a journalist that "some people noted a certain discrepancy in our ages . . . . A bridegroom of course is not usually thirty years older than his father-in-law."10

"Martita revered Don Pablo," Moscoso remembered. "And he revered her. But I believe that his purpose in marrying her was to leave his legacy, his artistic fortune, to her." [11] Pablo Casals died on October 3, 1973, at the age of ninety-six. There was no question in anyone's mind that the festival, then in its sixteenth season, would continue. Marta, who years later married Casals protégé Eugene Istomin and was named artistic director of the Kennedy Center for the Performing Arts, agreed to carry on her beloved husband's work.

*   *   *

The Ogilvy-Moscoso-Puerto Rico relationship lasted until 1968, when the Ogilvy account was terminated by the Ferré administration after the victory of the pro-statehood New Progressive Party. "It was the most bitter tragedy of my career," Ogilvy related.[12] "I had been emotionally involved in helping to solve the problems of Puerto Rico, to the extent which is rare in the advertising business . . . . I had made a modest contribution to that progress." And perhaps just as important to Ogilvy, Moscoso had become the most stimulating client he had ever had.

In 1962, Moscoso, as head of President Kennedy's Alliance for Progress, asked Ogilvy if he could do for Latin America what he had done for Puerto Rico. Would he attend a meeting of the Alliance's advisory committee and tell them the story? When Ogilvy entered the committee room, his mind darted back to his first meetings with Moscoso and the seemingly impossible task they had undertaken. "My joy at being back in his service was so overwhelming," Ogilvy wrote, "that tears welled up in his eyes."

*   *   *

The story of Puerto Rico's renaissance gained a political dimension. During the Cold War this small island became a "Showcase of Democracy"—a laboratory proving that poor societies can improve their lot under a democratic, free-enterprise system.

"I could not think of a better place to be," Vice President Richard Nixon stated on May 13, 1958. "Mr. Vice President, *ésta es su casa* (this is your home)," Muñoz Marín had responded.[13] Nixon had spoken from the heart: the Puerto Rico stopover followed an ugly incident in Caracas, where an angry mob shouting *Muerte a Nixon* (death to Nixon) almost overturned his limousine on its way from Maiquetía Airport to the American Embassy. "It was like being on the inside of a drum with someone pounding on it . . . a close call with death" Nixon wrote in 1990.[14]

In its issue of June 23, 1958, *Time* tied the Nixon visit to its cover story on Muñoz Marín, "Democracy Laboratory in Latin America." Puerto Rico, the article declared, had gained "a notably un-Latin reputation for incorruptibility among top officials," and it was governed by an enlightened leader. In the story, Moscoso was depicted for the first time as the man who was determined to "dragoon or inveigle" American capital to Puerto Rico.

"Tiny Puerto Rico," *Time* reported, which had "clawed its way in fifteen years to a nearly doubled standard of living [is] an exciting, sunny, scrubbed and cultured place to be." David Ogilvy could not have produced a better advertising copy to communicate the image of the new Puerto Rico. Far from Anita's ugly island of *West Side Story*, national media described it as "the place to be."

By that time Ogilvy passionately felt that the economic miracle was his as much as Moscoso's and Muñoz's. "My visits to Puerto Rico," he wrote nearly a half-century later, "were a mixture of hell and love. The hell was that I suffered from an incurable terror of flying." But once there, he and Moscoso would travel throughout the island visiting factories—as Moscoso had told him at the beginning, to see for himself the real-life fruits of his advertisements, the creation of jobs for flesh-and-blood men and women, schools for children, hospitals for the sick, housing for the poor. The love part, again just as Moscoso had told him, was the rewarding knowledge that he was doing more with his great talent than selling Hathaway shirts.

One Ogilvy-created Puerto Rico ad had Governor Muñoz Marín as the hero. The message was that as the number of factories established in Puerto Rico grew, the number of Puerto Ricans forced to migrate to the mainland inner cities would decrease—a matter of growing concern in New York, Chicago, and other urban areas. Ogilvy placed the Muñoz "political" ad next to the Ruml hard-sell ad in some publications.

If Ogilvy fell in love with Puerto Rico—or more precisely, fell in love with being part of Puerto Rico's finest hour—Moscoso fell in love with Ogilvy's elegant advertising. The ads usually ran two pages: a full-page photograph on the left, a strong headline near the center of the page, at the right a short text. One 1958 ad pictured a clearly Spanish-looking young woman in an evening gown holding flowers in her hands and turned towards an ornate interior patio: "Girl by a gate—in Old San Juan."

Ogilvy's text:

Time stands still in the Puerto Rican patio. That weathered escutcheon bears the Royal Arms of Spain. You might have stepped back three centuries. In a sense you did.

You start to wonder. Can this really be the Puerto Rico everyone is talking about? Is this the island American industry is now expanding to, at the rate of three new plants a week? Is this truly the scene of a twentieth-century renaissance? Ask any proud Puerto Rican. He will surely answer—yes.

Within minutes from this patio, you will see the signs. Some are spectacular. The new hotels, the four-lane highways, the landscaped apartments. And some are down-to-earth. A tractor in a field, a village clinic, a shop that sells refrigerators. Note all these things. But, above all, *meet the people.*

It won't be long before you appreciate the deeper significance of Puerto Rico's renaissance. You'll begin to understand why men like Pablo Casals and Juan Ramón Jiménez (the Nobel Prize poet) have gone there to live.

Moscoso was particularly delighted with an ad of the bare, whitewashed wall of the San José Church in Old San Juan, which dates back to 1532. It showed a lone figure, a young Puerto Rican nun, dressed in black against the stark background of the building's sun-drenched whiteness. Ogilvy's photographer, Elliott Erwitt, Moscoso recalled four decades later, "caught the candor in her face, a transparent innocence."[15] It was exactly the image and copy he wanted: refined, cultured, hopeful.

Other ads achieved similar impact. Moscoso especially remembered authorizing the expenditure of $66,000 for a two-page ad in *Life,* a photo taken from a helicopter of grammar school boys and girls exploding out of the school building, many running with their shoes in their hands. "It was a wonderful picture that caught the excitement and exhilaration of these hungry children, free at last, running home for lunch. The ad had a strong, uplifting effect, like seeing one of those movies in which you leave the theater treading on clouds because all of a sudden this is a wonderful world, you are divested of all your cynicism. . . . It was that kind of an ad."

Chapter 11

Tourism
The Fighting Word

When Muñoz Marín and the Populares first came to power in 1940, "tourism" was a fighting word. The word was politically associated with the conservative Coalition Party, which insisted that the island's only natural resource was its scenic beauty and balmy weather. The political and ideological left, however, viewed tourism promotion as an effort to whitewash the island's dreadful social and economic conditions. Some feared that San Juan would turn into "another Havana" infested with vice and mob-controlled corruption.

In 1934, the newly appointed governor, Blanton Winship, proposed a road beautification program to make the island more attractive to tourists. He was shocked by the negative reaction to his plan. The governor, critics said, should be worrying about the many thousands of Puerto Ricans living in cesspool slums.

Winship's appointment had deeply disappointed Muñoz and island liberals. They had expected President Roosevelt to name a New Deal reformer. They got instead a staunch conservative who preferred to promote tourism. Winship established an Institute of Tourism and hired a U.S. public relations firm that brought pretty American models to the island to be photographed in swimsuits on the beach—the same kind of promotions being done for Miami and Atlantic City. Winship then made matters worse: in order to finance his tourism plans, he suggested a sales tax on salt that was quickly approved by the Republican-Socialist Coalition majority in the legislature.

In the 1940 political campaign, Muñoz and the Populares used the regressive salt tax as a symbol of the Coalition's policies that victimized the large mass of Puerto Rico's poor. One of Muñoz's first acts after his party's victory was to repeal the tax. To further dramatize his aversion to the pro-tourism policies, and reacting to rumors of corruption, Muñoz had the slot machines removed from the night clubs and dumped into the sea.

But Moscoso disagreed with his party's rejection of tourism. Of course, the idea that tourism was by itself the solution to the island's ills was a pipe dream. But certainly, it would complement the industrialization program by creating thousands of good jobs. The opposition, Moscoso felt, was mis-guided. Indeed, having good tourist facilities on the island would make it more attractive to potential industrial investors and their families.

"Neither Fomento nor the planning board had a tourism development plan," Moscoso recalled years later. "We were never able to obtain from Muñoz the necessary directives as to how tourism was going to be devel-oped. In fact, it was very difficult to get him interested in anything that had to do with tourism."[1]

Moscoso had already succeeded in turning Muñoz around on several cru-cial policy issues. With tourism in mind, he was now determined to do it again. He began to work on a project several times bigger than that of the original Fomento plants: a $7.5 million investment in a luxury tourist resort hotel.

Moscoso and his team quickly learned that promoting Puerto Rican tour-ism would be no easier than promoting manufacturing. The obstacles were essentially the same. The elements required to run a profitable tourist op-eration were simply not present on the island. There was the imposing Condado Vanderbilt Hotel, built by the Vanderbilt family in 1918 in antici-pation of a tourist boom to be generated by the fact that Puerto Rico was allowed the option to remain "wet" during Prohibition. The local voters, however, unexpectedly chose to go "dry," and the hotel, unable to attract tourists, had to close. A decade later it was reopened sporadically by a wealthy Puerto Rican landowner, Manuel González, who bought it to use mostly for his personal social activities.

The only other tourist hotel was the Normandie, built and run by the eccentric Puerto Rican engineer Félix Benítez Rexach to look like its name-sake, the famous cruise steamship. It had an atrium with a large interior pool that bewildered visitors who wondered why there was an indoor pool in an island of perpetual sunshine. Mismanaged, the hotel hardly invited return visits. There was, in fact, much in Puerto Rico to discourage even an initial holiday trip. There were no organized tours, the taxis appeared un-safe, the drivers—as seemed the case with everyone else on the island—were unable to communicate in English, and restaurants were scarce.

But at the bottom, the biggest obstacle faced by tourism development was the emotional attitude of Muñoz and his administration. In 1944 the island's fire department chief, Raúl Gándara, who was close to Muñoz, publicly attacked Moscoso for suggesting that Puerto Rico could become a major tourist attraction. It was futile, he said, because the island could not compete with other, more attractive Caribbean destinations. Gándara also revived the old argument that it was morally wrong for Puerto Rico to "degrade itself by buying tourists." Moscoso decided to rebuke Gándara publicly. "A tourist is not bought, nor can a tourism industry buy him. One sells *to* a tourist—it's the tourist who buys."[2]

Moscoso's strategy was to break the cycle of negativism by proving that tourism was not only an economic development tool but also a likely source of pride for the island. It had been counterproductive in the past, he thought, to induce tourists to come to Puerto Rico when it was certain they would leave full of negative impressions. Moscoso decided to make a bold move: to build a world-class luxury hotel in one of the island's most beautiful spots.

To get this project through Muñoz and the Populares, Moscoso needed a credible disguise. This hotel, he said, would cater primarily to businessmen. Puerto Rico must at least provide visiting investors with a comfortable, attractive place to stay that had friendly service and clean, efficient restaurants. If the new hotel attracted tourists, fine, but its purpose was to serve as a Fomento tool. This was only partly true, Moscoso knew, but it worked. Muñoz and the legislature, despite misgivings, gave him the go-ahead.

Moscoso sent a letter to several U.S. hotel companies. The only answer that came in Spanish was signed by Conrad Hilton, owner of a growing hotel chain that included the Plaza in New York, where many of the first Puerto Rican migrants worked. Hilton, a native of San Antonio, New Mexico, had organized the Hilton Corporation that year, 1946, and was beginning to look for offshore ventures. His interest in Puerto Rico was his first. Moscoso invited Hilton to come to the island to discuss the possibility of leasing the new hotel from the Puerto Rican government. He also offered Hilton participation in deciding the size and type of hotel that could succeed in Puerto Rico and, most important, the site.

A group of Hilton executives came to Puerto Rico but after one week on the island told Moscoso that they had not found any suitable sites. Mariano Ramírez, Fomento's attorney, recalled years later how Moscoso remained silent for several moments, then said: "All right. Now, if you have a little time, I think you would enjoy seeing what I think must be one of the world's most ridiculous hotels."[3] Moscoso invited the bewildered Hilton people to drive over to see the Normandie. Ramírez, who went along with the group, recalled that "the visitors had . . . a good laugh when they saw the bizarre hotel, and they wanted to meet the 'genius' behind it." Félix Benítez, the owner, who lived on the top floor in what to Ramírez seemed like "Asian splendor," welcomed the group with his usual exuberance. Ramírez noticed that one of the Hilton men walked over to a window overlooking the nearby San Gerónimo fortress. "This is it!" he yelled, turning to Moscoso. "If you can get us that place down there—we have a hotel."

It was easier said than done. The spectacular site, a federal reserve since the 1899 Treaty of Paris, had been leased to a retired Navy officer who built his home there and surrounded it with a fifteen-foot fence. Commander James Barker, who had good connections with the administration of President Warren Harding, made a formal claim "for past services" and secured a lease from the Navy for ninety-nine years for a token one dollar a year. Through White House intervention on Barker's behalf, a line was inserted into the Navy's 1921 budget bill authorizing the lease, which Undersecretary of the Navy Theodore Roosevelt Jr. then signed. It was the most valuable land in Puerto Rico; the San Gerónimo fortress was at the eastern tip of the San Juan Peninsula facing the Condado area, which was then the island's premier residential area. It had a breathtaking view. Could Fomento pry this site from the commander? This was the question in Ramírez's mind as the group said goodbye to Benítez.

Ramírez's research found a possible opening. Eight years after signing the lease, Theodore Roosevelt Jr. was named governor of Puerto Rico. He quickly realized that giving away this beautiful fortress and valuable land had been not only absurd but possibly illegal. The fortress was a part of the island's historic patrimony as were the Spanish fortifications that surrounded San Juan, initially linked by underground tunnels to the huge, majestic San Cristóbal Fort. Roosevelt took the case against Barker and the Navy up through the federal court system but eventually lost. Now Moscoso and Ramírez approached Barker and much to their surprise found that the long legal battle to retain the site had worn him out. He was willing to negotiate. Within a week the land was expropriated, and the court fixed a cash payment of $464,000 for the sixteen acres leading to the fortress.[4]

Opposition came from an unexpected source, however. Believing that Moscoso was building primarily a business hotel, Senate President Muñoz and Governor Jesús Piñero had endorsed the project. But the usually supportive Dr. Rafael Picó, the planning board president, now insisted that Puerto Rico had much more pressing social needs; instead of Moscoso's hotel, he argued, the rum tax rebates should go to schools and hospitals. This was the familiar argument against Moscoso from his own party's liberal wing. But this time the attack came from one of Tugwell's prize administrators known for his pro-development, pro-industry attitude. Hadn't Moscoso, Picó asked, learned his lesson pouring millions into the early, unprofitable Fomento-owned factories? Why not build a more modest, less costly hotel?

Moscoso needed a special strategy to convince Picó. Although the relation between Moscoso and Governor Tugwell had cooled appreciably in the final year of his governorship, mostly due to Tugwell's opposition to tax exemption, Moscoso decided to write to him, thinking that no one could influence Picó better than his mentor. The hotel project, Moscoso wrote to Tugwell, was moving forward; Hilton had agreed to run it on a profit-sharing basis, studies were being made to determine the size, and the Hilton people were scouting for architects. "The only fly in the ointment seems to be Rafael Picó," he wrote.[5] Citing Pico's "obsession" with building schools and hospitals, Moscoso commented wryly: "where on Earth he is going to get the money to run them is still a moot question." Moscoso concluded his plea: "I am sure Rafael will listen to your opinions whereas he would probably not listen to mine." Tugwell responded, "I don't know why he should take my advice."[6] But the strategy worked. Picó decided to table his opposition, and Moscoso finally got the green light.

He dispatched Ramírez and Guillermo Rodríguez to New York, the former because of his meticulous attention to detail and sound judgment, the latter because of his well-earned reputation as a tough negotiator. In two weeks and after lengthy dealings with two teams of New York lawyers, Ramírez and Rodríguez concluded the Hilton contract. When Moscoso received their reports, he became increasingly aware of the acute difficulty of his position: both sides—not just the government, but the Hilton people themselves—were increasingly worried about the risks. Even though Hilton's initial investment would be low—$500,000, compared to the government's $7.5 million—the firm worried about potential losses. If they reached $250,000 in one year, Hilton wanted the option to pull out of the deal. After intense discussions, Moscoso finally told his negotiators to accept Hilton's demands. There had been, as expected, hard exchanges over the profit allocation; two-thirds would go to Fomento. The split would depend, however, on what they called the "gross operating profit." Accountants for both sides would have to determine exactly what this included. One addition involved Hilton's agreement to pay annually 5 percent of the value of the machinery and equipment provided by the government.

Then it was a matter of size and design. Market studies led Moscoso and the Hilton people to conclude that a 300-room hotel was needed. But what about the architectural style? Hilton's architects submitted plans for a Spanish colonial-style building with red tiles. "This is no San Antonio," Moscoso shot back. The hotel must reflect, he said, a distinctive new Puerto Rico design, not a familiar reproduction of traditional Spanish or American Southwest architecture. The Puerto Rican firm of architects, Osvaldo Toro and Miguel Ferrer, and engineer Luis Torregrosa Casellas submitted a design that Moscoso liked immediately; it was functional, clean, modern, and all the rooms had ample terraces that faced the ocean. With misgivings, the Hilton people accepted it.

Moscoso named his brother-in-law, Roberto Sánchez Vilella, head engineer in charge of the hotel's construction at a salary of $9,000 a year. Sánchez, Muñoz's principal lieutenant, had just resigned abruptly from his post, apparently overwhelmed by the pressures of the job. Moscoso, of course, was aware that Sánchez had been one of his most persistent critics; the two men rarely agreed on anything, and their styles and attitudes were diametrically opposed. But Sánchez, a brilliant mathematics student at Ohio State University and painstakingly precise and cautious, was the man Moscoso needed to find hidden flaws and pitfalls.

The need for extreme care in this particular project was driven home to Moscoso by the unusual degree of attention it was attracting in the island media. The project was branded "Moscoso's Folly." The misgivings that Rafael Picó had expressed were now exaggerated and converted into a symbol of a "runaway Moscoso" intent on throwing good money away in fantasy projects. This criticism was not new, of course, but now Moscoso experienced a barrage of attacks, especially from the newspaper El Mundo, although Moscoso thought he had a reasonably good relationship with publisher Angel Ramos. After all, Ramos had agreed to serve on Fomento's Tourism Advisory Committee.

The hotel would fail, article after article declared with total confidence; one columnist speculated that it would become a hospital, while another suggested that it would be turned into a prison. It would be Fomento's most expensive "white elephant," the media forecast.

The animosity, Moscoso knew, was certain to grow, for he was now thinking of something even more controversial: legalized gambling. The fundamental task of the new luxury resort was to prove to potential investors that hotels could be built and run profitably in Puerto Rico. And the key to profits, he was convinced, was having a casino within the hotel.

"I don't know how I survived that period," Moscoso said, referring to spring of 1948; on top of getting Muñoz and the Populares to accept tax exemption for new industry and hotels, he also shocked them with the pro-

Moscoso's decision to spend an unheard-of $7.5 million to build the luxury 300-room Caribe Hilton Hotel was denounced by the media as "Moscoso's Folly;" they predicted that the hotel would fail and the building would be converted into a prison. But the hotel was enormously successful, launching Puerto Rico's tourism industry. For Conrad Hilton, seen here with Moscoso laying the first stone for a hotel expansion, it was the beginning of Hilton International.

posal to legalize gambling. This was, for many of the intellectuals and poets in Muñoz's inner circle, the last straw. At one of Muñoz's late-night tertulias, Moscoso recalled, University of Puerto Rico Professor Antonio Colorado, a short, slight man with a powerful voice and acerbic wit, became so agitated that he suddenly climbed on top of a piano and proceeded to voice his outrage. Was it not enough, he shouted, that Moscoso wanted to bring to Puerto Rico the vulgarity of the Miami and Havana tourism strips without also the criminal underworld through gambling?

That was the tone of the attack at a Popular Party legislative caucus called by Muñoz to consider Moscoso's gambling bill. The virulent assault launched against Moscoso by Colorado was now taken up by senate leader Samuel Quiñones, the chain-smoking lawyer and writer who had joined Muñoz in founding the party in the 1930s. Quiñones was normally soft-spoken, thoughtful, a compromiser; he was often used by Muñoz to mediate internal political conflicts. Now Quiñones's emotional opposition to the gambling bill had a chilling effect. "My good friend Samuel Quiñones," Moscoso recalled, "got up on the tip of his toes and gave me the lambasting of my life. I never heard more horrible things said about me. It was for him almost a religious issue; what I was proposing was simply sacrilegious—I was corrupting the very soul of the Populares. I sat there quietly and took it, my only hope being that at the end Muñoz's intuitive pragmatism would win the day."[7]

It did. When Muñoz's turn came to express his view, he acknowledged each of the many opposing arguments. But the bill, he pointed out, had been carefully crafted by Moscoso and his consultants to protect Puerto Rico precisely from mob control; the gambling licenses would be restricted to casinos located inside tourist resort hotels; the games and the personnel would be heavily policed by government inspectors; all casino employees would be required to have a government permit before starting to work. More important, there would be intense scrutiny of all applicants for casino licenses, including each of the major stockholders of the hotel. This, Muñoz argued, was the real issue: does the Government of Puerto Rico trust itself to administer this program—does it trust its own integrity, its honesty? "With Muñoz's simple, obvious logic," Moscoso said, "he pointed out that it takes two to consummate a bribe, and since he was confident that the Puerto Rican government would not accept bribery, the underworld would simply stay away. And, of course, the government always held the power to take away the license at the first sign of corruption." There was still another safeguard: Muñoz and the party legislators wanted to make clear that the purpose of gambling was not to make the island the mecca of professional gamblers but to attract mostly recreational gamblers. So the bill prohibited any mention of the casinos in either the hotels' or the government's advertising. Furthermore, the hotels were required to make casinos as inconspicuous as possible; they would not be seen from anywhere in the lobby. Finally, although the hotels enjoyed tax exemption, the casinos themselves would be fully taxable. The casino revenue would be divided three ways: one-third for the government, one-third for the hotel, and one-third for the University of Puerto Rico. The gambling bill was passed and signed by Governor Piñero on May 15, 1948. But what Moscoso called a "wrenching experience" was not over.

It became evident that the hostility against legalized gambling remained very near the surface. The following year, Muñoz, as the new governor, rejected Moscoso's regulations for casino licenses. Muñoz demanded that only those hotels committing themselves to major investments in improvement and expansions could qualify for the licenses. Moscoso asked banker Esteban Bird, the president of his Tourism Advisory Board, to try to get Muñoz to approve the regulations. In what the press described as a friendly meeting, Bird argued that the unintentional effect of Muñoz's requirement would be to favor large hotel corporations and discriminate against mid-size and small hotels. This clearly violated Muñoz's commitment to promote local investments. Although Fomento had received ten petitions in the eight months since the law was passed, only one had been approved.[8] Muñoz relented, and Fomento quickly proceeded to grant five more licenses.

*   *   *

Moscoso organized another spectacular party to inaugurate the glittering, ultramodern, ten-story Caribe Hilton. It was a celebration that rivaled the Muñoz inauguration festivities. In the second week of December 1949, four hundred guests were flown from the United States; again Moscoso used the opportunity to host businesspeople, bankers, and potential industrial investors. There were so many guests that Moscoso and his organizers had to divide the festivities into two days; it was, the *New York Times* reported, a "Hollywoodian opening" well represented with movie and radio personalities. The master of ceremonies was the Puerto Rican-born Broadway actor and director and later Oscar-winning movie star, José Ferrer. But the focus once again was on Puerto Rico's industrialization program. The "Caribe Hilton opening was exploited to the hilt in order to promote Operation Bootstrap," the *New York Times* reported.[9]

Moscoso was finally on his way to getting Puerto Rico into the tourism business. The previous year he had convinced the legislature to officially declare tourism an industry, thus making the tax exemption law applicable to hotel investments. By late 1949, Moscoso was driving toward the construction of two additional hotels, both smaller than the Caribe Hilton, one in Mayagüez on the western coast, the other in the beautiful central mountain town of Barranquitas. They were being built with public capital, although he had also begun negotiations with the Hilton organization to run the fifty-room Mayagüez hotel. There were plans for a $1 million upgrade of the old Condado Vanderbilt Hotel, now called the Condado Beach Hotel, to add eighty-five rooms. American media reports even spoke of a renovation of the odd Normandie Hotel. Still, with all this new construction and expansion, the total number of hotel and guesthouse rooms in Puerto Rico did not reach one thousand.

The morning after the Caribe Hilton's magnificent, joyous inauguration, Fomento attorney Mariano Ramírez walked into the lobby looking for one of Moscoso's special guests, the economist Leon Henderson, the man who had accompanied Tugwell when he sauntered into the Moscoso drugstore in Ponce a decade earlier. The outspoken Henderson walked over to a man standing alone at the other end of the lobby who appeared to be in an ugly mood. Henderson whispered to Ramírez that the man was Henry Crown, a Chicago multimillionaire who had recently bought the Empire State Building and was a director of the Hilton International Corporation. "What's wrong, Henry?" Henderson asked. "Drink too much last night?" "No," Crown answered. "It's that I'm worried. I told Hilton that he was making a big mistake getting into this. I voted against it. He didn't believe me and he will live to regret it, mark my words." [10]

Crown's dark view of the potential of tourism was shared by another person who did not see much of a future in island tourism, Puerto Rico's top economist, Dr. Harvey Perloff. Several months after the Hilton's inauguration, Perloff's major work, *Puerto Rico's Economic Future,* was published. The author devoted less than a page to tourism. As a creator of employment, Perloff predicted, "the tourism program can be expected to be of relatively limited significance." [11]

Perloff was right in that tourism would never become Puerto Rico's principal source of employment; Moscoso completely agreed. But the great concern over Moscoso's Folly proved wrong. The Caribe Hilton was to become, from the start, the single greatest success story of Operation Bootstrap.

Rafael Fábregas, the young accountant recruited by Moscoso for the Puerto Rico Development Company, recalled receiving the first check from Hilton. Never before had he held a million-dollar check in his hand. The Caribe Hilton became the flagship for the new Hilton International. Its year-round high occupancy, reputation for quality service, and excellent restaurants served as a model for the expanding global chain and for the other luxury hotels built on the island. In stark contrast to Moscoso's early factories, none of which ever fulfilled the high expectations, the hotel rapidly exceeded the most optimistic projections. It became the development company's biggest source of income from its investments. In fact, the income nearly covered PRIDCO's total operating expenses. [12]

Moscoso, who "was never one to stop calling a spade a club if that would help him get a hole dug with it," [13] got away with the biggest risk in his Fomento career. Puerto Rican tourism took off following the hotel's inauguration. The number of tourists (nonresidents staying at a hotel) doubled from 37,670 in 1952 to 71,678 in 1957 and again to 145,863 by 1960. Tourist expenditures exploded from $3.5 million in 1952 to $29.4 million in 1960. [14] More important, the hotels registered an 81.6 percent year-round occupancy rate.

Yet outbreaks of criticism persisted, except that now the reason was the hotel's spectacular success. Anthropologist Oscar Lewis in his work *La Vida,* a chronicle of Puerto Rico's La Perla seaside slum along the foot of the Old San Juan walls, had one of the characters lament the contrast between the extravagant hotel and the nearby squalor. A similar comparison was made by some members of Congress who visited the island to determine congressional funding to attack local poverty and unemployment. They wondered why Puerto Rico had spent millions in this luxury pleasure palace. Moscoso

Teodoro Moscoso and Conrad Hilton nailing a plaque to a palm tree at the Caribe Hilton hotel in 1955. The resort hotel built and owned by Fomento launched the Puerto Rican tourism industry in spite of the misgivings of many Popular Democratic Party leaders.

was upset by a newspaper story that reported he was "tongue tied" when Congressmen Stephen Young contrasted the Caribe Hilton to El Fanguito. No, Moscoso answered, he had forcefully informed Young that "public housing projects will not permit you to build hotels, but hotels will generate the income that will permit you to build public housing, or to not have to build them."[15] Tourism generated by the Caribe Hilton, he said, will in turn generate $15 million in government revenue.

As Moscoso had anticipated, the success of the Caribe Hilton triggered a hotel building boom: the San Juan Intercontinental out in Isla Verde near the airport, Lawrence Rockefeller's resort at Dorado, and the $4.6 million La Concha in the Condado, another Fomento hotel.

*   *   *

With each new victory, however, the fear of what Moscoso was doing to the island's mores and values increased. The accusation continued that Fomento was undermining the island's culture, a source of deep irritation to Moscoso. According to historian Arturo Morales Carrión, "the acquisitive society fathered by the industrialization would be too strong for the deeply humanistic values of the PPD's public philosophy."[16]

In moments of particular frustration, Moscoso would tell his colleagues in Fomento what he would not dare say before Popular leaders. Scott Runkle, his public relations director in the early 1950s, recalled a day when Moscoso returned from a meeting in which he was accused of insensitivity to the fact that building Puerto Rico was not just a matter of erecting factories. "I remember him crying out in anger: 'Puerto Rican culture? What culture?' Or words to that effect."[17]

Moscoso's irritation stemmed from his belief that he, as much as any other Puerto Rican, was making an authentic contribution to the island's culture. Real cultural development, Moscoso kept insisting, had to go beyond the island's folklore, native foods and dances, or the popular *santeros,* carvers of primitive religious statues. It included not only the Casals festival but also saving architectural jewels such as Old San Juan. In fact, nothing gave him greater satisfaction than being the catalyst in the magnificent restoration of this historic city through a Fomento project headed by the agency's director of tourism, Stanley Robbins.

*   *   *

Getting Robbins to Puerto Rico, as with many others who joined Moscoso's program, was the result of a fortunate accident. A position in the U.S. Virgin Islands with the Caneel Bay Plantation resort having fallen through, Robbins contacted Esteban Bird, a member of Fomento's tourism advisory board. Bird immediately phoned Moscoso with a two-word message: "Hire him!" Moscoso did.

Robbins had a long career in Latin American foreign policy—including Roosevelt's Good Neighbor policy—and in the travel industry. More important for Moscoso, he had worked also on the nation's oldest architectural restoration program, the reconstruction of Williamsburg, Virginia, that began in 1926. Robbins had visited Puerto Rico several times and realized the enormous potential of developing the centuries-old section of San Juan into a historic site. There was no doubt in Moscoso's mind that he represented exactly the kind of tourism developer that Fomento needed. The problem was the salary. Robbins requested $25,000 a year, more than three times what Moscoso himself earned at the time. Bird decided to call an extraordinary meeting of the Tourism Advisory Board in which Robbins made a presentation of his ideas for getting Puerto Rico's tourism off the ground once the new hotel opened. The board was impressed, and his appointment and salary were approved.

Early the next morning, casually browsing through the island's most powerful newspaper, *El Mundo,* Moscoso was flabbergasted. The popular political columnist Eliseo Combas Guerra made a scalding attack on Moscoso. Combas described the meeting of the day before in lurid tones, decrying that Robbins was being paid much more than any other public servant and that Moscoso was the culprit. Moscoso was accustomed to Combas's biting yet often humorous columns attacking his "extravagance," but this time he could not restrain himself. One of the tourism board members who voted in favor of hiring Robbins at the $25,000 salary was *El Mundo* publisher Angel Ramos. There was no way that Combas could have known about the meeting and the salary decisions unless his boss told him.

"I called Mr. Ramos at his home," Moscoso said. "I don't believe he had gotten out of bed yet. Unfortunately, I used language that is not my custom. It was very bad; I think he was stupefied. In any case, he resigned from the tourism board."[18]

Robbins began by making an inventory of Puerto Rico's potential tourist attractions. He spent several weeks traveling through the island, talking to University of Puerto Rico professors and to a number of Americans who were scattered throughout the island, questioning them on what would appeal to the American traveler. Puerto Rico's great resource aside from the beaches and scenery, he reported to Moscoso, was the old city of San Juan: the massive, imposing fortresses at both ends facing the Atlantic—El Morro and San Cristóbal—the narrow cobblestone streets lined with ornate Spanish balconies, the cathedral, the quaint del Cristo chapel. But Old San Juan, aside from the state and municipal government buildings and several stores and restaurants, was in fact a slum. Behind the facades of the old buildings were decrepit mazes of rooms and patios where in past centuries one or two families had lived—but that now housed ten or more. Many of the buildings were abandoned and occupied by derelicts.

Robbins proposed for old San Juan something similar to the Rockefeller family's restoration of Williamsburg. Moscoso loved the idea and suggested approaching the Rockefellers to see if they would allow Fomento to contract a team of Williamsburg experts. Utilizing his contacts at Williamsburg and his good relations with the Rockefellers, Robbins got a positive response; the team soon arrived in Puerto Rico. The obvious first step was to protect the old city by declaring it a historic zone where all construction and physical changes would be carefully controlled by a government agency. Restoration, Moscoso learned, was not a simple matter of repairing and painting over; precise studies had to be made to determine the original structural plans and the decorations and colors of the buildings. At Williamsburg, where five hundred buildings had been restored, a special laboratory was set up to analyze the original paints on the buildings. The Williamsburg team assisted Robbins and Moscoso in preparing legislation to protect the historic zone. It was approved; the planning board was designated as the monitoring agency.

During that period, Moscoso proceeded to reconstruct such buildings as the Casa Cabildo across the street from the cathedral and the small, popular Parque de las Palomas overlooking La Princesa prison and San Juan Bay.

Robbins resigned as head of tourism in April 1951 and returned to the U.S. mainland, but he remained a consultant to Moscoso until mid-1954. The restoration of Old San Juan received its next powerful boost on June 1955 with the creation of the Institute of Puerto Rican Culture. Its mission was to "conserve, promote, enrich and divulge the cultural values of the people of Puerto Rico." Muñoz himself proposed the bill. It sparked a firestorm of partisan controversy by pro-statehood advocates led by Luis Ferré, himself a major patron of the arts who later founded the Ponce Museum of Art. Ferré opposed the bill as a manifestation of Muñoz's and the Populares' "deep-seated nationalism." The drive to glorify the island's culture, he charged, was in reality a subliminal campaign to prepare the island for eventual independence.

The appointment of thirty-four-year-old Ricardo Alegría as executive director of the new institute proved to be a boon for the restoration project. Alegría pursued cultural development with the same drive and intensity Moscoso had for tourism and industrialization. Puerto Rico's leading archaeologist, with degrees from the University of Chicago and Harvard, Alegría promoted restoration through a series of incentives including tax exemption. He organized a team of local architects and historians to assist property owners in careful rebuilding, and he established a warehouse for hard-to-find materials. Under his relentless drive, Old San Juan was transformed dramatically. Many of the restored buildings were converted into elegant homes, galleries, or museums. Alegría continued his work as an archaeologist, publishing several books and numerous articles on the island's pre-Columbian history. Writing in the late 1970s, he declared that the Institute's greatest accomplishment, however, was to help Puerto Rico overcome its traces "of inferiority complex." No Puerto Rican, Alegría wrote with satisfaction, is now ashamed to say that he is proud of his culture and his identity.

*   *   *

Besides the Old World charm of the old city, there were other major factors for the extraordinary growth in tourism after the inauguration of the Caribe Hilton. In his last press conference before leaving the island, Robbins announced a crucial victory for Puerto Rico: the Civil Aeronautical Board had authorized Eastern Airlines to fly the San Juan-New York route, which up to then had been monopolized by Pan American.[19] The competition brought an immediate benefit as Eastern announced a round-trip fare of

$64.50, $10 lower than Pan American's fare. Travel between the U.S. East Coast and Puerto Rico, on a per-mile basis, was now among the cheapest in the world. Fomento statistics from the 1950s showed that 90 percent of the tourists came from the U.S. East Coast and that 80 percent of all mainland travelers earned annual incomes in excess of $10,000.[20]

Ogilvy's tourism advertising took full advantage. The big, beautiful photographs that dominated his ads dramatized the island's European heritage. Puerto Rico was a relatively inexpensive way to travel to a foreign country, culturally speaking, in the safety and convenience of remaining under the American flag.

Moscoso was the catalyst for another cultural project to which he remained intensely dedicated throughout his life. Adding to the Old World feel of San Juan was *La Casa del Libro,* an antique book and manuscript museum on Cristo Street. The man behind the project just happened to come to Puerto Rico on a holiday visit and was convinced to stay.

In early 1955, Elmer Adler, a recently retired Princeton University professor, walked into the University of Puerto Rico museum. He was a renowned connoisseur of old books and fine printing and had headed Princeton's Department of Fine Arts. Having arrived on a cruise ship, he and his wife toured Old San Juan and then took a taxi out to Río Piedras to visit the university's museum. Ricardo Alegría, yet to be named to the Institute of Culture, was then museum director. While accompanying Adler through the exhibits, Alegría mentioned that Puerto Rico was in need of vastly improving the quality of its printing and that the visitors should meet Fomento's Teodoro Moscoso and his deputy, the artistically inclined Guillermo Rodríguez.

Moscoso was fascinated by the scholarly Adler and urged him to accompany him to La Fortaleza to meet Governor Muñoz. After a long, interesting discussion, Muñoz, Moscoso, and Rodríguez asked Adler and his wife to establish residence in Puerto Rico and to enjoy retirement while helping the island develop the craft of fine printing. Adler answered that it made little sense to start such a project without first educating the public on the history and tradition of printing. Of course, he was delighted by the idea of spending the winter months on the island; perhaps, he declared, he could start by establishing and directing a fine printing educational program in San Juan.

The idea that emerged from the meeting was *La Casa del Libro.* Adler selected a run-down building on Cristo Street near the Capilla del Cristo. Moscoso proceeded to purchase the building and to restore it. He also convinced the legislature to appropriate $20,000 yearly and organized a group of volunteers to run it under the guidance of Guillermo Rodríguez, who, thanks to Adler, had developed what turned out to be a lifelong passion for calligraphy. Moscoso recruited members of his clan to sit on the board: Martin Clapp, Fomento's controller; attorney Max Goldman, head of the governor's tax exemption office; one of the Caribe Hilton architects, Miguel Ferrer; and another architect, William Reed, who was with the Rockefellers' homebuilding company, IBEC.

Adler and his wife decided to move permanently to Puerto Rico and live in an apartment above the museum on Cristo Street. He had already donated his collection of old and fine books to Princeton; now he convinced the university to donate any duplicate books to the new museum. For Moscoso and his associates, *La Casa del Libro* became more than a labor of love. Moscoso threw himself wholeheartedly into the project as if it had been the promotion of a Fortune 500 industry. "This was not merely a hobby for us," Moscoso recalled. "This became a serious Fomento project. Why would an agency whose job was industrial development get involved in a book museum? It was, of course, a respite from the pressure of convincing businesspeople to invest in Puerto Rico, of dealing with machinery and factories: we had a need to put a humane physiognomy to our industrialization program."[21]

Through Moscoso's and his committee's fund-raising activities, the collection grew in size and importance. In his will, Adler created an $85,000 endowment and donated an additional $15,000 to purchase books and documents. Valuable gifts were received from various sources. The Nebraska Consolidated firm that owned the large grain mill, *Molinos de Puerto Rico*, donated two royal decrees issued by Queen Isabel of Spain authorizing Christopher Columbus to provision his ships for his second voyage to the New World with grains owned by the royal family and stored in Seville and Cadiz. It was during this 1493 voyage that Columbus discovered the island of Puerto Rico. By the 1980s, the museum held one of the world's largest collections of fifteenth-century Spanish books and had become the principal museum of rare books and documents in Latin America.

Moscoso's dedication to *La Casa del Libro*, the restoration of Old San Juan, and the Casals festival belied the popular image, among friends as well as foes, that he was a one-dimensional man exclusively concerned with Puerto Rico's material development. "I guess," he commented years later, "that the one reason that Fomento got so involved in projects like *La Casa del Libro* was that it proved that there was a spiritual side to my life."

Part

Four

The Soul and Muscle of Bootstrap

Don Luis, please, stop pushing Gandhi at me!

Moscoso to Muñoz Marín, 1958

Chapter 12

The Price and Wages of Success

Moscoso's and Ogilvy's success in radically changing Puerto Rico's image and the news stories about the island's phenomenal economic growth revived in the U.S. labor movement the claim that Puerto Rico was using cheap labor to steal jobs from American workers. Although Muñoz had assured organized labor that Fomento was not based on sweatshops, the fact remained that the government of Puerto Rico periodically went to Congress to defend the island's flexibility in the application of the federal minimum-wage legislation. For Muñoz, with his strong pro-labor roots, this was another ideologically difficult sacrifice in behalf of Operation Bootstrap.

For Moscoso, though, it was not a sacrifice but common sense dictated by reality. Tax exemption, of course, was the most powerful incentive offered by Fomento. But to take advantage a company had to make a good profit, and for most of the industries coming to the island this depended on the ability to pay lower wages than on the U.S. mainland. Muñoz and Moscoso argued that it was not a cheap-labor policy because Puerto Rico's goal was to raise salaries as fast as the island's particular conditions allowed. But they argued before both Congress and organized labor that with unemployment in the 15 percent range and per capita income still one-third that of the U.S. mainland, they needed time to catch up.

The applicability of the U.S. Fair Labor Standards Act to Puerto Rico dated back to the New Deal. However, from the beginning, when the minimum wage was twenty-five cents an hour, it became evident that the effect of imposing this same rate in Puerto Rico would be disastrous. In 1940, the U.S. Labor Department was authorized to name a tripartite committee with the power to recommend a lower minimum wage for those island industries able to prove that it was essential for their survival. It was called the "flexible wage system" and mandated two criteria: that the applicable wage not be so high as to curtail local employment nor so low as to give Puerto Rico a "competitive edge" over the mainland.

By 1955, the AFL-CIO was determined to eliminate this Puerto Rican advantage. Moscoso and his economists now faced a major crisis, worse than they dared to admit publicly. Defending minimum-wage flexibility required a high degree of understanding of Puerto Rico's economic problems. Political considerations and controversies, such as whether Puerto Ricans were or were not second-class citizens, only served to confuse this highly complicated issue. Moscoso's economic think tank produced ample evidence that virtually every cost item in running a manufacturing operation in Puerto Rico was higher than on the mainland. One vital lesson that everyone in Fomento had learned was what the agency's staff economists called the "psychological cost of capital," that is, to take the risk of investing in Puerto Rico, a company needed a much higher expectation of profit than on the mainland. Some Fomento economists believed that once salaries in Puerto Rico reached mainland levels—as all other production costs were higher on the island—this would mean the demise of Bootstrap. As the dilemma headed toward a crisis, it was the foundation garment industry that finally brought the issue to the forefront.

Operation Bootstrap first achieved the "critical mass" needed for economic takeoff in the brassiere industry; that was the point where the sheer size of the industry promotes itself and where a particular manufacturer cannot afford not to have a plant at a particular site in order to compete with those that do. The brassiere plants in Puerto Rico went from six in 1950, employing six hundred workers, to twenty-six in 1955, with more than three thousand employees.[1] Fomento witnessed what seemed like a stampede.

The president of the International Ladies Garment Workers Union, David Dubinsky, who was highly influential among Democrats in Congress, led the campaign against Puerto Rico. Testifying before a Senate committee, Dubinsky argued that the island had already taken 20 percent of all brassiere-manufacturing jobs in the United States in large part, he said, because the flexible system for wages set up in 1940 was not working as stipulated by the law. The tripartite committee reviewing salaries on the island was excessively lax and slow in pushing salaries up to reach the mainland minimum-wage level.

Muñoz led the battery of Puerto Rican officials and private-sector representatives testifying in defense of the existing system. He insisted that there was absolutely no discrepancy, that Puerto Rico's government, Congress, and the labor movement all wanted to push up salaries as fast as possible.

The problem was how to achieve this goal. Puerto Rico needed flexibility, he said, precisely to reach the levels of worker productivity and employment that would permit it to attain minimum-wage parity with the mainland. And to ensure that this happened as soon as possible, Puerto Rico had enacted its own minimum-wage law.

Muñoz and Moscoso saw how much power Dubinsky held over minimum wages in Puerto Rico. After his persistent lobbying, the Senate approved an amended bill that decreed a series of fixed increases through January 1, 1958. During fall 1954, Dubinsky's pressure on the Labor Department already had driven up the minimum wage of brassiere workers in Puerto Rico from thirty-three to fifty-five cents an hour. Dubinsky's congressional testimony, the Fomento economists argued, was simply wrong: the flexible system was not pushing salaries down, it was pushing them up. Back in 1951, island brassiere workers were earning 25.8 percent of what mainland workers earned. In June 1955, that wage was up to 46.6 percent, the Robert A. Nathan Associates 1955 study found (213). The economists added that the system, contrary to what Dubinsky alleged, was working exactly as intended by Congress.

The 1955 Senate action sent shock waves through Fomento. There was the fear that the Senate's large automatic increases would at best stop the industry's growth and at worst drive it out of the island. As the Nathan Associates report pointed out, this was indeed "a very serious challenge to the flexible system in effect since 1940." But Congress was doing more, the study stressed. It was directly attacking the core of Bootstrap, calling for the implementation of the 1940 rule stating that Puerto Rico could not use its lower minimum wage as a competitive advantage. What was Operation Bootstrap if not precisely the promotion of Puerto Rico's competitive advantage? Furthermore, the report continued, a policy designed to avoid the "curtailment of employment" made no sense on an island that needed to create hundreds of thousands of new jobs to reduce its massive unemployment.

The Muñoz-Moscoso appeal to Congress convinced the members of the House of Representatives not to approve the Senate amendments instigated by Dubinsky. In the end, Muñoz's emotional argument that "the lowest salary is no salary" proved effective in describing an island with unemployment four times higher than on the mainland. But as the Nathan study urgently warned Muñoz and Moscoso, the Senate action was an ominous signal that the flexible system itself was in danger. While the House kept the system intact for the moment, it created a special committee to study whether Dubinsky and the other critics were correct. The Nathan report further warned that organized labor's campaign would gain strength as Fomento achieved greater success: "As industries expand, they must increase their sales on the mainland markets and the competitive problem will become more widespread and more acute. Complaints that specific Puerto Rican industries are enjoying an unjustified competitive advantage will grow rather than diminish" (7).

It was evident to Muñoz and Moscoso that to avert disaster it was crucial to somehow win Dubinsky over to Puerto Rico's side. But was this, in fact, a possible mission? If it was politically difficult for Muñoz and the Populares to reconcile their "pro-labor" and "pro-union" mystique with their ongoing battle against federal minimum wages, how were they going to convince the crusty, old, Russian-born warrior? Muñoz and Moscoso decided to try.

Muñoz got himself invited to address ILGWU's annual convention held on May 18, 1956, in Atlantic City, New Jersey. Looking directly at Dubinsky, he repeated his old argument: "I want to tell you most emphatically that a low wage policy is not part of Operation Bootstrap. Wages in Puerto Rico still are lower than here, but that is because of the stage of development of our economy and in spite of the clearly defined and well established policy of the Commonwealth government. People are not for industry. Industry is for the people. . . . This [achieving mainland-level wages] will take some time, but you can be certain that the time will be as short as a strong purpose and a dedicated will can make it."[2]

Wanting to gain additional credibility with Dubinsky, Muñoz invited him and the ILGWU to increase their organizational efforts in Puerto Rico. He pointed with pride at the delegation of Puerto Rican migrants employed in garment factories in New York and other cities. Then, again addressing the speech to Dubinsky, he repeated his invitation: "The presence of a strong ILGWU organization in Puerto Rico will help us immensely in this effort."

Dubinsky readily accepted. He sent a Spanish-speaking organizer to the island who proved to be exceptionally effective. At the same time, Dubinsky's organizers began working out an arrangement with mainland firms allowing the union automatically to represent workers in the firms' new Puerto Rican operations in a system called "double contract." Muñoz and Moscoso expected that Dubinsky's involvement with the island would make him appreciate its economic development hurdles. Dubinsky, however, proved unrelenting on the minimum-wage issue. He continued to pressure Congress about wages in Puerto Rico.

*   *   *

By 1960, Moscoso felt that he needed to have someone "in charge of Dubinsky." He assigned the task to a young economist whom he recruited in New York to head Fomento's Industrial Services Division. Leo Suslow received a Ph.D. from Colgate University, worked and traveled extensively throughout Central America, and was the agency's spokesman with the textile industry. An intelligent, personable, streetwise, and at times irreverent young man with a quick sense of humor, Suslow got along well with American labor leaders. More important—and this is what made him right for the Dubinsky assignment—he was just as mentally tough.

Suslow arrived in New York thinking he had a confirmed appointment with Dubinsky; the secretary, however, casually informed Suslow that Dubinsky had left for an AFL-CIO meeting in Miami. Suslow suppressed his annoyance and decided to follow Dubinsky to Florida and eventually tracked him down in the Turkish bath of the Empress Hotel. Looking through the fogged glass panes, he finally spotted Dubinsky's short, muscular frame. He tapped on the glass; Dubinsky waved for him to come in. "What the hell," Suslow cried, trying to motion to him that he would wait outside, but Dubinsky insisted. Suslow removed his clothes and went inside: "I sat there for about two minutes and I was beginning to die," he recalled decades later. "'Let's get the hell out of here,' I told him. 'Stay,' he said, 'this is good for you: you've got a cold, I can hear it.' 'No, no,' I said, 'I can't take it anymore. Mr. Dubinsky, we have important things to talk about.' 'Don't worry, don't worry,' he said." Suslow finally escaped, and Dubinsky followed. "He turned to some fellow and said, 'Take care of him.' The guy laid me down on a table and started breaking my bones, kneading them, I never heard such cracks in my life and I kept saying to myself, 'It's six o'clock in the morning, I haven't slept in two days, what the hell am I doing here?' Then I looked up, and there was Dubinsky, showered, all dressed up. He said, 'All right, let's go downstairs and have cup of coffee; let's talk.'"

Dubinsky, it turned out, considered himself an expert on Puerto Rico. He didn't want to hear the arguments used by the island government and the garment industry against full federal minimum wages on the island. He had participated personally in the Labor Department's tripartite hearings that set the minimums for the brassiere industry. Don't bother to repeat all of this, Dubinsky told Suslow. It was not, the Fomento emissary said to himself, an auspicious beginning to his crucial mission.

Suslow decided to repeat Muñoz's pitch. We are both on the same side, we are pro-labor, pro-worker, so let's work together. Puerto Rico's leaders were living up to their promise that industrialization would not take place at the expense of mainland workers. Runaway industries had been turned away. Muñoz had included in the island's constitution a pro-labor bill of rights, including the right to organize and to collective bargaining. Certainly the ILGWU's experience in Puerto Rico, Suslow went on, had proved that Muñoz and Moscoso were friendly and supportive of honest unions, especially unions as anticorruption, antiracketeering as Dubinsky's. An unrealistic wage policy in Puerto Rico would only drive the textile-industry jobs to those regions of the United States that were most antilabor or to a foreign country with real starvation wages.

Suslow kept going back to the question of honesty. It was 1960; both Muñoz and Moscoso, he reminded Dubinsky, had begun to speak out forcefully against the real threat of corruption in the labor movement in Puerto Rico—the incursions by Jimmy Hoffa's Teamsters Union. In fact, it was Suslow's job to ensure that no Fomento plant engaged in illegal or unethical antilabor practices. "Dubinsky knew that neither Moscoso nor any of us would tolerate any implication by management to buy off a union," Suslow recalled. "I mentioned to him that whenever I was approached by an industrialist who thought that he had to do business in Puerto Rico as in some states and big cities or foreign countries, he got himself into trouble."

The argument won Dubinsky over: "All right, all right," he said, "let's settle on a figure."

This meant that Dubinsky was willing to suspend his latest drive to get Congress to eliminate or radically change the flexible system. Instead, he wanted to negotiate with Suslow, as Muñoz's representative, a new increase in the minimum wage applicable to Puerto Rico. He threw out a number: "Does that sound reasonable?" Suslow, convinced that he had just won a major and perhaps decisive victory for Fomento and Puerto Rico, restrained his excitement, answering quietly that he had to check.

*   *   *

Moscoso was elated. Suslow had achieved the nearly impossible, and it had been partly due to his sincere pro-labor attitude. Suslow often took issue with the Fomento economists who equated each increase in the minimum wage with a loss of jobs. This was much too simplistic, he argued; the unions had a powerful point when the jobs created by increased consumption and the general lifting of the standard of living were factored in. Fomento, Suslow insisted, had to understand much better the motives and objectives of organized labor.

"It was not that the labor leaders did not trust Moscoso," Suslow recalled. "On the contrary, Moscoso came across as a man truly dedicated to all Puerto Ricans, not just the employers. He would say to union leaders:

'Look, I have to create jobs for unemployed Puerto Ricans so that they can eat a good meal every day. If what I'm doing is not right, you tell me what you want me to do.' These were tough men who had fought many battles, but I think that they would walk out of a meeting with Moscoso saying, 'This guy is really committed. Are we going to sink that island?'" What Moscoso needed, Suslow said, was acceptance that some sort of accommodation would have to be made with the unions. Perhaps in his heart of hearts he would have preferred not having to deal with them. Suslow's job was to constantly remind Moscoso that the worst possible Fomento policy was to ignore the unions.[3]

The Dubinsky agreement allowed Bootstrap's takeoff to continue into the 1960s. Total employment climbed rapidly: 114,000 new jobs were added to the labor force from 1960 to 1965. Leading the surge was precisely the apparel industry: of the 100,591 manufacturing jobs in 1965, 39,828 were in apparel and other textile-related industries.[4]

The success in avoiding uniform application of the federal minimum wage to Puerto Rico was one of two events crucial to Puerto Rico's economic development that took place during the 1950s; the other one was the massive migration of young Puerto Rican workers to the U.S. mainland. As a Nathan Associates analysis pointed out, Puerto Rico averted a catastrophic increase in unemployment in the early part of the decade as a result of the migration of working-age Puerto Ricans. Regardless of whether the government of Puerto Rico should promote the exodus of Puerto Ricans—indeed, whether the government was already secretly engaged in the anti-patriotic policy of driving Puerto Ricans from the island—became still another highly controversial issue. And once more, the accusing finger was pointed at that loose cannon—Teodoro Moscoso.

Chapter 13

Migration

To New York and Brazil

Moscoso's admiration for Muñoz was based in large part on Muñoz's willingness to sacrifice both ideological and political sacred cows in order to sustain economic development. Whether it was tax exemption, legalized gambling, or fighting for minimum wage flexibility, Moscoso had faith that Muñoz would sacrifice short-term political expediency for the long-term welfare of the island.

But there was one area in which Moscoso deeply believed that Muñoz fell short: his unwillingness to confront the insular Catholic Church on the issue of birth control. Moscoso, like almost every economist and social scientist who had addressed the issue since 1900, believed that unless Puerto Rico aggressively addressed its overpopulation, everything else amounted to "whistling in the wind." Muñoz would not yield to Catholic pressure to repeal the April 1937 island law legalizing birth control. Indeed, in his early writings back in the 1920s and 1930s, Muñoz recognized that the island was critically overpopulated. But at the same time, as much as Moscoso and others pushed him, he would not actively promote birth control clinics.

If birth control clinics and outreach programs were not possible, the only obvious alternative was massive migration. But Muñoz's and the Populares' attitude toward migration was the same as toward birth control: neutrality—to neither discourage nor promote it. Puerto Ricans began to move in large numbers to the U.S. mainland at the end of World War II. From an average annual outflow of 904 from 1930 to 1940 it jumped in 1946 to 39,911 and fluctuated between 24,000 and 35,000 in the next five years. Both statehooders and independentistas, eager to prove that the island still suffered from colonialism, branded Muñoz's much-heralded peaceful revolution as a hoax, as merely glowing statistics made possible by pushing poor Puerto Rican families off the island and into the decrepit slums of Spanish Harlem.

As the debate over Puerto Rican migration heated up, divergent viewpoints about its pros and cons began to come from key figures close to Fomento—the economists Rafael de J. Cordero and Roberto de Jesús and even Fomento cofounder Rafael Fernández García.

Cordero, the veteran economics professor and auditor of Puerto Rico, had been one of Moscoso's early mentors, a man whose views on the island's economic realities, especially the overwhelming impact of the population explosion, deeply influenced Moscoso's thinking.

However, while Moscoso had begun to think more and more about a structured Puerto Rican migration program as a way to defuse the population bomb, Cordero arrived at the conclusion that it was a bad social and economic policy for Puerto Rico to encourage migration. In an article published in 1952, he wrote that migration gave the island only temporary relief and that it was not the escape valve it was made out to be.[1] First, studies demonstrated that the educational level of the migrants was higher than that of the remaining population. Therefore, it made no sense for Puerto Rico to invest in educating and developing the skills of young people if they were going to take their productivity outside the island. Cordero asked: "Can a poor country permanently incur in these costs without receiving the benefit of their productive labor?"

In any case, he argued, it was likely that many of the migrants would return when the U.S. economy slowed down, and Puerto Rico would be back where it started. Cordero threw further cold water on Fomento: a good part of the island's current growth, he said, was a result of war-related spending, including payments of as much as $100 million a year to World War II and Korean War veterans. Still, the island's yearly per capita income was only $300.

Even if the 1952 high level of migration continued, Cordero insisted, the only realistic policy to combat the island's monstrous population problem was for the government to carry out a birth control program of "sufficient dimension and intensity." Moscoso agreed that reducing the island's natural growth (66,750 in 1952) through government-sponsored birth control programs was the real solution. But who was going to convince Muñoz and the Populares?

Like so much in island politics, the debate over migration became a question of semantics. Muñoz insisted that the government's migration policy was neutral. But when a government makes it as easy as possible for its people to migrate, when it trains them, gives instructions in new living conditions, provides basic English classes, battles the airlines to keep the fares low, and establishes employment offices at their destination, isn't it in effect sponsoring a policy that encourages migration?

From Moscoso's point of view, this was another superficial political debate. No one could stop Puerto Ricans from buying plane tickets and going to New York; they were American citizens. But the stark reality was that the giant movement of Puerto Ricans out of the island was an unexpected blessing, and the first person in Puerto Rico who should have recognized it was precisely Rafael de J. Cordero.

Moscoso himself had Cordero's article published in the October 1952 issue of the Fomento magazine. In the next issue he published a sharp reply by the equally well-respected head of the Budget Office, Roberto de Jesús. Cordero's description of the migration as antisocial and antieconomic, de Jesús argued, had an important flaw: it ignored the fact that the flow of Puerto Ricans between the island and the mainland was two-way.[2] In 1952, 277,000 islanders went north, while 217,000 returned, many bringing back skills, experience, formal education, and a work ethic acquired on the mainland. So it was inaccurate, de Jesús wrote, to say that the migration was draining Puerto Rico of its most productive population; on the contrary, it was adding to the island's productivity. Furthermore, he went on, while it was true that most migrants were more skilled and better educated than the remaining population, it was reasonable to expect that as the migration continued, the less skilled and less educated would follow. As for Cordero's fear that once the U.S. economy slowed down, the migrants might return to the island, de Jesús pointed out that there would still be strong incentives for Puerto Ricans to stay on the mainland, especially because the economic conditions there were bound to remain better than in Puerto Rico. Other factors undoubtedly were the unemployment and other welfare benefits available only in the United States.

The basic point of de Jesús's answer to Cordero, however, was that the rapid increase in migration had indeed become a blessing of great significance for Puerto Rico. De Jesús began his article: "The first of January of 1953 there were in Puerto Rico 3,883 fewer people than in the first of January of 1952." Also, for the first time, de Jesús continued, the island's birth rate dropped below 40 per thousand: down to 37.2 in 1951 and to 35.1 in 1952. While recognizing that demographic predictions for the United States as well as for Puerto Rico had often been wrong, de Jesús ventured the "cautious opinion" that full employment would continue in the United States, thus Puerto Ricans would continue to migrate. The result in Puerto Rico during the next decade was likely to be a stable or moderately growing population.

*　　*　　*

The start of the Korean War on June 25, 1950, created a tight labor market on the U.S. mainland. It had the double effect of making Puerto Rico more attractive for labor-intensive light industry and the mainland more alluring to unskilled Puerto Rican workers. By 1952, the total annual outward flow of migrants had risen to 59,103.

For Moscoso's cold economic planners, this was similar to the $160 million rum tax rebate windfall during World War II. It gave Operation Bootstrap a breathing period. If the migration continued, perhaps Moscoso and Fomento could begin to win the race against Puerto Rico's unemployment.

Moscoso, meanwhile, understood the human factor involved. "It was heartbreaking," he later recalled.[3] "We saw these thousands of Puerto Ricans going from an exotic culture to a hostile environment for which they were not prepared, to a city where many found discrimination. We saw them getting off the chartered airplanes in New York, out into the freezing temperature, without coats, some without even jackets." This was a dilemma for the government of Puerto Rico. Because it could not prevent Puerto Ricans, American citizens, from moving to the mainland, the least it could do, Moscoso argued with unusual emotion, was to prepare them for the move and, once there, help them to adjust. Muñoz agreed and asked Moscoso to deal with the problem. "It was another vacuum that Fomento moved into."

Although worker migration was indisputably an area under the jurisdiction of the Puerto Rico labor department, Moscoso decided to set up offices on the U.S. mainland to assist recent Puerto Rican arrivals. He named "a jíbaro from Caguas" by the name of Adrian Higgs, son of an American soldier who arrived with General Miles in 1898 and decided to stay on the island, to head the new program. The Boston-educated young Higgs had exceptional mechanical skills and had just returned to Puerto Rico when Fomento lawyer Mariano Ramírez discovered him. He was ideally suited to provide Fomento factories with much-needed technical assistance, Ramírez told Moscoso. However, on an impulse, Moscoso selected him to run a "Fomento Puerto Rico employment service."

The outgoing, friendly Higgs immediately set up makeshift educational centers throughout the island where potential migrants got a quick course on what to expect in New York and the other large American cities, plus a smattering of basic English. His next assignment was to convince the U.S. Labor Department's employment service to include Puerto Rico in its programs. To complement this, Moscoso had Higgs set up programs at the Fomento regional offices in New York, Chicago, and Los Angeles. "We had serious problems at the beginning with the mainland employment service," Ramírez recalled. "Moscoso stepped on many toes in Puerto Rico. Now he stepped on the United States Labor Department's toes." Higgs, however, succeeded in working out an agreement with the department to include Puerto Ricans in the "expanding circle recruitment system."⁴

Although the vast majority of the migrants ended up in Spanish Harlem and South Bronx, Fomento made a big effort to find job opportunities in other states. Fomento's office in Chicago learned of a plan to bring over three thousand unskilled workers for a $500 million expansion of Minnesota's iron-mining industry. In addition, there were job opportunities for five hundred construction workers. The Fomento office began recruiting islanders, warning them that "this is hard work that requires a good physical condition."⁵ The applicants were also advised that they should be no less than five feet five inches tall and weigh more than one hundred fifty pounds. Fomento found that Puerto Rican workers were already finding their way throughout the country. There were clusters of workers in such cities as Cincinnati and Lorraine, Ohio; Milwaukee, Wisconsin; Gary, Indiana; and Salt Lake City as well as Detroit and Chicago.

Now the idea was to establish Fomento's own expanding circle around a nucleus of Puerto Rican families. The Salt Lake City office found such a nucleus. In the mining towns of Copperfield and Dinkeyville, thirty miles southeast of the city, were seventy-six Puerto Rican families who had been living and prospering since they decided back in 1944 to accept the offer of a Kennecott recruiter who had come to Puerto Rico.

This was clearly an experience radically different from the depressing, violent *West Side Story*. Moscoso ordered a detailed study of these early migrants. Forty of the families owned their own homes, all with television sets; all the families owned automobiles. The families were mostly small compared to those on the island, although one couple had eleven children. Most of the men had married Puerto Ricans; several married Italian or Mexican women. They all had achieved a significantly higher standard of living than the average island family and a yearly family income of $6,000. Although they all came from rural Puerto Rico, according to the Fomento report, they had become reasonably fluent in English and were well integrated into the community, participating in church and civic activities. Their success as mine workers was confirmed by their job seniority; one Puerto Rican from Mayagüez, Jesús Ortiz, had become an instructor in other Kennecott mines.

There was, however, a sour note. The company was so pleased with the original group it had recruited from Puerto Rico that it decided to recruit four hundred more. But instead of recruiting on the island they went to New York to offer the jobs to Puerto Rican migrants already there. The company soon discovered that these Puerto Ricans were different—less goal-oriented, less willing to relocate and settle, and some apparently came thinking their new jobs would be a pleasure trip. There was, the Fomento study showed, a somewhat distressing difference in the work ethics and attitude of many Puerto Ricans who had first migrated to New York.

* * *

Meanwhile, Moscoso convinced Muñoz to institute a formal, well-financed program for migrant education and assistance. A migration division was created in the insular labor department under an assistant secretary of labor with the added responsibility of carefully supervising the contracts and working conditions of the seasonal migrant farmworkers. By the end of the 1950s, the migration division's staff was working in 115 cities and towns throughout the United States.[6]

As much as the new migration division attempted to assist workers and their families, however, the mass migration of Puerto Ricans was considered a major national tragedy by many American social scientists. The United States, of course, was a country of immigrants from foreign countries and migrants within its own borders. In the 1950s, more than thirty million Americans moved within a state or from one state to another. There had been a huge migration of blacks from the rural South to the industrialized North after World War II. But now the highly publicized arrival of large numbers of Puerto Ricans seemed to catch even New York City unprepared. Culturally, they were foreigners like immigrants in the past, but they were also American citizens who qualified for welfare assistance.

One sensationalist New York newspaper headline about the 1946 increase in migration screamed: "Tidal Wave of Puerto Ricans Swamping City." Two years later, another New York paper reported that there were already 710,000 Puerto Ricans in New York, when in fact there were 180,000. Some New York commentators saw a "conspiracy" led by left-wing Congressman Vito Marcantonio to bring swarms of Puerto Ricans to New York to feed and oil his political machine. Others saw the massive migration as driven exclusively by the desire to live on welfare in the United States. "In the last 20 years," one organization said, "some 60,000 of these Brown Brothers have been funneled into our town, mostly in East Harlem."7

*   *   *

Moscoso began asking: Why New York? Why not promote migration to a friendlier environment with lots of space—say, Brazil? It was the interior secretary in the Roosevelt administration, Harold Ickes, who put this idea into Moscoso's head a decade earlier. He suggested to the House Interior Committee that it explore the possibility of setting up Puerto Rican colonies in Central or South America. Enthused, Moscoso and Rafael Fernández García prepared a long memorandum filled with Puerto Rico's dreadful demographic and social statistics and urging Ickes and Congress to pursue the idea. To ensure that Ickes got the memo, Moscoso asked Interior Undersecretary Oscar Chapman to deliver it personally. Although Chapman replaced Ickes when he resigned in 1946, and in spite of getting such important members of Congress as Senator Charles Bell and Representative Fred Crawford to support the idea, it lay dormant until 1951, when a Brazilian economist visited Puerto Rico.

Dr. Rómulo Almeida came to the island to attend a United Nations economic congress. During a meeting with insular government officials including Fernández García, he mentioned Brazil's programs to promote immigration of skilled workers and farmers. After returning to his country, he wrote a letter to Fernández García informing him that he had been appointed economic advisor to President Getulio Vargas. Moscoso and Fernández decided to use this letter to probe the Brazilian government about its interest in the establishment of Puerto Rican agricultural colonies in the country. But first, they needed Governor Muñoz's personal approval.

Would Muñoz want to enter into negotiations with the Brazilian president? As both Moscoso and Fernández were to find out, everything having to do with Brazil took a curious twist. President Vargas ruled Brazil as "an outright—but amiable—dictator" from late 1930 to 1945, when he was overthrown by the army.8 Instead of retreating into a life of undisturbed comfort, he decided to run for the senate. He then ran for president in 1950 and was overwhelmingly elected in what was regarded as an unusual but legally conducted election. This made him a constitutional president, not the right-wing dictator with whom Muñoz earlier would have refused to deal.

For tiny Puerto Rico, with its 2.2 million people tightly packed into 3,540 square miles, the possibility of working out something with Brazil seemed, according to Moscoso and Fernández, too good to be true. Here was the fifth largest country in the world, more than twice as large as the next biggest in Latin America, Argentina. Brazil was a country known for its unusual, at times even bizarre, politics and leaders but with truly staggering economic potential. It had one more plus: a friendly culture, to a large degree free from class and racial tensions. Moscoso and Fernández could only marvel at the statistics. More than half the country had a population density of less than one person per square kilometer; three-fourths of the entire country had a density of less than five persons per square kilometer. At the same time, Fernández pointed out that with a total population of 50 million—unlike almost all the rest of Latin America—Brazil represented a big enough internal market to ensure agricultural as well as manufacturing success for the Puerto Rican colony's enterprises.

Muñoz authorized Moscoso and Fernández to inform President Vargas through economist Almeida of his strong interest in Puerto Rican immigration to that country. In July 1951, Moscoso sent Fernández to Brazil on a forty-day visit that included meetings with members of the government and the private sector and with agricultural experts. Also, he was to explore several sites for the colony, both north and south of Rio de Janeiro.

Fernández carried a letter from Governor Muñoz Marín to the Brazilian president. While very interested in the project, Muñoz wrote, he was nevertheless acutely aware that a "migratory movement of the kind that your country and mine envisage, requires careful consideration and delicate adjustments."[9] Puerto Ricans who live throughout Central and South America are known for their hard work and respect for the law. They have contributed to the economic and cultural development of their adopted countries. Dr. Fernández García, Muñoz assured Vargas, "is authorized to discuss the diverse aspects of this project with the officials whom you consider convenient, and on his return to Puerto Rico he will submit a report that will receive the most careful consideration on the part of our Government."

Fernández García arrived in Brazil sensing that his was a mission of historic importance to Puerto Rico. As his aircraft flew from Caracas to Río, he was able to experience the country's immensity. He had the eerie sensation of flying for seemingly endless hours over virgin land with no sign whatsoever of human life or habitation.

Fernández now also experienced firsthand the peculiarities of the Brazilian work style. On arrival he learned that his host, Almeida, was not waiting for him and instead had left on a three-day trip. Americans in Puerto Rico tended to criticize the islanders for their excessive informality in keeping appointments and their inability to follow a time schedule—the exception, of course, being Fomento. In Brazil, Fernández found that government employees started work late in the morning. Their supervisors would not appear until one or two o'clock in the afternoon. He was not able to hold more than one meeting a day and often had to wait two or three days for the next one.

But Fernández managed to meet with numerous government officials, farmers, engineers, and academics. He visited several colonies of European immigrants, talked extensively with the families, and compiled a great number of statistics—the composition of the family units, the exact measurements of their homes, the furnishings and appliances, a precise breakdown of the farms, the number of milk cows, bulls, pigs, chickens, and roosters. He focused on one colony of Dutch immigrants, carefully analyzing the economic and technical assistance received from the Brazilian and Dutch governments. The immigrants, he reported, seemed healthy and happy. Why could there not be another equally successful colony of Puerto Ricans?

Finally, after inspecting potential sites for a Puerto Rican colony north and south of the capital, he believed he had found a zone with all the basic requirements: extensive and uninhabited land available at low cost and flat enough for mechanized agriculture; a proper climate for tropical products; abundant rain or easy irrigation; proximity to a large population center; and available communication links.

Going over soil analyses, Fernández learned that an area south of São Paulo along the Ribeira River was among the most fertile in the region. He was delighted to discover in São Paulo's office of vegetable production an even more detailed study of several valleys along the river. One of these captured his attention: it was 12,500 square kilometers, over one-third bigger than Puerto Rico, and had only 80,000 inhabitants. He learned that this zone attracted early European immigrants but was abandoned because it was not apt for coffee plantations. The area did produce corn, sugar, bananas, and rice. Brazilian engineers pointed out that the valley led to the Bay of Cananeia, which offered superior conditions for a magnificent port. Further interviews with local farmers showed Fernández that the main reason the valley was not fully developed was the lack of adequate transportation to the port. Nearby, he was told, was a highly successful Japanese colony producing large quantities of tea for Holland, Canada, and the United Kingdom. Rainfall and temperature tables demonstrated that the climate was similar to that of the small, mountain town in central Puerto Rico, Aibonito.

* * *

Fernández returned to Puerto Rico eager to get to work on the project. He was known for his low-key, scholarly, controlled demeanor, and everyone at Fomento took notice of his enthusiasm. Fernández displayed more optimism about the Brazilian venture than he had on any earlier projects. He envisioned a project of a magnitude previously not dreamed of even in Moscoso's unbridled imagination: the creation of an idyllic, small Puerto Rico where at least three hundred thousand islanders would find a promised land of security and comfort.

Fernández prepared a draft of a sixteen-point agreement to be entered into by the governments of Brazil and Puerto Rico. He proposed that Brazil purchase and make available to Puerto Rico 6,000 square kilometers of land. Puerto Rico would create a company—a public corporation—to bring the immigrants from the island and administer the colony; Puerto Rico and Brazil would share equally the cost of the extensive infrastructure-building. The Cananeia port area would be converted into a free port in which the Puerto Rico company would promote industry. Fernández went on in great detail, including provisions that allowed Puerto Ricans to take their kitchen appliances without paying duties, the establishment of a one hundred thousand-ton quota for refined sugar to sell to the Brazilian government, and specific authorization for the Puerto Ricans to fish in the Ribeira River.

Fernández informed Muñoz and Moscoso that he had discussed the sixteen-point plan with President Vargas, who suggested that the government of Puerto Rico officially submit it. The total cost for Puerto Rico over a ten-year period would be $100 million: fifty thousand families would live in farms averaging thirty-five *cuerdas*. Although Fernández attempted to restrain his enthusiasm in his long report to Muñoz and Moscoso, it clearly broke through. Unlike the current "depressing" emigration of many young skilled Puerto Ricans workers to the United States, he wrote, entire families would move to Brazil to create a flourishing Puerto Rican community. Furthermore, unlike the current unplanned, uncontrolled exodus, "the effect of this emigration to the economy of Puerto Rico will be stimulating."[10]

But Fernández García, even with Moscoso's full support, could not get Muñoz to focus on this historic plan. Muñoz was now totally involved in an even more important historic project—getting the people of Puerto Rico and the U.S. Congress to approve the 1952 constitution for the island and a new political status.

Meanwhile, President Vargas also had his own distractions. His 1950 triumphant return to power deteriorated into tragedy. He had won the elections easily but now found the country much more difficult to govern without returning to iron-fist rule. His enemies, led by the fiery editor of the

newspaper *Tribuna de Imprensa*, Carlos Lacerda, became increasingly stri-
dent and fearless. The sixty-nine-year-old president seemed confused and
vulnerable: "Vargas, who appeared to be losing his grip, did not seem to
know what was going on in his own palace, which fairly boiled with graft,
intrigue and corruption," wrote the veteran Brazilian journalist.[11] The nightmare led to a tragedy; one of Vargas's sons sued the belligerent newspaper
editor for slander, and the following year, assassins attempted to kill the
editor. He survived, but a popular former air force officer who served as his
bodyguard was killed. Lacerda accused Vargas's son of the plot. On August
24, 1954, a group of military officers gained entrance to the presidential
palace and demanded Vargas's resignation. Vargas withdrew to a nearby
room and killed himself.

The grandiose project to create a Puerto Rican paradise in Brazil died
with him.

Chapter 14

Winds of Change

In mid-1950, Moscoso decided that it was time to begin planning his retirement and to pave the way for a new generation of men and women to take over Fomento.

Running the agency had become much more complicated as well as exasperating. Fomento was promoting oil refineries, high-technology electrical assembly plants, and pharmaceutical companies. But while Fomento had kept up with the sophistication and expertise needed to function in the new promotional environment, the rest of the Puerto Rican government agencies had not. Moscoso found it more difficult to push to perform at the higher levels necessary to attract the industrial giants. At times he felt as if he had to carry on his own shoulders not only his own agency but also practically the entire Puerto Rican government. It was increasingly hard for him to contain his frustration.

For example, many of the large, new industries that aimed to come to Puerto Rico required a vast and rapid upgrading of the island water and sewer authority's treatment plants in order to meet legal standards for toxic waste disposal. An impatient Moscoso could not understand why this government agency, a public corporation with the ability to sell bonds and regulate the cost of water and sewer services, could not move faster. As much as he complained and pushed, Fomento promotions began to back up due to the failure of the rest of the government. He asked himself: Fomento was modernizing Puerto Rico, but who would modernize the government of Puerto Rico?

The nagging philosophical differences with Muñoz never really subsided. There were the recurring, largely symbolic incidents involving a small statue of Mahatma Gandhi. Often, when Muñoz wanted to tell Moscoso to slow down, to stop and think of the broader social implications of a program, Muñoz would reach for the little statue, which he kept on his desk, and simply push it toward Moscoso. Finally, at one meeting, Moscoso reacted badly: "Don't, Don Luis. Please stop pushing Gandhi at me!" As much as Moscoso admired Gandhi's great leadership in freeing his people from colonialism, he thought that his romanticized vision of an India totally free of modern industrialization was a sure prescription for poverty. Ask Nehru, Moscoso wanted to shout back at Muñoz. But no, it was futile to continue this debate with Muñoz. Instead, he would make a gradual exit from Fomento. First he would convince Muñoz to allow him to run the agency from the New York office. He would train one of his lieutenants to run the Puerto Rican operation, and eventually, if the successor lived up to expectations, Moscoso would propose the person as the new administrator of Fomento. But first, Moscoso had to convince Muñoz that Fomento was so strong and efficient that it no longer needed him.

For an island so long paralyzed by a "prevailing sense of hopelessness," the feature article in the 1962 Britannica Yearbook was the ultimate compliment. Puerto Rico, it reported, was "the most hopeful example in the Americas of how to develop an underdeveloped community in the clean atmosphere of freedom."[1] Puerto Rico had become a sort of senior member among developing societies. The article added: "The results of Fomento's work are spectacular." The Bootstrap program drove up the island's net income by 700 percent in just two decades, from $225 million to $1.5 billion. Per capita income went from $121 to $571. Most of the growth came from private investment. In 1959, half of the island's $116 million gross fixed investment was private; a decade later its gross fixed investment of $300 million was two-thirds private.

In 1959, Fomento had broken through the "100 hundred plants in a year barrier;" 111 new factories had begun operations. The total was now 631 industries in operation or being established. The Fomento staff had grown to three hundred. One of the bright statistics gathered by Hugh Barton and his economic staff of forty professionals was that of Fomento's cost effectiveness. As of 1950, Operation Bootstrap had generated thirty times more additional government revenue than the total government expenditures for the program.[2] This, Moscoso and Barton hoped, would end the misconception that tax exemption was a cost to the insular treasury. Puerto Rico was now beginning to move into big-league, big-investment industrialization, such as petroleum refining and processing; one of the new capital-intensive industries was the $50 million Commonwealth Oil refinery twenty miles west of Ponce. This plant in turn attracted a $28 million Union Caribe plant. There were many other heavy industries on the horizon.

"Fomento was going pretty much as I wished," Moscoso said years later.

"If anything, the rate of industrialization was too fast. That became the new criticism: we were modernizing Puerto Rico too quickly, the social structure was being demolished with nothing else to take its place. My answer was: look, the Planning Board was created to plan, the Department of Education to educate. I was hired to industrialize. '*Cada palo carga con su vela*.' Each mast must hold its own sail."

Coming on the heels of the expansion of the main airport's facilities, the introduction of jet travel suddenly allowed the island to overcome one of the great, historical obstacles to its development. The travel time from the U.S. mainland to San Juan was cut to less than half. Moscoso's advertising and promotion, which at the beginning misleadingly made it seem that Puerto Rico, U.S.A, was within easy reach, was now accurate. Strong airline competition, meanwhile, aggressively pursued by Fomento, provided excellent transportation for cargo as well as passengers. Another positive break was the closing of American tourism in Cuba following the January 1959 overthrow of the Fulgencio Batista dictatorship and the Fidel Castro takeover. Puerto Rico's tourism got an unexpected boost. One of Moscoso's principal sources of frustration in the 1950s had been the slowness in attracting private hotel investment, even after the Caribe Hilton's resounding success. By 1958 there were only 1,155 tourist hotel rooms, including the new Lawrence Rockefeller-owned resort in Dorado. Now jet travel and the Cuban Revolution ignited a hotel construction boom. By the end of 1960, there were nearly 3,000 rooms. Total annual visitors from the mainland numbered 400,000 and contributed $58 million to the economy. Puerto Rico experienced a virtual tourism gold rush; investors could not build hotels room fast enough. The big problems facing Puerto Rico in the early 1960s became hotel overbooking and poor service by hurriedly trained hotel workers.

*   *   *

In attempting to convince Muñoz to let him move to New York, Moscoso did not want to reveal his weariness. Instead, he approached Muñoz positively. Moscoso was now publicly predicting the agency's continued promotion of up to two hundred new plants a year, reaching a total of 2,500 by 1975, even accounting for the ones that would be closed along the way. This in turn was the basis for Muñoz's prediction in his 1960 message to the legislature that the island's net income would triple by the end of the decade. At this stage Moscoso would be more useful ensuring that enough new promotions entered the conveyer belt at the New York office. If any new problems developed at the Puerto Rico end, he would jump on one of those new jet planes and fly back.

Moscoso had another argument in favor of moving to New York. As he looked at his travel records for the past few years, he found that he spent more time on the U.S. mainland than at home. He regretted not having been more of a part of his son's and daughter's upbringing. Now, he simply wanted to "come home every night."

He decided to consult Roberto Sánchez Vilella, his brother-in-law and now secretary of state and Muñoz's right-hand man, knowing that if Sánchez disapproved, Sánchez might kill the idea with Muñoz. Sure enough, Sánchez objected. The head of a top insular agency could not work in New York. There was no precedent, and there were too many meetings in Puerto Rico that Moscoso could not miss. What about scheduling all the meetings on the same week of every month? Moscoso countered. As they discussed the proposal, Sánchez asked if he was willing to fly to San Juan twice a month. Of course, Moscoso answered. Write everything down on paper and I'll take it to Muñoz with my recommendation, Sánchez added. Muñoz approved it on a trial basis; if it didn't work, Moscoso would have to return.

For Moscoso, however, there was no returning. He had already selected the person to take over the Puerto Rican operation—the tough-minded young economist who was in charge of the New York office, Rafael Durand. Moscoso felt that Durand was perhaps too much of an introvert but was a fast learner, a sponge for new information. Moscoso considered another young administrator, Danilo Ondina, who, like Durand, was not the outgoing salesman type but a good planner and solid thinker. They would make a good team, Moscoso believed, greatly facilitating his exit. But Ondina took himself out of the running, accepting a high executive position in one of the island's principal banks, the Banco de Ponce. Durand would be Moscoso's successor.

*　　*　　*

It was a good omen for the big move to New York. Over lunch with Arthur Ochs Sulzberger, who three years later, in 1963, was named publisher of the *New York Times,* Moscoso mentioned that he was frantically looking for an apartment in mid-Manhattan. How much are you willing to pay? Sulzberger asked. Fomento was going to pick up part of the rent but it could not be terribly expensive, Moscoso answered. One quick phone call by Sulzberger to the newspaper solved the problem. There was an apartment at 875 Fifth Avenue owned by a retired General Electric vice president who was spending the year abroad. It was a bargain at $500 a month.

"Getting the apartment was pure luck," Moscoso said, "but it was also the result of one of the most important bonuses of working in Fomento—

the network of friendships made through the years, getting to know people of importance, with power, who can do things." More than any other Puerto Rican including Muñoz, Moscoso developed a network of friendships throughout the United States that he used fully throughout his life. Like his mother, who loved the adventure of moving to new houses, cities, and countries and immediately surrounding herself with new friends, Moscoso now looked forward to this new chapter in his life. The city, however, was hit by a snowstorm the day he and Gloria moved into the apartment. The following day they went out into the street. "The city was silent. There was no traffic, there were no people. We walked maybe twenty or thirty blocks without meeting anyone." This peace and quiet in Moscoso's life would be short-lived.

The Battle for Democracy in Latin America

The task we set for ourselves in the Alliance for Progress, which is the development of an entire continent, is a far greater task than any we have ever undertaken in our history.

President John F. Kennedy, 1962

Ted Moscoso . . . accomplished so much in such a short time in Washington despite the many obstacles confronting him.

Senator Hubert H. Humphrey, 1964

Chapter 15

Moscoso in Venezuela

If Moscoso was hungering for new challenges in his life in 1961, he was about to embark on an unexpected three-year, heart-stopping roller-coaster ride in Latin America and Washington. On March 21, he received a letter from Undersecretary of State Chester Bowles addressed to Fomento's New York office. He had suggested Moscoso's name to President John F. Kennedy for the post of American ambassador to Venezuela. Bowles knew Puerto Rico well. He had visited the island several times beginning in 1955 as Muñoz's guest. An admirer of Operation Bootstrap, he had encouraged Senator John F. Kennedy to visit the island in 1958 to meet Muñoz, Moscoso, and other Puerto Rican "miracle-workers." After Kennedy's election, Bowles was one of the president-elect's advisors who promoted the "democratic left" of Muñoz, Rómulo Betancourt of Venezuela, and José Figueres of Costa Rica; he also promoted the Bootstrap development model as the basis of a new U.S. policy toward Latin America. After a lengthy discussion with Gloria, Moscoso wrote back to Bowles offering himself for the appointment.[1]

Venezuelan President Rómulo Betancourt had spent years of exile in Puerto Rico. He was a man of exceptional courage who was now determined to lead his country to democracy. Betancourt had to face not only the traditional opposition from the right but also the new threats from the radical left. Fidel Castro and Ernesto "Che" Guevara were proclaiming that the Cuban Revolution would convert Latin America into "many Vietnams." Oil-rich Venezuela was the first battleground.

As a candidate, Kennedy followed the advice of Bowles and others and relied heavily on Muñoz Marín and the Puerto Rican experience in democracy and rapid economic development in forging a new American policy toward Latin America. He appointed Moscoso to a task force on Latin America headed by the old New Dealer, Adolf Berle, who had long been engaged in Puerto Rican matters. "Kennedy," Arthur Schlesinger Jr. wrote, "whose friendship with Muñoz began with the Puerto Rican trip of 1958, fell heir to [Muñoz's] ideas and relationships."[2] The essential thrust of these ideas consisted in converting U.S. policy and power into an agent— instead of an opponent—of fundamental social and economic reform in Latin America through support of leftist democratic leaders precisely like Venezuela's Rómulo Betancourt.

Meeting with President Kennedy on May 2, Moscoso became acutely aware of the extraordinary difficulty and importance of his assignment. One day before his Senate confirmation on April 18, a contingent of 1,400 U.S.-trained Cuban exiles invaded Cuba. The Bay of Pigs fiasco critically damaged Kennedy's credibility in calling for a new "alliance for progress" between the United States and Latin America. There was no doubt in Moscoso's mind that Kennedy's personal interest in Latin America was real and deep— deeper than within his own administration, as Moscoso was to discover, beginning with the State Department hierarchy. Nothing would dramatize the shift in U.S. attitudes toward Latin America as much as Kennedy's strong and sustained support of Rómulo Betancourt. While never a doctrinaire Communist, the young Betancourt had joined the Costa Rican Communist party during his exile there. Now Kennedy trusted Muñoz's and Moscoso's assurances that he had, indeed, evolved into a democratic leader. Success in the democratization of this resource-rich country, the scene of the ugly mob violence against Vice President Richard Nixon in 1958, was crucial to Kennedy's ambitious hopes of radically changing the Latin American perception of the United States. But there was also Kennedy's determination to prove himself in the Cold War. "The Alliance for Progress," Schlesinger wrote, "represented the affirmative side of Kennedy's policy. The other side was his absolute determination to prevent any new state from going the Castro road and so give the Soviet Union another beachhead in the hemisphere" (773).

In its 130-year history as a soverign nation, Venezuela had never witnessed the constitutional transfer of power from one elected president to another. "President Kennedy," Moscoso recalled years later, "made it clear that I had a defined objective."[3] It was to prove, in the Venezuelan ideological battlefield, that the Alliance could work, that Betancourt could survive both the reactionary military-backed oligarchy and the Fidel Castro-backed guerrilla insurgents. The specific goal was to use American policy and power to help Betancourt achieve his big reforms and thus demonstrate that the United States was really committed to democratic revolution. As Moscoso walked out of the Oval Office, he felt that he had a mission vital to this young administration and this young president. Just how vital would be brought home to him the moment he arrived in Caracas.

*   *   *

When the news of Moscoso's appointment reached the Venezuelan capital, demonstrations flared up throughout the city. A motion was introduced in parliament calling on the government to reject the appointment. A Communist legislator denounced what he described as an attempt by the United States to end Puerto Rico's fight for independence. Another member of parliament from the *Unión Republicana Democrática* party joined the attack. Moscoso did not represent either the United States or Puerto Rico, he cried, since Moscoso turned his back on the island's demand for freedom. Acceptance of Moscoso, he said, was acceptance of Puerto Rico's "perfumed colonialism,"[4] the name Castro and his followers gave to Muñoz's commonwealth status. Since his student days, Castro had been a pasionate advocate of Puerto Rican independence. More to the point was the graffiti that appeared throughout Caracas declaring *Muerte a Moscoso:* Death to Moscoso.

The embassy staff in Caracas took the graffiti seriously enough to urge Moscoso to delay his arrival until the orchestrated demonstrations and protests subsided. In an office provided at the State Department in Washington, Moscoso took a crash course on Venezuela's economic and political crisis.

Betancourt's first two years in office had been beset by a severe recession. Dictator Marcos Pérez Jiménez had embarked on a spending extravaganza during his last years in power by building spectacular public works projects. His administration, riddled with corruption, left behind a gigantic public debt. President Eisenhower's oil import restrictions were another crippling blow to the economy. Betancourt's election, furthermore, provoked a panicky flight of Venezuelan capital. The one thing Moscoso could do immediately was to stem the flow of capital by dramatizing the Kennedy administration support of the Betancourt government. From Washington, he began calling on his network of friends on Wall Street, including George Wood, chairman of the First Boston Corporation, and the respected liberal economist Robert Nathan. An economic mission arrived in Washington from Caracas; Moscoso became the contact with international credit institutions. It was determined that a line of credit of $600 million would create investor confidence in Venezuela. Moscoso found that oil-rich Venezuela had little experience in dealing with credit institutions.

Finally word arrived from Venezuela that even though the government expected more street demonstrations, Betancourt personally guaranteed the

Moscosos' safety. On May 14, 1961, Moscoso, Gloria, and their son José arrived in a commercial aircraft at Maiquetía Airport, where they were met by a delegation of government officials, military and police officers, and embassy personnel. The unusual importance the media assigned to him was evident by the number of reporters and photographers who surrounded the group, insistently asking Moscoso about Puerto Rican independence. Moscoso, prepared, brushed off the questioning, pointing at Puerto Rico's exercise in self-determination in freely selecting commonwealth status.

The Moscosos were rushed to waiting automobiles accompanied by forty heavily armed police officers. Several hundred other police were posted along the route to his residence. A military helicopter was on standby in case street demonstrations prevented the drive to Caracas. One top police commandant told the press that this was the "most extensive display of military protection since the visit of Vice President Nixon."[5] Unlike the Nixon visit, however, the Moscosos' ride was uneventful.

Nine days later, in what the local media described as an unusually elaborate ceremony at Miraflores, the presidential palace, Moscoso presented his credentials and an autographed copy of President Kennedy's book, *Profiles in Courage,* to the Venezuelan president. Betancourt's stoic expression changed to a smile as he accepted the gift.

Moscoso was certainly not the stereotypical "ugly American" diplomat who did not understand the local culture or speak the language. The question about Moscoso was whether he was an "American" at all. Years later, Moscoso referred to this implied ambivalence in his identity: "When I was in Latin America, I felt like a North American: when I was in Washington, I felt like a Latin American."[6]

At one meeting with Venezuelan officials soon after his arrival, Moscoso compounded the confusion as to his role and his loyalty. He took two embassy economists to a meeting with a man whom he admired, Minister of Mines and Hydrocarbons Juan Pablo Pérez Alfonzo, who had made his mark as the principal proponent and later cofounder of the Organization of Petroleum Exporting Countries, OPEC. In January 1961, OPEC held its second conference in Caracas under his leadership.

At the meeting with the oil minister, Moscoso became annoyed with the manner and tone of his two seemingly hostile economists. At one point, one of the economists raised his voice and banged the table with his fist. Moscoso lost his temper and ordered the embassy economist to shut up. Jumping to his feet, he ended the meeting and apologized to the oil minister. The next day he was informed that the economist had asked to be transferred to another post. This made him angrier, and during a luncheon with a reporter for the *New York Herald Tribune,* Moscoso let off steam: "These men were . . . yes . . . disrespectful to that minister . . . they pounded the table and made demands."[7]

Moscoso received a call the next day from the State Department. The *Herald Tribune* and other newspapers had published front-page stories about the incident. In Venezuela, the story caused a sensation. One newspaper carried a screaming headline: "Moscoso Criticizes Functionaries of the U.S. Embassy in Caracas." The story enhanced his standing with the Venezuelans. As Moscoso's son, José, commented: "My father was really seen as a Venezuelan minister without portfolio, working directly to help modernize the country."[8] But this was precisely the perception of the new ambassador that troubled members of his embassy staff in Caracas and his diplomatic superiors in Washington. "I think I did not make many friends with the Foreign Service that day,"[9] Moscoso admitted. The State Department professionals now had reason to question Moscoso's deepest loyalties.

Two weeks later, Moscoso was involved in another incident that produced more sensational headlines in the Caracas papers. This time, however, it was more than his loyalty that was questioned by Washington—it was his sense of survival.

Ignoring that to enter the campus of the state university in Caracas was a provocation to those responsible for the *Muerte a Moscoso* graffiti, Moscoso accepted an invitation to the opening of an exhibit of modern American architecture at the Caracas School of Architecture. The elderly Spanish-born chauffeur, who usually talked endlessly, was now quiet and appeared apprehensive as he drove the ambassador's Cadillac limousine into the campus.

The mood at the event was cheerful, and after the presentation the professors invited Moscoso to visit the faculty facilities up on the eighth floor. At about supper time, the time he usually arrived home, he started to leave. Gloria would surely worry if he delayed longer. But the professors and other guests urged him to remain. A half-hour later, he made another attempt to leave and was again urged to stay. This time he started to get suspicious. Finally, he was informed that he could not leave the building. A mob of radical students had occupied the first floor and was attempting to get into the elevators to come up after him. His car had been burned. The chauffeur had escaped unharmed, but when he attempted to rescue the briefcase that Moscoso left behind, a student had yanked it from his hands. A jeep appeared and apparently attempted to push Moscoso's car off the campus. Near one of the exits to Roosevelt Avenue, the jeep stopped, and students set the car on fire.

The mob that occupied the first floor of the building was shouting anti-American slogans and *Muerte a Moscoso*. The university's chancellor, Francisco de Venanzi, emerged and with other university officials was doing his best to prevent the students from entering the elevators. The Caracas district governor, Alejandro Oropesa Castillo, one of Betancourt's closest political collaborators, finally arrived with a police contingent. Up on the eighth floor, the professors received word that Moscoso could be brought down. He was pushed into an elevator filled with police and taken out of the building. The militants were held back behind a cordon. With hysterical cries of *Linchemos a Moscoso*—"We will hang Moscoso"—still ringing in his ears, he was pushed inside a waiting car that sped away.

When Moscoso arrived at his residence, Gloria told him to phone Betancourt immediately. Betancourt was beside himself with anger. "He gave me a dressing down," Moscoso confessed later.[10] "He shouted, 'Do you know that I am the President of this country? Do you know that I don't dare enter the University grounds? And you, the American Ambassador, go in there with no security.'" Betancourt could not believe that Moscoso was so foolhardy as to play into the hands of the extreme left, giving it a golden opportunity to achieve what it had attempted in the anti-Nixon riots: to cripple Venezuelan-American relations.

The next day, the Venezuelan media were filled with stories reporting that the attack was not a spontaneous demonstration but had been organized by a Communist professor and two well-known radical student leaders, all directed by the Communist member of parliament.

In the State Department, there was still another reason to be concerned about the judgment of the intrepid—or naive—Puerto Rican. Moscoso had not only entered the campus without security but also had left in the car a briefcase brimming with confidential reports prepared by one of the embassy's technical advisors, Irving Tregan. Moscoso intended to read them carefully that night at home. He had assigned Tregan to study and evaluate the operation of the key economic ministries, to analyze their efficiencies and make recommendations for improvement. Tregan's reports, meant for Moscoso's eyes only, were brutally candid in describing deficiencies in operations and personnel. Moscoso had told Tregan that he did not need to be diplomatic, as Betancourt personally requested these evaluations. Now, in the hands of the extreme left, the reports became more ammunition against Betancourt and the United States.

Moscoso's worst fears were realized. The contents of his briefcase surfaced at the August 1961 meeting of the Organization of American States at Punta del Este, Uruguay, to formalize President Kennedy's ambitious Alli-

Moscoso spent only five months as U.S. ambassador to Venezuela in 1961, but they were months filled with action-packed excitement and drama as he worked closely with President Rómulo Betancourt to establish democracy in that nation. One of the highlights of his stay in Caracas was the visit of one of Moscoso's political heroes, Adlai Stevenson, here with him and Gloria Moscoso.

ance for Progress. Che Guevara, in military uniform, led the Cuban delegation. He said the Alliance was doomed to failure. It was "a device designed to separate the people of Cuba from the other peoples of Latin America, to sterilize the example of the Cuban Revolution and, finally, to domesticate the people of the hemisphere to the orders of imperialism."[11] Guevara repeated Castro's famous pronouncement that the "Andes will be the Sierra Maestra." According to an American delegate, it was a "chilling prophecy ringing in the ears of the delegates." At the climax of his speech, Guevara announced that he was going to reveal concrete evidence of how the Kennedy administration had already succeeded in domesticating one Latin American government, one Latin American leader. Displaying the Tregan reports, Guevara declared that this was conclusive proof that Rómulo Betancourt and the government of Venezuela were controlled by the Yankee ambassador. While the Castro delegation knew that it could not derail the signing of the Alliance for Progress Charter, it believed that the revelation would undermine its credibility.

In Venezuela, however, Betancourt turned the tables on Castro and Guevara. Cuban possession of the Tregan documents, the Venezuelan newspaper *El Mundo* reported in big headlines, constituted devastating confirmation that the anti-Betancourt movement had become a tool of Soviet-Cuban propaganda. On August 16, Venezuela's *El Mundo* reported: "Russian Espionage in Caracas: Secret Documents given to Castro."

Moscoso's own consternation that his foolish action had compromised the U.S. mission at the Alliance conference was relieved when the head of the delegation, Treasury Secretary Douglas Dillon, assured him that Guevara's attack had little impact on the Latin Americans. Nineteen Latin American nations, all except Cuba, went on to sign the Alliance for Progress Charter.

*   *   *

On the evening of October 26, 1961, the embassy in Caracas received a wire message from President Kennedy. It was for Moscoso. Kennedy wanted him to run the Alliance for Progress. "I regard this," the president said in the cable, "as one of the most important jobs in the United States government today and have complete confidence in your capacity to undertake it successfully."[12]

Moscoso took the message to the privacy of his library; he needed time to think. Outside the library, he could hear staff members milling around. The content of the message, delivered to him only moments earlier by a marine, had somehow gotten out to the staff.

Moscoso's thoughts first went to Rómulo Betancourt and how deeply and personally involved he had become in helping the Venezuelan leader—his friend, Muñoz Marín's friend. Moscoso had arrived less than six months earlier and was accomplishing Kennedy's specific mission to help Betancourt survive his full term in office. But then he felt another strong emotion. Yes, he had this sense of obligation and deep bond with Betancourt, but also with all Latin America. With the president's message in his hand, Moscoso said to himself: I am, after all, a Latin American. Of course he was a U.S. citizen and openly proud of it. But his upbringing, his native language, his culture, all made him a Latin American. He had an understanding of Latin Americans that was extremely difficult, perhaps impossible, for North Americans to acquire, even those as liberal and open-minded as Adolf Berle or Richard Goodwin. He understood Latin America's faults—the tendency toward exploitation, greed, selfishness. How many of the men who signed the Punta del Este Charter really understood what they had signed? How many really intended to remake their societies after centuries of a repressive social and economic structure cast by millennia of cultural formation on the Iberian Peninsula? But at the same time, he also valued the resourcefulness of the Latin American masses. Give the people a chance, give them the tools, and look what they can do for themselves. Look at what the Puerto Ricans did for themselves.

Since his appointment to Venezuela, he loved to ask State Department specialists on Latin America if they had read José Enrique Rodó's book *Ariel.* You must, he preached, for no one will ever understand Latin American intellectuals and political leaders without understanding the effect of this thin volume published in 1900, which became "the pillow-book of a generation of Latin American youth."[13] It was, Moscoso thought, a historical accident. Rodó was born and lived almost all his life in the same small country in which the Alliance for Progress was launched, Uruguay.

The book, *Ariel,* had become the intellectual wellspring of anti-Americanism in Latin America. The essential argument was that American culture represented a historical retreat in world civilization: the triumph of the material, utilitarian savage over the human spirit. Americans were the Calibans of civilization.

There was one way that he could help the United States in Latin America, Moscoso thought: by promoting and communicating a simple idea, stated by many others but never understood by the State Department "realists," that culture, more than politics, economics, and military hardware, is the key to reaching the Latin Americans. He recalled an incident back in 1953 when he arrived at the airport in Lima, Peru. In the same airplane was Henry Kaiser, the famous and admired American industrialist who played a gigantic role in World War II in building 1,490 ships in as little as four and a half months. Moscoso was surprised that this industrial genius was arriving unnoticed and was met only by a couple of U.S. embassy employees.

A short distance away, however, there was a big crowd of Peruvian youths pressing toward another aircraft that was taxiing in. Moscoso could see behind one of the windows the face of a man "with a beautiful moustache." When the man stepped out, Moscoso recognized William Faulkner. He was mobbed by the youths, books and pens in their hands, begging for his autograph.[14] This, Moscoso now said to himself, is the key to reaching Latin Americans. The Alliance, of course, was about democracy and social justice, land distribution, tax reform—but those same students who considered *Ariel* their gospel, the same who joined in spitting at the vice president

A crowning moment in Moscoso's career was his appointment by President John F. Kennedy as coordinator of the Alliance for Progress at the White House on November 6, 1961. A year later, Kennedy described the Alliance as "probably the most difficult assignment the United States has ever undertaken." Moscoso's two years of running the Alliance were a heart-stopping, roller-coaster experience of accomplishment and exhilaration but also one of disappointment and frustration.

of the United States, who cried *Muerte a Moscoso,* would peacefully rush to the American embassy or any other building hosting a reading or conference by William Faulkner.

But there was another stab of doubt that he had never experienced before. He thought of the president's words: "I regard this as one of the most important jobs in the United States government today." Can I do the job? Am I up to it? The hell with it, he said as he opened the doors of his library and found his entire staff smiling widely, approaching to shake his hand and celebrate. It had not crossed their minds that Moscoso, the fearless human dynamo, would not leap at the enormous challenge.

Moscoso made his decision: he would accept the helm of the Alliance for Progress. That evening Secretary of State Dean Rusk phoned Moscoso. Would he fly to Washington as soon as possible to meet with President Kennedy?

Chapter 16

The Alliance for Progress

President Kennedy put any final doubts to rest during their meeting. The president greeted Moscoso amiably and offered him a drink, which the nervous Moscoso gladly accepted. Richard Goodwin, who wrote Kennedy's Alliance for Progress speeches, was there but only for a few minutes. Moscoso explained some of his lingering misgivings to the president. But Kennedy felt that his work in Puerto Rico's development, his help in building an economic system from scratch, and his understanding of Latin America's problems qualified Moscoso to lead the Alliance. "He just said that I had to take this job, that he had discussed it with several people, and that he felt that I was the obvious choice," Moscoso recalled.[1] On November 6, the White House press office announced his appointment.

The Alliance committed the United States to providing "more than a billion dollars during the twelve months which began on March 13, 1961" as the first installment of a pledge of more than $20 billion in direct assistance and institutional financing over the next ten years.[2] Many in Congress saw the Alliance as an extraordinarily generous foreign aid program that should accommodate the United States' own economic interests and Cold War strategy. However, the $20 billion was only 10 percent of the total amount deemed necessary to jump-start the economies of the Latin American partner countries and to bring about social reforms. The remaining 90 percent was to come from the Latin Americans themselves, according to the accords signed at the Punta del Este conference that launched the program. The individual Latin American monetary commitments, however, had yet to be agreed upon or budgeted. The accord was in fact more rhetoric and hope than developmental nuts and bolts.

Moscoso was surprised and disappointed when informed that his title would be "Assistant Administrator of the Agency for International Development." He was one of AID's four regional administrators working under

After his appointment as head of the Alliance for Progress in 1961, Moscoso thought he had convinced President Kennedy to give the Alliance administrative autonomy with its own identity, as was the case with the Peace Corps. Moscoso's "conspiracy" was frustrated by Secretary of State Dean Rusk. Here they are seen meeting in 1961.

AID's director. This was a far cry from Kennedy's description of his assignment as one of the most important jobs in the U.S. government.[3] Indeed, Kennedy also made it clear that Moscoso would be in charge "of the entire Alliance for Progress effort." Did the State Department really expect him to run and represent the Alliance for Progress before all Latin America and to be in charge of a plan to overhaul nineteen national economies while carrying the bureaucratic title of assistant administrator of an agency deep within the bowels of the department's bureaucracy? That, in Washington terminology, was a "non starter" if he ever saw one.

This was one battle Moscoso won over the objections of the State Department. Although he remained an assistant administrator of AID, he was finally given the more impressive additional title of "coordinator of the Alliance for Progress." The new title, however, did not make much of a difference. William Rogers, Moscoso's special counsel at the Alliance, wrote: "When

Teodoro Moscoso was sworn in by President Kennedy . . . the Latin American Bureau he was supposed to administer was an organizational shambles. . . . Space, secretaries, regulations, all cried out for attention. No one was certain even where the offices would be located."[4]

Moscoso set out to make the Alliance administratively autonomous, much like the Peace Corps run by Kennedy's brother-in-law, Sargent Shriver. Moscoso wanted an agency that was administratively and physically separate from AID and even the State Department. State Department officials who had suspected that the Puerto Rican was naive enough to take the president's high-flung Alliance rhetoric literally were right. According to the State Department, Moscoso's idea was so outlandish that it would immediately fall on its face. It was absurd to run the equivalent of a separate State Department just for Latin America. The extraordinary scope and complexity of Kennedy's Alliance required not a separate agency but precisely a program under tight departmental control.

The president was scheduled to make his first trip to Latin America on December 15, 1961. He and Mrs. Kennedy were to stop overnight in Puerto Rico on their way to Venezuela and from there go on to Colombia. Moscoso was asked to accompany them. As the expert on Puerto Rico and Venezuela, Moscoso's first assignment in Washington was to help make the preparations for the trip. Now he would have the personal opportunity to argue his case for a Peace Corps-type Alliance agency at least physically—if not officially—separated from the State Department.

There were great concerns over the president's security. Richard Goodwin and Deputy Assistant Secretary of State Morales Carrión, another major Puerto Rican appointment in the Kennedy administration, strongly supported the trip. Secretary Rusk questioned Moscoso extensively on President Betancourt's ability to control subversives in Caracas. Clearly, a repeat of the ugly and dangerous riots that marred Nixon's 1958 visit to Caracas would prove mortal to the Alliance.

The trip was a big success. In the outskirts of Caracas, Kennedy was taken to a rural community where Betancourt was carrying out a land reform program. Along the way, Moscoso and Goodwin rehearsed Kennedy in pronouncing selected key words in Spanish. However, he decided not to read his short speech but to attempt to communicate directly with the poor farmers. Moscoso saw how relaxed and natural the young president felt in what should have been an exotic setting for a politician from Boston. Kennedy spoke with his usual elegance but, it seemed to Moscoso, with unusual conviction and emotion. He used the language of the democratic left: land reform, tax reform, real distribution as well as creation of wealth. Moscoso was moved; there could be no question that the president really believed in the Alliance's idealism. Betancourt leaned toward Moscoso and said: "He is talking not just to these *campesinos,* but to all *campesinos* in Latin America."[5]

In Bogotá, Colombia, the crowds were also large and emotional. President Alberto Lleras Camargo, who unlike Betancourt spoke fluent English, turned to Kennedy to assure him that the people were cheering him "because they believe you are on their side."[6] Incredibly, not a single violent incident occurred during the entire trip. The meetings with the three leaders of the democratic left—Muñoz, Betancourt, and Lleras—dramatized how far U.S. policy had moved from the days when American presidents pinned medals on the uniforms of detested Latin American dictators.

Moscoso first brought up the subject of the Alliance's organizational autonomy on the flight from Washington to San Juan. Asked to sit next to the president during parts of the flight in order to go over the briefing books on each country, Moscoso broached the subject. Kennedy was sympathetic. Moscoso explained how Fomento's ability to promote its own distinct identity had worked in favor of Puerto Rico's Operation Bootstrap. Moscoso wanted to achieve the same esprit de corps, the same intense pride and loyalty in each of the Alliance employees. An OAS artist, Moscoso continued, had prepared an excellent logo for the Alliance; it depicted a hand-held torch within a forward-thrusting triangular arrowhead design. Moscoso would display the logo in all Alliance projects throughout the hemisphere, and all Alliance employees would wear it as a lapel pin. The president clearly liked Moscoso's enthusiasm.

The president and Richard Goodwin also discussed the need to make the Alliance more responsive and efficient. "I think he [Kennedy] had an idea of setting up the Alliance as a separate entity that would give it much more freedom and flexibility from the whole bureaucracy. Just before his death, he was talking very seriously about creating the post of Undersecretary of State for Latin America. We had discussed it the day before he went to Texas," Goodwin recalled.[7]

After Bogotá, the last stop on the trip, the president told him to proceed with his plan for a separate Alliance agency, Moscoso asserted. Kennedy assured him that he would put it in writing after his return to Washington. "As a result of the decision, while flying back to Washington I began to work out the strategy of getting out from under the wing of the State Department."[8]

Moscoso's first task was to get his Washington staff under one roof. Again, he had a stroke of luck. After informing his assistants of the president's approval, they quickly located a newly vacated building on Pennsylvania

Avenue. It was at the right location and of the right size. Moscoso visualized a large Alliance flag flying prominently from the building to be seen by the millions of visitors to the nation's capital. He ordered stationery printed with the Alliance logo. Most important, as he and his people rushed forward with his plan, Moscoso was constantly reassured of his special relation to the president. Kennedy phoned him frequently and on several occasions invited him to spend the evening with him and members of his family. All this made Moscoso feel secure in his defiance of the State Department. But he noticed an increase in media criticism of his program. There were stories and comments that the Alliance was disorganized and simply not moving forward. Moscoso decided to turn this criticism in his favor, using it to prove that the Alliance desperately needed emancipation from the stifling State Department bureaucracy. It was all true, he complained to reporters; he was having a terrible time simply organizing the offices, getting desks and secretarial help. Highly motivated, newly recruited professionals were unable to get work done. But the negative stories boomeranged. The image of the Alliance in disarray merely fortified the stereotype of a Hispanic who had the ability to sell the Alliance but not to run it.

Another communications strategy backfired; this one originated in the White House. The decision was made to organize another high media event to commemorate the first anniversary of Kennedy's first announcement on the Alliance made on March 13, 1961. The media, however, focused instead on the Alliance's shortcomings. So strong were the criticisms that the *New York Times* came to its defense, editorially pointing out that "it is a bit unfair to pick . . . [on this] ten-year program that only now is getting under way. Pessimism and cynicism at this moment are worse than unrealistic; they can strangle the Alliance before it gets a chance to take form and gather momentum."[9] The newspaper's warning was to prove prophetic.

For Moscoso, the most damaging event took place at a White House meeting called by the president in late February 1962. In attendance were Assistant Secretary of State for Latin America Robert Woodward, AID Director Fowler Hamilton and other AID officials, Richard Goodwin, and Moscoso. The purpose was to prepare for the first-anniversary events, but the meeting rapidly became a heated discussion about what had gone wrong. Reports of what took place at the meeting quickly circulated throughout the AID offices. The reports in turn sparked the most negative media coverage yet: both *Time* and *Newsweek* magazines ran stories describing the Alliance as a program in shambles, with 225 Washington employees scattered throughout the city in four separate buildings. Many of the 1,060 field workers were considered unqualified; the *Newsweek* article stated that "nine out of ten mission chiefs will have to be replaced."[10] *Newsweek* reported that when the president finally turned to Moscoso, he answered: "Sir, this sort of thing is too silly to discuss in front of the president, but the facts are that I have no secretaries. I have an agency spread all over town and the bureaucracy is getting me down." There was a moment of stunned silence at the meeting. White House aide Arthur Schlesinger later noted that the president reacted to Moscoso's statement by calmly, matter-of-factly suggesting that he hire Kelly Services temporary workers. "I doubt if there is any precedent," he wrote, "of a President concerning himself with such matters, but it reflected Kennedy's willingness to give attention to even the most minor point and give a most sympathetic hearing to the most absurd complaint." Schlesinger added that Moscoso made matters worse by complaining that he was unable to get a relatively minor administrative official transferred from another AID office to the Alliance. The president, Schlesinger noted sarcastically, then "immortalized the particular gentleman" by ordering that he be relocated.

That Moscoso had brought up such complaints at a meeting with the president became an albatross around his neck. "The story," Schlesinger noted, "was famous in AID." Decades later, a former AID official who was not at the meeting but who recalled the negative impact within the agency commented: "I think that Moscoso never recovered. It was the number one topic of conversation in AID and the rest of the State Department. It hurt Moscoso's reputation in Washington."[11]

The State Department now had its opportunity to squash Moscoso's scheme for an independent Alliance. He had scheduled the long-awaited move to the new building for the following weekend. Everything was ready; office materials and personal effects were stored in labeled boxes, desks and other furniture stacked in the hallways. The day of the move, however, Moscoso received a telephone call from new Undersecretary of State George Ball. Do not proceed with the move, Ball flatly ordered Moscoso. Stunned, he began to inform Ball of the president's personal approval after the visit to Bogotá. Ball interrupted: "Just stay put, and do not call the president on this. He agrees that he cannot have two Departments of State."[12]

Moscoso's immediate reaction was personal. There was, he felt, a condescending tone mixed with anger and arrogance in George Ball's voice. In an article published in 1988, Moscoso wrote: "It crossed my mind to pack my bags and return to Puerto Rico, but I rejected the thought when I considered what leaving Washington 'in defeat' would mean to Puerto Rico and to me personally."[13]

It took Ball and others a week to decide what to do with Moscoso and his

Although Moscoso was second only to Luis Muñoz Marín as an architect of modern Puerto Rico, he deliberately avoided and discouraged media attention. So while Bootstrap received widespread media coverage in the United States and worldwide, Moscoso was often the "invisible man." Here is a rare portrait photo of Moscoso taken in the 1970s after his return to Fomento.

people. The staff was told to keep everything in boxes, ready to move. Finally, on March 3, the order was received to move to the third floor of the old State Department building. To make room, those occupying offices were "given 30 minutes to clear out 'and no arguments,'" *Newsweek* reported in its issue of April 9, 1962. Some in Moscoso's staff, caught in the confusion, their work paralyzed, along with the furious State Department people forced out of their offices, now cast in cement their view that it was all Moscoso's fault. Meanwhile, Moscoso expressed to *Newsweek* his sense of resignation: "I'll go on with this bureaucratic millstone around my neck as long as I can."

*   *   *

Moscoso's decision to remain in Washington meant resignation, even submission, but not surrender. "There comes a time when you give up fighting the bureaucracy and if you can't beat them, well, you join them," he concluded.[14] As he had done in Fomento, he set out to attract a staff of exceptionally motivated assistants. William D. Rogers, associated with Puerto Rico for years through Abe Fortas, left his position as a partner of the law firm of Arnold, Fortas, and Porter to become a special counsel. William Dentzer, Moscoso's special assistant, became a key link to official Washington, working for White House assistant Ralph Dungan and for AID administrator Fowler Hamilton. William Haddad, a crusading New York journalist married to a granddaughter of Franklin Delano Roosevelt, joined the team to head the public affairs program. Robert Goldman, who later headed the Anti-Defamation League of B'nai Brith International, joined as a speech writer. And Moscoso called on his old Fomento network. First Boston Corporation Chairman Robert Wood, who soon after was named president of the World Bank, agreed to join a special advisory committee. Economist Alvin Mayne, a former Puerto Rico Planning Board economist, came on full-time and became especially active in assisting the Dominican Republic. Hubert Barton, Moscoso's alter ego in Fomento, now out of the cloud of Communist affiliation in the State Department, joined for special assignments.

There were important accomplishments in the critical though mostly unseen task of building the institutions Latin America's economy needed. Moscoso asked Enrique Campos del Toro, the man who organized and ran Puerto Rico's first savings and loan bank, to duplicate his success in the region. Nearly one hundred were established by the mid-1960s, generating millions in local savings used to build new private housing.[15] There was also success in organizing credit unions: by 1963 there were 2,500 of them with nearly 600,000 members. Working with George Meany and the AFL-CIO, training was provided for Latin American labor leaders in union organization, in the techniques of collective bargaining, and in establishing cooperatives. In 1964 David Rockefeller organized the Council for Latin America, a new forum for ongoing coordination between American businesses involved in Latin America and the Alliance team. That year the U.S. Chamber of Commerce issued a strongly supportive report with numerous recommendations to improve the Alliance.

Even those who criticized Moscoso admired his infectious enthusiasm and superior salesmanship. Schlesinger wrote: "Moscoso was unexcelled in communicating the political and social idealism of the Alliance to the Latin Americans, who had great faith in him, where he was well respected, and to his own staff."[16]

Moscoso also succeeded in his relations with key congressional leaders. Congress had rejected Kennedy's request for a three-year appropriation, thus denying the Alliance this modicum of stability and continuity. Conservative Congressman Otto E. Passman, chairman of the House Appropriations Committee, whom Schlesinger described as "a fanatical foe of all foreign aid," became an adversary of the Alliance. During the congressional hearings, Passman kept Moscoso on the witness chair for days, barraging him with questions.[17]

The result was that the funds destined for Latin American programs and projects were delayed. Meanwhile, Moscoso came under pressure from the increasingly impatient Latin Americans. Some congressmen, in turn, echoed this impatience. At one congressional hearing, a congressman who had recently returned from Bolivia, considered the most backward country in Latin America after Haiti, pointed out that during the previous year several million dollars were approved to build a much-needed airstrip. Bolivian leaders complained bitterly to him that work on the airstrip had not begun. The congressman visited the site and saw for himself that they were right. Now he demanded to know from Moscoso why the delay. Patiently Moscoso described the great difficulties of building anything in a country with few engineers, technicians, or skilled workers. He fumed later to his staff that fifteen years after Congress approved it, the Dulles International Airport was still far from complete: "Americans invented instant coffee, instant soup, instant everything—now we're expected to build instant airports in Bolivia."[18]

Still, Moscoso was able to produce impressive numbers: by October 1963, Alliance funding had built 8,130 schools, 139,800 houses, 685 sewer systems, 900 hospitals, and benefited 14,746,000 people with the Food for Peace program. The Alliance clearly was gaining momentum. Three years after it was launched, $4.5 billion in direct U.S. aid plus an additional $1 billion in institutional financing had flowed into Latin America. The Latin American governments themselves had spent between $22 billion and $24 billion in Alliance-related programs. Four years into the program, the Alliance had provided 7,000 miles of roads, irrigation for 136,000 new acres of farmland, 530,000 kilowatts of electric power, classrooms for 1 million students, 450 new health facilities, and granted $200 million in financing for 5,000 industrial firms and $250 million for credit to 450,000 farmers.[19]

Moscoso had succeeded in inching forward the bureaucratic monster in Washington, even though each request for AID funds required the approval of fourteen different U.S. agencies plus three interdepartmental committees created precisely to expedite the requests. But even more daunting, he had begun to move the other bureaucratic monsters within each of the nineteen Latin American nations.

To assist him in this enormous task Moscoso counted on a committee of OAS and Latin American economists—dubbed the "nine wise men"—to approve each country's developmental plan. Moscoso saw the group as a master planning board for all Latin America. It was headed by Chilean economist Raúl Sáez; Harvey Perloff, who had prepared Puerto Rico's first five-year economic development plan in the late 1940s, was one of the U.S. representatives.

The president mentioned to Moscoso his desire to move an old friend, former MIT economics Professor Richard Bissell, from the CIA into Alliance work. Bissell was one of the architects of the Bay of Pigs attack—and he became one of its political casualties. However, aware that Bissell had worked on the Marshall Plan, Moscoso enthusiastically offered to provide him a temporary office to prepare an analysis of the plan's lessons applicable to the Alliance. He wanted guidelines on how to make the Alliance a truly multinational program by shifting leadership and responsibility from Washington to Latin Americans. The president liked the idea.

One evening, Moscoso unthinkingly asked Bissell to accompany him to a fine French restaurant, the Left Bank, where they would dine with Sáez and other members of the Alliance planning committee. When Moscoso walked into the restaurant, Bissell at his side, he saw the faces of the Latin Americans freeze. Bissell's involvement in the Bay of Pigs had been highly publicized. One of the Latin Americans present was Cuban economist Felipe Pazos, who went into exile after being replaced by Che Guevara as the head of Cuba's Central Bank. Moscoso realized he had committed an embarrassing faux pas. The last thing these Latin Americans wanted was to be seen in public with one of the authors of the Bay of Pigs. Pazos was visibly uncomfortable. Others followed. "We finally sat down," Moscoso recalled years later, "to a very, very cold evening."[20]

Bissell's study, however, contributed to what had become Moscoso's principal goal: convincing a highly skeptical State Department and the president to fundamentally change the structure of the Alliance to make it a true partnership with Latin America. "It was not clear," William Rogers wrote, "that Latin America wanted a truly multilateral effort, but in Washington there was an agreement, in 1963, to find out."[21]

That the Alliance simply could not succeed until it became truly "Latin-americanized" was the thesis of two other reports prepared independently by Brazil's former President Juscelino Kubitschek and Colombia's former President Alberto Lleras Camargo, two of the region's top political leaders. These reports were also critical of the snail-paced Alliance programs, but they proposed exactly what Moscoso and his people were actively promoting in Washington—the creation of a Latin American-controlled Alliance board of directors. While uniting the economic and political-diplomatic components, the board would effectively run the program and have virtual control of its funds.

What began as discussions "within a small circle in AID and State," Rogers wrote, now engaged "widening circles in the Department and the White House." The issue was no longer the fate of the Alliance, but whether the United States was willing to submit its own national interest to the decisions of this new body. This raised the difficult and emotional issue of American sovereignty. "The United States would be committing a hoax if it embarked on the venture half-heartedly," Rogers added.

In November 1963, in São Paulo, Brazil, acting on the recommendation of the U.S. delegation headed by Averill Harriman and with the sole opposition of Kubitschek's successor, João Goulart, the OAS's Economic and Social Council created a new body, the Inter-American Committee for the Alliance for Progress, CIAP. It was not all that Moscoso and some of his people in the Alliance had hoped for in passing responsibility to the Latin Americans. The United States retained ultimate authority for final disposition of its own contribution to the Alliance. But it was, for Moscoso, a crucial step forward.

Moscoso became so ill during the CIAP meetings that he was unable to get out of bed to attend several sessions. He was aware that the campaign to select the head of CIAP had begun, and he wanted to be in the center of it. "The lobbying that went on was incredible, absolutely incredible," he commented.[22] It was evident that the quality of the leadership, the international prestige of the person selected to head the CIAP, was vital. But Moscoso was looking beyond. The leader had to be more than an economist or a developmentalist; he had to be a visionary dedicated to an economically and politically integrated Latin America, the dream of Simón Bolívar. That person existed, Moscoso had decided: the brilliant Argentinean Raúl Prebisch. "Prebisch was perfect for the job because he was not only a great economist, but also a political animal—he had charisma and he was a diplomat." Also, Moscoso thought in private, having Prebisch at the helm meant that the opportunity was at hand for him to make a graceful exit.

Although it was less than two years since he had left Fomento for Venezuela and less than a year at the Alliance, Moscoso rationalized many reasons for returning to Puerto Rico. Wasn't it time he put his family first? His wife, Gloria, had followed him from Ponce to San Juan in the early 1940s, leaving behind a life of security and comfort; she had spent two decades hardly seeing him at night or on the weekends, tending to unexpected dinner and house guests, bringing up the children by herself. Moscoso was still reproaching himself and would for the rest of his life for his absence from José's and Margarita's childhood. During the Venezuelan stay, Gloria had constantly worried about the ever-present threats of *Muerte a Moscoso*. She was also unhappy in Washington; everyone in the city seemed to be, like themselves, transient.

In December 1962, as that frustrating, emotionally draining year came to an end, Moscoso stole time for a Christmas trip to Puerto Rico. He went to see Muñoz, his mentor, to let off steam. Moscoso pulled out press clippings severely criticizing the Alliance's slowness and administrative difficulties: "Many aid experts," an April *Newsweek* article read, "call it the sickest agency in Washington . . . we ought to rename it the Alliance without Progress." A March *Time* headline read: "*Alianza, Si, Progreso, No.*" Yet, Moscoso lamented to Muñoz, there were encouraging signs that the Alliance was meeting one of its principal objectives. Eight countries had exceeded the goal of 2.5 percent annual growth.

By now determined to leave, Moscoso could dedicate himself to what might well be, after all, his most lasting contribution: the installation of Raúl Prebisch as the head of the new Alliance. Moscoso never got the opportunity to convince Kennedy before the fatal trip to Dallas on November 22, 1963.

Moscoso's days running the Alliance, however, were numbered. "I knew that he [President Kennedy] was dissatisfied with the administrative ability of Moscoso," Robert Kennedy wrote.[23] "He'd hate to get rid of Moscoso— he liked him, and of course, he knew Latin America liked him—but he didn't feel it was going very well. He was quite eager to get some better personnel to run it."

His brother, Kennedy went on, had attempted to convince Sargent Shriver to take over the entire AID program. Shriver declined after making a study of the agency and determining that he could not run it without precisely the same administrative autonomy and flexibility Kennedy had given him in the Peace Corps: Moscoso's exact argument.

*　　*　　*

Arthur Schlesinger sent Richard Goodwin the transcript of an announcement made that day by President Lyndon Johnson. Schlesinger scribbled at the bottom: "R.I.P. . . . the Alliance for Progress, born October, 1960, died, December 14, 1963."[24]

The new president, in his first administrative change following Kennedy's assassination, announced the removal of Teodoro Moscoso as head of the

Alliance for Progress and of Edward Martin as assistant secretary of state for inter-American affairs. Ambassador to Mexico Thomas Mann was named to both posts. Goodwin's reaction was bitter. Back in 1961 Kennedy had removed the conservative Mann from that same post precisely to make way for the Alliance.

"There is real gloom among advocates of the Alliance for Progress," Goodwin wrote in his diary and later published in his *Remembering America.* "Mann is a colonialist by mentality who believes that the 'natives'—the Latin Americans—need to be shown who is boss. He is a tough-line man— a man who feels the principal job of the United States in Latin America is to make the world safe for W. R. Grace and Company. He is not much of an administrator but is tough, arrogant, and opinionated. In other words he has all the worst qualities coupled with a basic lack of belief in the Alliance for Progress" (245).

Moscoso believed that Goodwin's emotional reaction was much too harsh. He did not see Mann as a doctrinaire colonialist but simply as a conservative Texan who could not help coming across as condescending toward Latin Americans. As ambassador to Mexico in 1962, he had demonstrated something less than diplomatic tact in distributing a pamphlet entitled *Mann and Marx.* William Rogers wrote: "Mann had no natural instinct for the vocabulary of idealism which had come so naturally to Kennedy and his appointees . . . a more dramatic shift in tone and style of U.S. Alliance leadership would have been difficult to imagine."[25]

Official Washington and the media reacted as if Moscoso and Martin had been ignominiously fired. Johnson, however, softened the blow by naming Moscoso U.S. representative to CIAP, a post with ambassadorial rank. Moscoso accepted, convincing himself that there was one paramount reason to remain in Washington: to urge Johnson to accept Prebisch as the head of the Alliance's new overseeing body.

Mann promised Moscoso that he would recommend Prebisch to the president. He kept his word. Several days later, while having dinner at home with friends, Moscoso received a telephone call from the LBJ Ranch—it was the president. Returning to the dinner table, Moscoso could not restrain himself from passing on to his dinner guests the good news that he expected Johnson to announce his endorsement of Prebisch as early as the next day. One of the guests, however, was *New York Times* correspondent for Latin America Tad Szulc. Years later, Moscoso confessed that he assumed that Szulc, whom he considered supportive of the Alliance, would wait for the official announcement. The following day, however, the story appeared on the *Times* front page under Szulc's byline. The journalist was simply following the dictates of his profession. But Moscoso never forgave him.

Enraged by the news leak, Johnson changed his mind and withdrew his support of Prebisch. Embarrassed and guilty, Moscoso flew to New York to personally apologize to the Argentinean. They were both crushed. Instead, former Colombian ambassador to the United States, Carlos Sanz Santamaría, was selected to head the CIAP.

"The Szulc story" and Johnson's inevitable reaction, Moscoso lamented, was a turning point in Latin American history that seriously hampered plans for regional integration. While in Paris in 1962, he had visited Jean Monet, the father of the European Common Market; he came away from the meeting convinced that a once-in-a-lifetime opportunity was at hand for Latin America's integration if the right person, Prebisch, and the right circumstance, the Alliance for Progress, coincided. Now, he was convinced, the moment was lost.

* * *

Moscoso resigned as U.S. representative to the CIAP on May 4, 1964. His departure, according to a *New York Times* editorial, was the final blow to what remained of the original Alliance idealism. U.S. policy had returned to its old "pragmatism," a euphemism that meant renewed tolerance of military coups and rightist regimes. The editorial recognized that Moscoso "served as [the Alliance's] midwife and nursemaid, shepherding it through its difficult beginnings." The *Washington Post* declared, "The resignation of Teodoro Moscoso is a twin loss. It deprives the administration of one of its most sympathetic and sophisticated advisers on Latin affairs and its deprives the Alliance of one if its most dedicated administrators and advocates." Senator Hubert Humphrey, who supported Moscoso throughout, said in a Senate speech that he deeply regretted the departure of a man who, along with President Kennedy, deserved the greatest credit for launching the Alliance. It was a tribute to the man, he added, that he accomplished "so much in so short a time in Washington" despite the many obstacles confronting him.

"The spirit of the Alliance," Moscoso said years later, "died with Kennedy, no doubt about it."[26] Shortly before the trip to Dallas, Kennedy told a convention of Latin American newspaper editors that "the task we set for ourselves in the Alliance for Progress, which is the development of an entire continent, is a far greater task than any we have ever undertaken in our history." For the rest of his life, Moscoso was to ask himself: was the Alliance for Progress, from the start, an impossible dream?

Part

Six

The Age of Section 936

Section 936 was not a giveaway, a loophole for U.S. corporations. It was to help our economy, particularly creating jobs, at
a moment when we were in a deep and serious crisis.

Salvador Casellas, Puerto Rico Treasury Secretary, 1973–76

Chapter 17

A Superport and a Confession

It was New Year's Day 1973. Moscoso and Gloria were enjoying the Christmas holiday in Río de Janeiro with their daughter, Margarita, her husband, and the couple's young children, Patricia and Sergio. The telephone rang. It was Muñoz's familiar voice. Return to Fomento? That's absurd, Moscoso objected. But according to Moscoso, the seventy-five-year-old Muñoz "got himself on the highest demagogic pitch I had ever heard . . . and by the end of the fifteen-minute conversation, I decided not to fight him any longer and to go back to Fomento."[1] Gloria could not believe that he had relented; holding back tears, she accepted his decision, as always.

Moscoso, in fact, was pleased by Muñoz's call. Since his return to Puerto Rico in 1964, after his resignation from the CIAP (Alliance for Progress), he had worked in the private sector, first as chairman of the executive committee of the Banco de Ponce's board of directors and later as chairman of the board of the Caribbean Oil Refinery Company, CORCO, the island's largest oil refining and petrochemical company. At first, heading CORCO gave Moscoso the satisfaction of spearheading another transformation in the island's economy. Backed by the firm's huge investments, Puerto Rico became one of the world's largest producers of petrochemical products.

Again, it was the island's special political status that provided the incentive for this billion-dollar industry. As of 1959, the U.S. government had prohibited the importation of foreign crude. President Dwight Eisenhower's Mandatory Oil Import Program was meant to safeguard national security by protecting the nation's oil industry, which was threatened by the growing competition of much cheaper oil from the Middle East and Africa. Puerto Rico, due to its unique status, was given special quotas to import foreign crude. Fomento successfully argued that it needed the quotas to attract job-creating investments. The quotas were in fact a powerful lure because they gave island-based refineries and petrochemical industries a substantial cost advantage over mainland producers.

Moscoso saw his job at CORCO as an extension, in the private sector, of his Fomento career. The petrochemical industry, he was convinced, allowed Puerto Rico to overcome one of its greatest obstacles to economic development. Except for the newly discovered copper deposits in the center of Puerto Rico, the island had no other exploitable natural resources. Plastic, he now preached with his old enthusiasm, was the "raw material of the future," with literally unlimited potential for new investments and jobs. "There is hardly a recent invention in the United States Patent Office which in some way is not connected with the creation of some kind of plastics."[2]

Moscoso also put to use his flair for dramatic public relations. He had CORCO technicians prepare a huge diagram depicting the company's phenomenal growth and its vast potential development. He called it "The Dream Sheet." It listed five "core plants," twenty-four satellite plants, and eight consumer-products processing plants. The total investment of $908.8 million would create forty thousand jobs. By April 1969, four years after joining CORCO, thirteen of the projects were in operation and another six in the engineering phase. By February 1973, Fomento had promoted a total of forty-nine new industries in petrochemical and allied products with a total investment of $1.2 billion. Moscoso as well as the head of Fomento, Rafael Durand, were convinced that thanks to the petrochemical industry, the original dream of Operation Bootstrap—almost full employment—was finally in sight.

By early 1973, however, after nine years in the private sector, Moscoso was eager for another change in his life. The relentless, driving, pushing style he used in Fomento and the Alliance for Progress created serious frictions with some members of CORCO's top management. The company itself was caught in a cultural war between conservatives who wanted to return to its safe roots as mainly a petroleum refiner and progressives who were driving to implement Moscoso's Dream Sheet.

CORCO chemist Dr. Barney Baus, a young progressive who worked closely with Moscoso in the development of new industries, recalled seeing a change in him. "I can't really say that I ever saw overt manifestations of his unhappiness. He was too positive a person to show it. With all his problems and difficulties with [CORCO president] Norman Keith, Moscoso's attitude was to continue to barrel forward, looking for answers and solutions. But he was definitely unhappy."[3]

Muñoz's insistent request that Moscoso, at age sixty-two, return to Fomento—although his better judgement gave him endless reasons for refusing—was in fact the excuse he needed to leave the private sector and go back to what was his true vocation, public service.

Since his return from Washington, major changes had taken place in Puerto Rican politics. Muñoz had retired from the governorship in 1964 and hand-picked as his replacement his trusted lieutenant, Roberto Sánchez Vilella. Sánchez was elected governor that year and almost immediately the Popular Democratic Party began to disintegrate. Muñoz, who had moved to Rome, was forced to return to the island and take command of the party he had founded. But it was too late. Hopelessly split, with Sánchez Vilella running on his own ticket against his old party, the Popular Party went down to its first defeat in 1968. Industrialist Luis A. Ferré, in his fourth try for the governorship, finally won.

When Ferré and his New Progressive Party took over the governorship in 1969, the key question was whether an ideological crusade for statehood would be launched, even though Ferré had stressed that a vote for him was not necessarily a vote for statehood. At stake was Operation Bootstrap, which was based on the island's unique political status within the United States. Statehood meant the end to U.S. tax exemption and the end of the Fomento program. But throughout his four years in office, Ferré walked a tightrope between his ideological commitment to statehood and Puerto Rico's economic dependency on manufacturing. Tampering with Fomento would inevitably slow down the island's economic development. When it came down to a clash between ideology and economic reality, Ferré opted for reality and signed the industrial tax exemption grants that Fomento requested.

Ferré and his party campaigned vigorously in favor of the application of federal minimum wage regulations to the island. But confronted with hard studies that predicted a massive loss of jobs in the apparel and footwear industries if the insular minimum wage was raised, Ferré made the difficult decision to continue Muñoz's old battle in favor of wage flexibility. Reversing course, he asked Puerto Rico's resident commissioner in Washington, Jorge Córdova Díaz, to also campaign actively against the elimination of wage flexibility. Again, the ideological commitment to statehood posed a political dilemma: creating more unemployment by enforcing federal minimum wage rates would obviously reduce Ferré's reelection opportunities in 1972.

The survival of the Fomento program under the Ferré pro-statehood administration was critical for another reason. It proved to investors that despite the change in ruling parties, Operation Bootstrap continued.

"Development of new industry takes time . . . that puts a premium on

Moscoso's biggest accomplishment in the 1970s, running Fomento, was the enactment by the U.S. Congress of Section 936 of the Internal Revenue Code, Operation Bootstrap's most important industrial incentive. During the crucial negotiations in Congress in 1974, Moscoso confers with Senator Edward Kennedy (right), Puerto Rico's Treasury Secretary Salvador Casellas (left), and the island's Resident Commissioner, a member of Congress, Jaime Benítez (second from left).

continuity of policy and personnel in an economic development organization," Moscoso wrote in 1984. "Much of Fomento's success is attributable to its initial quarter century of policy and operational continuity."4

*   *   *

In November 1972, the Popular Democratic Party was returned to power. A thirty-six-year-old Ponce attorney, Rafael Hernández Colón, who surprised everyone by emerging as the party's president after its shocking 1968 defeat, replaced Luis Ferré as governor of Puerto Rico. Hernández, who served as senate president in the previous four years, brought a new generation of professionals to his administration, yet he queried Moscoso about his willingness to return to Fomento. Moscoso's initial reaction was negative—until he received Muñoz's phone call in Río.

"Getting back to Fomento turned out to be traumatic," Moscoso later admitted.5

He soon realized how much Fomento had changed in the previous decade. It had become bigger, slower, and bureaucratic; it was grossly overstaffed. The agency still attracted bright, eager, young professionals, but Moscoso found veterans from his earlier days who had mentally retired years ago and were living on past glories. The first time around, having built Fomento person by person, program by program, he ran it as if it were his own company. Now, he said, "I found myself unable to make decisions that twenty years earlier I had made with a snap of the fingers."

Fomento employees, Moscoso discovered, had what was comparable to tenure. Hiring and firing required a long and cumbersome process that in the final analysis was more in the hands of a bureaucrat in the central personnel office than under management control. Repeating to himself the old *jíbaro* saying of pragmatist resignation — *hay que arar con los bueyes que tenemos* (we must plow with the oxen that we have) — Moscoso forced himself to stop reminiscing about the good old days and plunge into his new assignment. He was pleased to be able to put together a new team headed by Amadeo Francis, the respected economist who first joined Fomento in 1955, and José Rivera Janer, a dynamo of energy with a knack for public relations in the old Moscoso style.

In addition to the cumbersome new Fomento regulations, Moscoso was confronted by another obstacle: a powerful and popular environmental movement that drew considerable support from politicians and the island media. A significant part of the environmentalist leadership also had a pro-independence ideological agenda. Up to now, the political left had not succeeded in undermining Fomento's pro-American, pro-capitalist development. But the new interest in environmental protection gave the *independentistas* a strong tool, which they used against Fomento's two major projects — mining and the petrochemical industry — each of which had significant environmental impacts.

The first battleground for the new ideological conflict was the proposed AMAX and Kennecut copper mining and smelting complex in the central mountain region of Utuado and Adjuntas. At more than $600 million, it was heralded as one of the biggest investments in island history. In the past, the *independentistas* would have opposed the project as classic colonialism. The extraction of copper and to a lesser amount gold fit the old pattern of economic exploitation of a colony's wealth and natural resources. But the anti-mining campaign, which soon began to gain popular and political support, was made to appear exclusively environmental. The project, the opponents argued, would permanently devastate agricultural land, contaminate the air, and poison the underground water supply.

Fomento answered that the predictions of ecological devastation were false. The agency stressed the significant economic boost that the project would provide to one of Puerto Rico's most economically depressed areas. The Utuado-Adjuntas region was not apt for successful commercial agriculture, and the few existing coffee farms yielded only subsistence incomes. All this, Fomento pointed out, drove many young people to abandon the area; Utuado's population had declined by nearly 25 percent since 1940 and Adjuntas's by 18 percent. The economic benefits, meanwhile, would be enormous: the mining companies expected to extract $3 billion worth of copper and $400 million worth of gold, create thousands of direct and indirect jobs, and contribute $700 million to the insular treasury in different forms of revenue.

The opposition grew. *Misión Industrial,* a tight group of environmentalists officially linked to the island's Presbyterian Church but with close ties to the local Independence and Socialist Parties, succeeded in organizing civic groups against the project. Meanwhile, an increasing number of academicians, scientists, professionals, politicians, journalists, and labor unions joined the anti-mining crusade.

Although the mining project received at some point the endorsement of all four of Puerto Rico's elected governors, the environmentalist-led opposition succeeded in killing it. It was a stunning victory over what was considered Fomento's unstoppable Bootstrap juggernaut. The agency suffered its first big defeat on the island. There would be others.

*   *   *

In January 1973, as Moscoso assumed command of Fomento determined to regain the agency's old influence and power within the administration, the environmentalist movement, still gloating from its victory against the Utuado mining, was poised for another battle. This time, its target was a bigger and more controversial Fomento project: a huge oil depot with docking facilities deep enough to service supertankers.

The so-called superport was precisely the kind of idea that excited Moscoso, making him feel as if the 1950s Fomento spirit had returned. Thirty-nine miles west of the town of Mayagüez on the island's west coast is a small, flat island named Mona. Nearly halfway between Puerto Rico and the Dominican Republic, the dot-sized island is in the center of a major shipping lane for petroleum tankers coming from South America, Africa, and the Middle East on their way to U.S. refineries around Houston and Louisiana. There was a need for deep-water port facilities along that route. Fomento learned that a group of businesspeople and technicians were quickly putting together a superport project in Louisiana that would probably preempt the need for a similar port in other areas. The agency and Moscoso got into gear: whoever built the superport first was going to get the bulk of the business, he thought.[6]

Manuel Casiano, who headed Fomento during the Ferré administration, had initiated preliminary impact studies for a petroleum storage and transshipment terminal and a refining and petrochemical processing complex in the Mayagüez region. The studies confirmed that the biggest of the supertankers could navigate and maneuver there. A superport at Mona was possible.

* * *

Moscoso took over the project that could reduce the island's dependence on imported oil and, more important, result in a huge refining and petrochemical complex with all its job-producing and revenue-enhancing possibilities. "At CORCO," Moscoso said, "the capacity of the tankers was forty thousand to fifty thousand tons. A superport could handle the world's biggest supertankers of up to eight hundred thousand tons, and this would, of course, result in very big savings." When in 1973 he began to analyze the figures involved in the project, he quickly arrived at the conclusion that the economics were much better in Puerto Rico than in Louisiana. This enormous, complex project was so beneficial to the island that it would be a fitting finale to his long public career.

Isolated Mona Island seemed the ideal site also because the twenty-one-square-mile island was uninhabited. The island was well suited for one or two large power plants. This was of special importance to Fomento, because there were no power plants west of the Ponce area, even though that section of the main island was attracting a large number of new electronics assembly plants. Digital Corporation already had two factories in San Germán and Aguadilla that employed more than two thousand workers. Moscoso read extensively about the new technology developed by Sweden and Norway for underwater transmission lines. Moscoso anticipated resistance from occasional Mona campers and hunters or from Cabo Rojo fishermen who set out at midnight, when the Mona Passage becomes calm. Of course, the organized environmentalist groups backed by the island's extreme-left political movements would oppose a superport with the same zeal they had shown in their attacks against the copper-mining project. But Mona, after all, was nearly forty miles from Puerto Rico's populated coastline. Moscoso believed that his arguments in favor of this project were so strong that he could overcome the opposition. He was wrong.

"Knowing that the effect on the environment would be minimal," Moscoso said, "I could not imagine that preserving some fauna was to become more important than the livelihood of two or three thousand Puerto Ricans, who would be employed by this project. That was my mistake. It appeared that the iguanas in Mona were much more important than jobs for Puerto Ricans." The protest, as was the case with the mining project, grew with irreversible force.

The fear campaign reached the Dominican Republic, where government leaders expressed alarm at the possibility of contamination of its east coast by supertanker oil spills. Moscoso rushed to the Dominican Republic. President Joaquín Balaguer was concerned that the currents would deposit oil sludge on the beaches that his government planned to develop into major tourist resorts. On the contrary, Moscoso assured him, the superport would reduce the danger of oil spills, as the supertankers were considerably safer than the smaller and older tankers that presently were navigating the Mona Passage. He placed in front of Balaguer detailed drawings demonstrating that the latest technology "will allow us to virtually guarantee that there will be no spills, and if there are, we will have the sophisticated equipment to contain them." Balaguer, who was nearly blind, nodded his head. Moscoso gave him a brochure outlining the economic benefits of having a mammoth source of relatively inexpensive petroleum fifty miles from the Dominican coast. "I think that he was thoroughly convinced," Moscoso said. The Dominican president dropped his objection. But it was another matter to convince the Puerto Ricans.

The greater the opposition to the superport, the more determined Moscoso was to have it approved. Hadn't he won many other battles in the past? But now it seemed that everything had changed, including his own political party.

"From my point of view," said Lewis Smith, a former economist at CORCO who joined Fomento as head of the Office of Economic Research, "Moscoso had many more battles against the people in his own party than against the statehooders and *independentista* opposition. If we conclude that he was often frustrated the second time around, I think it was because of the wear and tear of swimming against the currents in his own administration. To cite one example: we, in Fomento, understood the great importance to Puerto Rico of the superport. The 500,000-barrel-a-day refinery would have produced 150,000 barrels of naphtha a day, 20,000 more than that needed to supply our entire petrochemical industry. I don't know if anyone else really understood this."[7]

Moscoso convinced Governor Hernández Colón to call an extraordinary cabinet meeting to unite the entire administration in a coordinated strategy in favor of the project. The governor scheduled a two-day, weekend retreat in a secluded area outside San Juan. Moscoso was pleased; this was the opportunity he needed to address all the questions and doubts about the superport in an informal, private setting, free of interruptions or deadlines. Also, this was the governor's opportunity to demonstrate his personal leadership in defense of Moscoso's now explosively controversial project.

At the appointed time, however, Hernández Colón had not arrived. His secretary of state and constitutionally the "vice governor," Victor Pons, received a message that the governor would be delayed and that the meeting should start without him. Pons, who managed the governor's political campaign in 1972, suspected that something odd was happening. Hernández Colón's delay in arriving at this crucial meeting did not seem accidental. Pons was not prepared to lead the discussion in support of the project, much less to provide the strong leadership and support it desperately needed. Approximately one hour later, he received another message that confirmed what he suspected: the governor would not attend. Hernández Colón's absence inevitably sent a message to his entire administration. As the meeting progressed under Pons's direction, the opposition grew in spite of Moscoso's arguments.

Lewis Smith, who accompanied Moscoso, recalled: "We were surprised by the level of hostility to the project. On the second day, the two most vociferous critics of the superport in the Popular Party, representatives Severo Colberg and Roberto Rexach Benítez, appeared; they had been invited by the governor. Rexach pulled out some papers and gave them to Moscoso. There were sixty-five questions about the superport. Without looking at them, Moscoso turned them over to me. 'Answer them tomorrow in writing,' he said. I will never forget the hours I spent answering those sixty-five questions: I still have nightmares about them." The answers had little effect. Later, at legislative public hearings on the project, two Popular lawmakers grilled Moscoso for four and a half hours. "They were clearly very hostile to Moscoso," Lewis said. "It could only be described as harassment."

*   *   *

International events, adding to local opposition, were to seal the fate not only of the superport project but of Puerto Rico's giant petrochemical industry. In the early afternoon of October 6, 1973, Egypt and Syria attacked Israel. It was the fourth Arab-Israeli war since 1948. This one, however, was different: in the words of Henry Kissinger, it was to "alter irrevocably the world."[8] Nowhere was this war to have a more devastating impact than in the small island of Puerto Rico and its 3.5 million people. Oil imported from Venezuela and the Middle East was Puerto Rico's *only* source of energy. All transportation to, from, and within the island depended on oil, and close to 80 percent of what Puerto Ricans consumed, including food, was imported. Virtually all manufacturing depended on sea and air carriers to bring the raw materials from overseas and to ship the finished products.

But most devastating was the impact of the oil crisis on the forty-nine refinery and petrochemical plants in operation on the island, by far Puerto Rico's largest industry. The effect of the Yom Kippur War and the oil embargo was to demolish the industry's economic feasibility: the favorable differential between low-cost foreign crude and high-cost domestic crude. Puerto Ricans, their government, and the major investors watched in helpless horror as OPEC increased the price of crude again and again: the advantage of between $1.00 to $1.50 a barrel became a disadvantage of between $3.00 to $4.00. Puerto Rico's industry faced unbearable losses and inevitable extinction.

The momentum of the island's economic growth, 7.3 percent in fiscal 1973, peaked by mid-1974 and then plunged. In 1975 the GNP declined by 2 percent. Operation Bootstrap came to a halt; twenty-three thousand manufacturing and thirty-four thousand nonmanufacturing jobs were lost from 1974 to 1976. By January 1976, unemployment was up to 21.9 percent. It was at a Great Depression level. Fomento economists insisted that real unemployment, assuming a labor-participation rate similar to that in the United States, was 40 percent. Government revenues plummeted. Although the constitution required the administration to balance the Commonwealth's budget, the revenue projections fell short by $200 million in fiscal 1975 and by an additional $350 million in the following years. Public debt leaped by 24.8 percent in 1974 and by 36.6 percent in 1975. Unless the governor took drastic action, Puerto Rico would be unable to meet its debt obligations for the first time in its history; a default would curtail its borrowing ability and steepen even more the island's economic free fall.

Governor Hernández Colón put into effect an emergency austerity program. He froze legislated government salary increases and raised taxes. In early 1974 he named a blue-ribbon committee headed by Yale economist James Tobin, a 1981 Nobel recipient, that urged even more conservative fiscal policies and stringent budget cost-cutting.

Hernández Colón's drastic actions stopped the economic plunge; the island avoided a disastrous default on its debt obligations. This earned him the admiration of the Tobin Committee. But the governor and the Populares paid a big political price. The painful austerity program triggered the bitter opposition of the island's labor movement. Government workers declared crippling strikes; a violent work stoppage by the electric power workers prompted the governor to call the National Guard to stop widespread sabotage of power lines. The media and political opposition dubbed a temporary income tax surcharge the *vampirita,* the little vampire. The phrase became the battle cry used to express the young governor's unpopularity.

Even though what was happening in Puerto Rico seemed like a bad horror movie, Moscoso came up with one bold move in a desperate attempt to save his superport project and the petrochemical industry. As the crisis that threatened CORCO, Phillips, Union Carbide, and the other oil industries was the result of the OPEC oil embargo, why not try to circumvent the embargo by appealing directly to the OPEC leadership and to the world's largest source of oil, Saudi Arabia? Moscoso's plan was to negotiate with the royal family a long-term contract that would guarantee Puerto Rico a stable supply of low cost oil. The original idea emerged during a visit to Puerto Rico of businesspeople from the United States, Europe, Japan, and the Middle East, including members of the Saudi Arabian royal family, all brought to the island by David Rockefeller. At a luncheon with the group hosted by the governor at La Fortaleza, Moscoso took the opportunity to describe his superport project. The Saudis expressed interest. Moscoso followed up aggressively, and several months later a letter was received from King Faisal inviting the Puerto Ricans to visit his country.

Moscoso's schedule in Saudi Arabia was filled with meetings with members of the royal household and Minister of Petroleum Admed Zaki Yamani. The superport project, Moscoso declared, would resolve not only the island's critical energy problem but also would give Saudi Arabian oil an additional, major entry into the U.S. markets under favorable conditions in competition with Nigeria, Libya, Algeria, or Indonesia. He returned to the island confident that an agreement was possible. The Arabs were indeed serious.[9]

In 1975 a second invitation for a visit in August came from King Faisal. Moscoso convinced the governor to make the trip. On arrival in Saudi Arabia, Hernández Colón, Moscoso, and their group were informed that King Faisal had left suddenly for Cairo to meet with the beleaguered Egyptian president, Anwar Sadat. Faisal's mission, the Puerto Ricans were informed, was to offer assistance with the reconstruction of the Egyptian military force following the Yom Kippur War. The king's brother, Prince Fahd, the royal family's oil expert and head of the Supreme Petroleum Council, would serve as host. After an overnight stop in Jidda, near Mecca, the group was flown to Riyadh for the formal meetings and then, in a long caravan of shiny black limousines, across the desert to the Persian Gulf, where Moscoso would show Hernández Colón a real-life superport. Moscoso knew from his first trip to the port that they would see schools of fish just below the surface of the clean, transparent water along the giant piers. There would not be a speck of oil or other pollutants in the water. If this does not demolish the anti-superport fear campaign, he thought, nothing will.

Moscoso suggested that the Saudis, in addition to the superport, should consider investing in the refineries and other port facilities. Extensive meetings were scheduled before sumptuous banquets in grandiose dining rooms. He recalled one of the meetings: "We were with Prince Fahd in this magnificent room decorated with the most ornate French-style furnishings I have ever seen in my life. The prince sat behind a desk that seemed to be solid gold. I'll never forget the telephone ringing—it surely was also solid gold." It was King Faisal calling from Cairo. Yamani whispered to the governor and Moscoso that the situation in Egypt was very bad and the king was informing his brother that he had committed economic aid to Sadat. How much? Moscoso asked. One billion dollars, Yamani answered casually. "One billion dollars, just like that—without having to consult with the Bureau of the Budget or testify endlessly at a legislature!"

Moscoso was intrigued by Yamani, the oil minister, who came across as gentle and benign, in striking contrast to his worldwide image as the power broker behind OPEC—the man who was bringing the entire industrialized world to its knees. Yamani quietly assured Moscoso that he merely followed the royal family's policies. At the same time, due to his Western education, he was distrusted by the radical anti-West Iranians and Iraqis, who called him a "despicable traitor" in the service of "imperialism and Zionism." This may be, Moscoso reflected in silence, "the single most powerful man in the world today."[10]

During an invitation to Yamani's palatial home, which to the Puerto Ricans became the cultural highlight of the trip, Moscoso had a chance to muse about the contrast between their host's colossal power and the genuinely warm, charming way in which he treated his guests. After the succulent dinner and the entertainment, provided by Yamani's two beautiful teenage daughters performing Arabian dances, the group entered into a relaxed after-dinner conversation. One of the Puerto Ricans turned to Yamani and asked: "Do you think the Arabs and Jews will ever get together?" Yamani's large black eyes widened in surprise: "What problem is there between the Arabs and Jews? We have no problem with the Jews. Our problem is with Israel." Then Yamani got up to dance with his daughters and to give a demonstration of what he called the "Dance of the Handkerchief."

The following day's schedule included the much-awaited visit to the area's superport. Walking fast, as usual, despite the furnace-like heat, Moscoso led the group of Puerto Ricans to the end of the dock. "There! There it is!" he said. But there was nothing to see.

Off in the distance, several tankers connected to pipes were being loaded. "Ted," someone shouted, "where's the superport?" "This is it!" he shouted back. "Is this what you brought us here for? What the hell, there's nothing to see!" Moscoso was now walking along the pier's edge, looking down at the water. Then he cried with great excitement: "There they are! Come here and look at this! Look at all those fish down there!" With sweat flowing freely from their faces, they all leaned over to look at the fish. "Don't they all look happy and healthy? See how pristine and clean the water is," Moscoso cried. "All those lies they are saying back in Puerto Rico about contamination! Where is the contamination? They are all lies." The group remained silent; his colleagues only wanted to return to the air-conditioned limousines.

In the last-ditch search for some magic formula to save the petrochemical industry, Fomento and Moscoso moved their campaign from Saudi Arabia to Washington. Oil industry executives were contacted, and it was decided to gamble that the U.S. government could be made to feel that it was "morally obligated" to save Puerto Rico's industry. The argument to be used by industry spokespeople was, "Because you, Uncle Sam, *lured* my company to invest hundreds of millions in Puerto Rico, now you have the moral responsibility to protect that investment." In testimony before the Federal Energy Administration, Robert West, CORCO's executive committee chairman, grimly insisted that the policy of "deliberate inducement" amounted to a "lure . . . to private capital to create employment in this island Commonwealth" and that because of it his company had constructed the world's largest aromatic plant in Puerto Rico and the twenty-fourth largest refinery in the United States.[11] Union Carbide's head of the Puerto Rico operations, Alex Regan, used the same argument: This "concentration of petrochemical capacity [in Puerto Rico] is not a natural phenomenon . . . but rather a result of conscious policy by the Puerto Rican and federal governments for over a decade to use the national petroleum policy to stimulate the economy of Puerto Rico."[12] Union Carbide built its giant plant in Puerto Rico, producing 20 percent of all the chlorine manufactured in the United States with the belief that the American government would not turn its back on both the investors and Puerto Rico, he stated. "It was in reliance on this competitive access that Union Carbide Caribe and other Island producers expanded their petrochemical operations by almost one billion dollars, with consequent benefit to the Commonwealth economy."

The last hope was now in the hands of President Gerald Ford, coincidentally one of Moscoso's classmates at the University of Michigan four decades earlier. After their college days, they had traveled together to Latin America when Moscoso headed the Alliance for Progress and Ford was a member of Congress. To increase his chances, Moscoso also appealed to Senator "Scoop" Jackson, the chairman of the Senate Interior Committee charged with U.S. energy policies. Jackson served with Moscoso on the 1964 Puerto Rico Status Commission, in which the senator's defense of the commonwealth status was taken as admiration for the Populares. Jackson wooed and eventually received the support of the Populares-controlled island delegation to the 1976 Democratic convention.

But Moscoso's relationship with Ford and Jackson had no effect. The island's appeals for special economic treatment because of its relatively high level of poverty and unemployment had little resonance in a Washington still reeling from the twin shocks of the energy crisis and the resignation of President Nixon. "Oil and energy," according to Daniel Yergin, "were already well on the way to becoming the hottest cauldron in national politics."[13] Like so much else after Vietnam and Watergate, the age when Puerto Rico had power brokers such as Abe Fortas who were able to influence the White House and Congress was gone.

"Fomento," Moscoso said at the close of his emotional testimony before the Federal Energy Administration, "cannot believe that the FEA will fail to act and save these industries from collapse."[14] It did. It seemed like a cruelly devilish prank. Having arrived so tantalizingly close to the payoff—the promised land of Moscoso's Dream Sheet—the island's petrochemical industry was doomed. With it, Moscoso's plans of a magnificent superport and a working Saudi Arabian connection also collapsed. Only the core Phillips Sun Oil refineries and the original, small Caribbean Gulf refinery that supplied the local market survived. The billion-dollar petrochemical complexes along the southern coast from Guayanilla to Peñuelas would become eerie graveyards of rusting stacks, tanks, and tubes. "Driving by Peñuelas," Moscoso confessed years later, "still almost makes me weep at the dream that was not realized."[15]

*   *   *

The long list of economic problems would cost Governor Hernández Colón his bid for reelection in November 1976. Puerto Rico's economy, however, was not totally abandoned by the fates in 1976. When the island seemed in danger of losing not only its biggest industry but also the enthusiasm and hope that had fueled its economic miracle, it was again blessed with a remarkable stroke of good luck.

Chapter 18

From 931 to 936

In early 1976, the word "fail" crept into Moscoso's vocabulary for the first time. Appearing before a committee of Congress on January 19, he was uncharacteristically grim in describing the four pillars needed to keep Operation Bootstrap alive—an aggressive family-planning program to arrest the population explosion, Fomento's ability to promote high-technology industries, greater financial resources for Fomento, and restoration of flexibility in the application of federal minimum wages to the island. "Without any one of the four," Moscoso said, "we will probably fail, and Puerto Rico will collapse into increasing misery and political turmoil."[1] His mood, of course, reflected the setbacks suffered in the previous three years. But none hurt more than a June 14, 1974, letter from Volkswagen.

When Moscoso and his staff were invited to Volkswagen's headquarters in Wolfsburg, Germany, to make a presentation for a huge assembly plant to be built somewhere within the United States, Moscoso believed that Fomento and Puerto Rico had a real opportunity to win over the competition. Fomento never worked harder on a promotion. Previous meetings with the Germans convinced Moscoso that the most significant obstacle was the rapid increase in ocean freight costs to and from the island. For a car manufacturer, this was a decisive cost factor. But Moscoso came up with still another of his creative and controversial gambles to overcome this seemingly insurmountable obstacle.

Why not, he asked Governor Hernández Colón, have the Puerto Rican government purchase the three financially strapped private ocean shipping lines? The island would then use this maritime link to the world as a tool to promote industrialization, beginning with the huge Volkswagen project. Once again his salesmanship prevailed. The governor and the legislature accepted this new bold adventure, and a government-owned shipping line, Las Navieras, was created. As he and Amadeo Francis, head of Fomento's mainland operations, prepared for their trip to Germany, they believed that Las Navieras made the Volkswagen project economically viable. They would guarantee to the Germans that the cost of shipping the cars to U.S. markets would be no higher than the cost of ground transportation from anywhere within the continental United States. Moscoso was prepared to offer still another incentive. Because the federal excise tax on automobiles would be rebated to the island's treasury, as was done with the rum produced in Puerto Rico, Moscoso could offer Volkswagen direct grants in the amount of these funds. Moscoso and Francis asked themselves, How could the Germans turn this down? They did.

The June 1974 letter brought the crushing news that the plant would be built elsewhere. The Germans made a long, exhaustive, finely detailed analysis of each one of the cost advantages and disadvantages of operating the plant on the island. It was not just the high cost of shipping; there were simply too many production costs that were higher in Puerto Rico that on the mainland.[2] Even the government's transportation subsidy and rebate did not erase the other big cost disadvantages. Although hourly wage rates were lower than on the mainland, other factors such as the high number of legal holidays in Puerto Rico ran up the cost of labor and reduced the wage differential.

The failure of the Volkswagen project, in Moscoso's mind, became much more than one more lost promotion. It had a chilling effect—something similar to Muñoz's wrenching meeting with Ben Dorfman three decades earlier. The letter, with German precision, questioned the essential viability of the entire Fomento program. There was no escaping the deadly logic. Tax exemption was worthless if salaries and other production costs were higher in Puerto Rico than in competing industrial sites. And they were about to go even higher. The federal government was about to increase the federal minimum wage, and this time it would be a particularly big blow to the island's industrialization. In 1974, the new Fair Labor Standards Act decreed that island wages would reach the federal minimum of $2.30 an hour by May 1976. As 92 percent of Puerto Rico's production workers were employed in industries with average earnings at or below the federal minimum, each across-the-board increase had, according to Moscoso, "a disastrous effect on our economy and our prospects for the future."[3]

But there was still more bad news for Fomento. In the 1970s, many Puerto Ricans who migrated to the U.S. mainland were returning to the island. From 1950 to 1970, the total net outmigration was 615,000; in 1971, it was zero. In the next three years, there was a net return of 143,000 Puerto

Ricans. The island was again experiencing an explosive population growth of 2.6 percent a year. The impact on Moscoso's battle against unemployment was immediate: the labor force reached 872,000 in 1975 and was expected to exceed 1 million within a decade. Meanwhile, adding to the joblessness was the decline of agricultural employment; there were 214,000 farming jobs in 1950 but fewer than 50,000 in 1975.

Moscoso's frustration grew. It angered him to see how the government continued to pour money into uneconomical agricultural projects. He asked his economists to prepare elaborate charts dramatizing how underfinanced Fomento was at this critical moment. One chart showed that from fiscal 1952 to fiscal 1975, the government spent a total of $840 million for agricultural development, compared to $416 million for industrialization. Yet agriculture declined in that period to only 7 percent of total employment and 5 percent of net income. Despite the statistics, the recommendation for the following year's budget was to allocate $85 million for agricultural development and only $25 million for industrial development.

On June 8, 1975, Moscoso finally released his frustration in a remarkably candid letter to Governor Hernández Colón, expressing views that he could not state publicly: "For 25 years I have *not* been telling the investors from the United States the whole truth about our economic reality. What we have told them is only as truthful as we have been able to prove. It is what we have not told them that troubles me and causes me solemn frustrations, if not anxiety."

Moscoso detailed a conversation with a member of the blue-ribbon Tobin Committee, then conducting a study of the island's financial crisis. Kermit Gordon, president of the Brookings Institution, asked Moscoso exactly what Puerto Rico was doing to continue its industrial program. Moscoso replied by letter that at the beginning of Fomento, it became evident that because the island did not have an infrastructure that could sustain economic development, Puerto Rico's essential attraction was low wages. But not any longer.

"Today," Moscoso continued, "we have overvalued the cost of our labor to the point where it does not compensate for the deficiency and high cost of our infrastructure and the disadvantage of our geographical position. . . . Needless to say, if there are no profits, tax exemption means nothing as an incentive to locate in Puerto Rico."[4]

He described a new report by the Arthur Anderson firm comparing the manufacturing cost of rum in Puerto Rico to that in Florida. "It takes seven workers in Puerto Rico to do the work of six in Florida." Why? "Here workers have an average of 59.4 days for vacation, holidays, sick leave, compared to 19 in Florida." Moscoso ended his letter: "To the industrialists whom I visit or who visit me, I will continue not telling them all the truth—until January 16, 1976. Then I will shut up."

Moscoso did not resign from Fomento on that date. As he had done so often before, he yielded to the governor's plea to remain until the end of his term, this time in December 1976. It was a fortuitous decision for him and for the island. Moscoso was to get an opportunity to leave Fomento on an unexpected high note. He was to play a crucial role in the approval of legislation by the U.S. Congress in 1976 that would rescue Bootstrap from the edge of the precipice and usher in a new stage of industrialization that would more than make up for the collapsed petrochemical industry. Puerto Rico was about to enter the Age of Section 936.

*　　*　　*

In his confessional letter to the governor, Moscoso omitted from his litany of frustrations what was in fact his and Fomento's greatest fear. By 1976, having seen so many of its investment incentives lost or diminished, Bootstrap was like a plane flying on only one of its four engines—tax exemption. But there was a devilish peculiarity to this incentive: it had a self-destruct mechanism, a built-in incentive to liquidate the Puerto Rican operation after the exemption period expired. In fact, about half the established plants closed down after eight or nine years of operation. Some closed due to the increases in the federal minimum wage or for other cost factors. But a large number did so to take advantage of the U.S. Internal Revenue Code liquidation provisions, Sections 931 and 332.

*　　*　　*

Since the original Puerto Rico Organic Act approved by Congress in 1900, the island was specifically exempt from all federal taxes. That is why Puerto Rico could offer 100 percent tax exemption, unlike any state of the Union. For tax purposes, Puerto Rico was treated as a foreign country. So, while American firms retained their profits in the island, they were tax-free. But when the profits were repatriated to the U.S. mainland, they became fully taxable. Sections 931 and 332, however, made an exception for industries located in U.S. possessions. It was precisely this exception that made possible Moscoso's 100 percent tax incentive. But to bring home the tax-free profits, the company had to liquidate its operations in Puerto Rico or other possessions.

The liquidation provision notwithstanding, Sections 931 and 332 were truly vital to Fomento; without them there would be no Operation Bootstrap. However, in 1962 Puerto Rico came within an eyelash of losing these two vital provisions. Fomento's attorney, Mariano Ramírez, received an urgent call from Washington. The House Ways and Means Committee had begun to consider eliminating Sections 931 and 332 as part of a larger tax reform package. "I rushed up to Washington to meet with our resident commissioner, Dr. Antonio Fernós Isern, who told me to forget about it, that there was nothing we could do to change the committee's mind," Ramírez recalled.⁵ As it turned out, the committee was upset at the American corporations that were using the sections to shift mainland profits to overseas corporations and thus improperly avoid taxes. "I told Fernós that this would kill our Fomento program . . . [but] his attitude seemed to me to be defeatist. I felt that Fernós was more interested in avoiding conflicts in Congress than in defending the industrialization program. For instance, every time some Congressmen complained to him about runaway industries, he called Moscoso and me to urgent meetings, in effect telling us to stop creating problems."

Fernós was right about the danger to the two sections. The House approved the reform bill that wiped out Sections 931 and 332. Alarmed, Ramírez and Fomento administrator Rafael Durand convinced Governor Muñoz to rush to Washington to testify at the 1962 Senate hearings and personally visit each of the Senate Finance Committee members. "We found two things," Ramírez said. "As in the House, the senators were extremely unhappy at what they perceived to be corporate abuse of 931 and its use as a loophole. They were abusive in their questioning of the corporation presidents and executives who testified. But they were also extremely deferential to Muñoz and sympathetic to Puerto Rico. We were convinced that they did not want to hurt the island."

When he returned to San Juan, Muñoz instructed Ramírez to remain in Washington to continue the lobbying. After four months, the efforts succeeded and the Senate retained the two sections; the House concurred. Years later, in his memoirs, the pessimistic resident commissioner, Fernós Isern, admitted the enormous importance of the victory: "I think we should recognize the generosity of the United States Congress for Puerto Rico in legislating especially as it did so as not to affect our economic development."⁶

* * *

Twelve years later, a new threat to Sections 931 and 332 surfaced. In 1974, Moscoso received a worrisome call from Resident Commissioner Jaime Benítez. Again, Sections 931 and 332 were in danger. Moscoso's worst fears were coming true. Benítez's office received a press release from the House Ways and Means Committee dated May 22 that listed a number of already-approved amendments to the tax code. Among them was the elimination of the benefits of the two sections. Puerto Rican and other possessions' corporations had deposited billions of dollars in tax havens around the world. The U.S. Treasury, already feeling the consequences of the oil embargo recession, was seeking to improve the country's balance of payments by forcing the 931 corporations to repatriate these funds.

Benítez, who was not forewarned of the Ways and Means Committee's actions, was outraged. He called Committee Chairman Wilbur Mills, who quickly agreed to allow Puerto Rico to present its case at the committee's May 30 session. Moscoso asked Benítez to fly back to the island as soon as possible. The following day at an emergency meeting held at La Fortaleza, the governor, Moscoso, and Benítez agreed that Salvador Casellas, the island's young treasury secretary, should appear early the next day before the committee. His assignment was to somehow stop or stall the committee and thus give Puerto Rico time to combat the mortal amendment.

Casellas was among the new generation of bright, well-educated Populares whom Governor Hernández Colón brought to his administration in 1973. Unlike previous treasury secretaries, Casellas fully supported Fomento's tax exemption development strategy. After graduating from Georgetown University and studying law at the University of Puerto Rico and Harvard, Casellas went on to a successful career as a corporate lawyer, specializing precisely in local and federal tax law. He had been the new governor's first choice to head Fomento. It was after Casellas declined, preferring to run the treasury department, that Hernández Colón invited Moscoso to return to his old agency. Casellas's support of Fomento was particularly vital to Moscoso. Many of the young men and women in the Hernández Colón administration, while respecting Moscoso personally, argued that it was time to move away from Fomento's model to a new developmental model. "All right," Moscoso would respond, "what model?"

"Because of what happened during those four years," Casellas recalled, "it was very fortunate, indeed, that I considered myself a Moscoso disciple. It was natural in the past for the treasury secretary to consider himself in a sort of adversarial position towards Fomento. But I was a true believer in the Fomento program."

On the day of the hearing Casellas felt nervous. He had never appeared before a congressional committee. But once he began his testimony, he sensed that he had captured Chairman Wilbur Mills's and Representative Al Ulman's attention. The principal point that Casellas underscored was that Congress, in effect, was making a fundamental choice for Puerto Rico between "the dignity of jobs" and the "dependence of welfare." This, coupled with his

A large part of Moscoso's success was the network of friends and admirers he developed over the year in the U.S. business community. Moscoso often called on them to help Puerto Rico. In 1990, Moscoso called on Lawrance Rockfeller, who had built the major hotel complex in Dorado, to assist in financing the Luis Muñoz Marín Foundation Library. Here Moscoso is seen with Rockfeller and his wife, Mary, on a visit to the Foundation in 1990. Also pictured is Foundation Executive Director Luis Agrait (second from left).

prediction of a renewed massive migration of poor Puerto Ricans to the mainland, had the greatest impact on the committee members. The purpose of his testimony, he said, was to ask the committee to suspend consideration of the amendment to Sections 931 and 332 until the governor, Moscoso, and Benítez had time to prepare Puerto Rico's formal and documented presentation.

Mills declared, just as he did back in 1962, that it was not the committee's intention to hurt Puerto Rico. The island government was asked to make its presentation four days later, on June 3. Mills also suggested a post-hearing meeting between Casellas and Chief of Staff of the Joint Committee on Internal Revenue Taxation Lawrence N. Woodworth. As soon as the meeting began, Woodworth mentioned that he would like to explore a "tax-bearing idea" that he had been considering. The idea turned out to be the seed of Section 936.

On May 31, 1974, Governor Hernández Colón sent a long, blunt memorandum to the committee:7 "without a doubt . . . we cannot subsist economically if the present interplay of Section 931 and 332 of the United States Internal Revenue Code and the Puerto Rican tax system is modified. This interplay is so crucial that any tampering with it is necessarily unacceptable. It is crucial, not only to the maintenance of the present level of economic well being, but is absolutely essential to the continued development of the Puerto Rican economy." The governor reiterated the argument Casellas had found effective: "It is our fundamental aim to create work and dignity for Puerto Ricans *in Puerto Rico*. We do not want our people to become basket welfare cases, dependent on Federal handouts as the only way to survive."

On June 3, Casellas returned to testify before the Ways and Means Committee accompanied by Moscoso, Benítez, and Ramírez. They began their testimony prepared for a long and difficult interrogation. Instead, as they concluded, Mills declared: "I am sure I express the opinion of the members of this committee when I say we certainly do not want to reverse the progress that you are making . . . . I have said on many, many occasions that sometimes there is a loophole in the law that you cannot fully close or eliminate without creating more problems in the process of doing so, than you have as a result of the loophole. This is, in my opinion, an example of what I have been talking about. As far as I am concerned, I am willing to forget about the whole subject matter."8

*   *   *

Ramírez, the veteran attorney, recalled: "I think that for as long as I knew Moscoso, and certainly after we got Muñoz to approve tax exemption in 1947, Moscoso talked about the 'British system.' He somehow got a copy of a Royal Commission Report on the tax advantages given to British companies investing in their colonies."

Now, Moscoso pulled out his old and tattered British tax report at the meeting in Woodworth's office. It turned out to be pretty much what Woodworth had in mind with his tax-bearing concept for Puerto Rico. The possessions corporations would be subject to federal taxation just as other American corporations located in foreign countries, but the Treasury Department would give them a "credit" equal to their tax liability. This would give Moscoso and Fomento absolute tax exemption now that the tax-free profits could be repatriated to the home firm without restriction. Liquidation of the possessions corporation was no longer required. "Right then and there," Casellas said, "we started the series of meetings with Woodworth, his staff, and United States Treasury Department representatives out of which came the final proposal for Section 936."[9]

The realization of what Fomento's people had always considered an impossible dream, however, was delayed for another year. In 1975, the revised section 931, newly designated 936, was included in that year's Tax Reform Act, but the bill died in Congress. Under the chairmanship of Representative Al Ulman, who replaced Wilbur Mills, the Ways and Means Committee reintroduced Section 936 in the 1976 tax legislation. On March 29, 1976, Moscoso, Benítez, and Casellas returned to Washington to testify again before Congress. This time their appeal carried an added sense of urgency. Puerto Rico was in the throes of the terrible energy crisis. Unemployment as of January was at 21.9 percent, the highest recorded level in island history. Inflation was running at 33 percent, 7 points higher than on the mainland. The island's gross national product had declined by 6 percent in the previous two years. Remarkably, Section 936, which was to generate almost continuous controversy in the future, sailed though Congress unopposed.

On October 1, 1976, the Tax Reform Act went into effect. For Moscoso it seemed truly heaven-sent. He was now counting the days left in the year so as to finally retire from Fomento and government service. On the last page of his desk calendar, the day he would definitely close his public career, he had scribbled Martin Luther King's electrifying exclamation: "Free at last, free at last. Thank God Almighty I am free at last!"

* * *

However, still another battle awaited Moscoso—this one against his trusted supporter, Treasury Secretary Casellas.

Moscoso insisted that the purpose of Section 936 was economic development, job creation. But Casellas, in his role as treasury secretary, insisted that Section 936 should also be used to raise millions of dollars in desperately needed tax revenues. Moscoso responded that if Puerto Rico used Section 936 as a revenue generator, it would critically blunt its effectiveness as an investment incentive. Casellas pulled a card from his sleeve: as a representative of the Puerto Rican government in the Washington negotiations, he said, he entered into an agreement with Woodworth and the U.S. Treasury Department staff to impose a "tollgate tax" of up to 10 percent of all the 936 profits repatriated to the mainland parent firm. It was crucial, Casellas argued, that Congress see immediate benefits to Puerto Rico through the tollgate tax. He estimated that in the first year the tax would bring $200 million to the islands's treasury. At the same time, it would provide an incentive to keep at least part of those funds on the island. Section 936 would survive, he insisted, only if Congress became convinced that Puerto Rico, not the corporations, was the primary beneficiary. "From the very first moment it was crucial to understand just why Congress approved Section 936," Casellas recalled. "It was not a giveaway, a loophole for possessions corporations. It was to help our economy, principally creating jobs, at a moment when we were in a deep and dangerous crisis. I argued with the governor and with Moscoso that without the tollgate tax, we were in danger of losing 936 rather quickly."

But Moscoso also had a card up his sleeve. Imposing the tollgate tax on industries that had been promised full tax exemption in a binding decree signed by the governor himself would constitute a breach of contract and would be challenged in the courts. Casellas countered that Moscoso erred in using the broken promise argument because all the U.S. corporations fully expected to pay taxes on the funds repatriated under the previous 931 provision unless they liquidated under Section 332.

Casellas soon learned what it meant to take on an infuriated Moscoso. "The opposition that my tollgate met, I have never seen before in my four years in government and I have never seen it since," Casellas told a news reporter in 1983. He witnessed in the legislature what he called "some of the most Byzantine attempts to kill the legislation."[10]

Moscoso assigned his two principal subordinates, Amadeo Francis and José Rivera Janer, to kill Casellas's bill in the legislature one way or another. Casellas did his own lobbying. Then, in an eleventh-hour move, he turned to his friend, Senator José Izquierdo Mora, who supported the bill but warned Casellas that there were only minutes left before the end of the session. Hurriedly, Casellas appealed to three minority senators, two of them *independentistas*. Just three minutes before the midnight closing of the session, one of the *independentista* senators, Rubén Berríos, moved to waive the reading of the tollgate tax bill. As midnight approached, the bill was approved by a voice vote.

Moscoso did not admit defeat. He called on his old Fomento colleague, Guillermo Rodríguez, president of the Government Development Bank, whose good reputation on Wall Street had been vital in maintaining Puerto Rico's credit rating. Certainly, Moscoso thought, Guillermo Rodríguez will convince Governor Hernández Colón to veto Casellas's bill. At dinner at La Fortaleza, Moscoso and Rodríguez thought that they had achieved their goal. Moscoso and Gloria left the next day for a long-planned trip to Europe, convinced that the Casellas bill was finally dead.

Casellas then received a curt note from the governor asking if he should increase next year's revenue estimate by the anticipated $200 million tollgate tax revenue. The governor was asking Casellas, in effect, to guarantee that his tollgate tax would raise this amount in one year. Casellas would not fall into the trap. He wrote back: "The answer is negative." The purpose of the bill was to motivate corporations *not* to repatriate their funds but to invest them in Puerto Rico's development. He was only able to reasonably estimate that his tax would produce from $35 million to $50 million a year.

The governor then called a meeting at his mountain retreat in Jájome. Moscoso, still in Europe, sent his top Fomento lieutenants to argue for a veto. Casellas asked Resident Commissioner Jaime Benítez to attend. The intrepid Benítez often annoyed the governor. The old educator at times referred to Hernández Colón, who was twenty-eight years his junior, as *ese muchacho*—that lad—and frequently interrupted him in mid-sentence. That evening, however, Benítez was exceptionally persuasive in favor of the tax. The following day, the governor signed the tollgate tax bill.

*   *   *

Section 936 changed the nature and structure of the Puerto Rican economy. Puerto Rico now had an incentive that made it exceptionally attractive to capital-intensive, high-technology industries such as electronics, computers, medical equipment, and pharmaceuticals. It launched Puerto Rico into a new world of knowledge-intensive services, such as telecommunications and finance. From "the brassiere capital of the world" in the 1950s, Puerto Rico became in the 1980s and 1990s one of the world's largest producers of medicines and wonder drugs; the island was now the "pharmaceutical capital." From garment plants, where thousands of women worked bent over bulky sewing machines, the Fomento factories now became showcases of state-of-the-art production. Surrounded by professional landscaping, they offered impeccably clean working areas, attractive cafeterias, large parking lots filled with late-model cars. These new factories had a seemingly unquenchable thirst for high-salaried Puerto Rican engineers, chemists, and physicists.

Treasury Secretary Casellas's much-opposed tollgate tax proved effective in inducing 936 corporations to retain their profits on the island; the tax rate, in fact, decreased accordingly. Partway into the 1990s, $15 billion in 936 funds were deposited in the island's banking system or invested in special funds set up by the government to promote hospitals, hotels, public housing, and shopping centers. The management of this money promoted a new service industry. Along San Juan's "Golden Mile" in the Hato Rey financial district, thousands of young Puerto Rican professionals were employed in the new investment banking firms.

Chapter 19

Bootstrap under Siege

For Moscoso, retirement in 1976 did not bring the total freedom that he longed for during his final months and weeks at Fomento. There were, instead, two new challenges to Operation Bootstrap that he could not ignore. The first came from Carlos Romero Barceló, a persistent critic of Fomento's industrialization program based on tax exemption, who was elected governor in 1976 under the New Progressive Party banner. The second challenge came in 1984, when President Ronald Reagan's administration asked Congress to repeal Section 936.

As mayor of San Juan from 1969 to 1976, Romero Barceló proved to be a charismatic leader. His aggressive style helped to project a macho image as a no-nonsense, no-compromise, hard-hitting, straight-talking politician.

Romero wanted Puerto Rico to become a state of the Union. He was convinced that he and his party had to destroy the "myth" that Puerto Rico needed Commonwealth status to survive economically. To make his point, he attacked Operation Bootstrap, especially targeting the tax exemption incentive. In 1972 and again in 1974, Romero published a ninety-page pamphlet titled *Statehood Is for the Poor*. "This is the reality," he wrote, "regarding 'Commonwealth status' and its 'advantages.' The truth is that it benefits directly the businessmen that come to Puerto Rico to make money paying low wages and not paying taxes . . . taxes needed to construct the schools for our children and the hospitals for our sick." That was why the "economic interests" opposed statehood and financially supported the pro-commonwealth party: "Not because statehood is bad for Puerto Rico and the immense majority of the poor Puerto Ricans. But because statehood is bad *for their pockets.*"[1]

Moscoso had one experience with Romero that revealed the depth of Romero's feelings. In 1972 Moscoso received an invitation to meet with Romero from Pedro Rivera Casiano, a successful entertainment impresario and advisor to the New Progressive Party on communications strategy. Romero went straight to the point; he told Moscoso that he came to the meeting because Luis Ferré, the founder of his political party, requested it, but if Moscoso thought he could change his mind on tax exemption and statehood, he was wasting his time. "He said," Moscoso recalled, "that our economic development was all wrong, completely irrelevant and unnecessary. All we had to do was to become a state and all the economic problems would be solved because the United States would not permit a beggar state. The enabling act would include measures to compensate for Puerto Rico's shortcomings."[2]

Moscoso decided to attempt a different approach; instead of opposing statehood, he argued that regardless of what Puerto Rico decided on its status—statehood, independence, or continued commonwealth—a long period of sustained economic growth was essential. "I told him that I did have, after all, some experience in Washington, and that I was convinced that Puerto Rico had to increase greatly its standard of living before Congress and the American people would accept the island as a state."

Romero rejected Moscoso's argument; it was, he said, the other way around. Puerto Rico must become a state in order to achieve economic development. Tax exemption, Romero went on, weakens the economy by denying the government revenue needed for services and infrastructure. Moscoso answered that without tax exemption there would not be any industries for Puerto Rico to tax. Yes, there would be, Romero retorted; the problem was that Moscoso neglected to use other inducements to attract industry. What inducements? Moscoso asked. As a state, the island would offer investors total political stability, as Hawaii did. All right, Moscoso countered, let's examine Hawaii: unlike overpopulated Puerto Rico, Hawaii achieved a high standard of living and a high per capita income within the federal tax system before becoming a state. No, Romero said, Hawaii's economy grew because of the great publicity achieved by statehood, which produced a tourism boom, and the same would happen in Puerto Rico. But Puerto Rico, Moscoso came back, unlike Hawaii, is surrounded with low-cost, beautiful Caribbean locations, all competing for tourists. Despite Fomento's efforts, he added, tourism still only accounted for less than 10 percent of the island's economy. It should be more, Moscoso added, but never like Hawaii.

Moscoso came away from the two-hour give-and-take having learned a valuable lesson. He did not, of course, change Romero's position, but he said, "I realized the great ability he had for supporting his arguments with wild or extreme points of view, with great energy and with no deviation possible from his mind-set. Perhaps that was what gave him most of his political appeal and power . . . the fact that he did not give in at all, at any time. He just fights and fights and never yields to the point of view of an opponent."

In 1977, Romero and the New Progressive Party controlled the governorship and both houses of the legislature. If they decided to go after the Fomento program, there was nothing in their way to stop them.

The triumph of the statehood New Progressive Party renewed Moscoso's sense of guilt. Up to what point was he responsible for the defeat of Governor Hernández Colón and the Populares and for this threat to the agency and the program he created? For it had been Moscoso more than anyone else in the Hernández Colón administration who insisted that, like Muñoz, the governor had to be willing to make apolitical decisions. Moscoso loved to recite anecdotes of Muñoz's political courage in supporting him in such controversial questions as tax exemption and legalized casino gambling. When Treasury Secretary Salvador Casellas, following the recommendations of the Tobin Committee, urged a series of tax increases in order to meet the government fiscal crisis, Moscoso gave Casellas vigorous support. At one meeting, Moscoso recalled that a "despondent governor turned to us and said: 'You know, of course, that this will cost me the election.'"

It seemed evident then that putting the island's economic recovery above Hernández Colón's political survival was the right thing to do. However, it was one thing for Moscoso to urge Muñoz to be courageous when it was a foregone conclusion that he would win the next elections and another to push valor on a governor facing tough opposition. It was now evident that young Hernández Colón, lacking Muñoz's enormous political power, paid the price in his defeat by Romero Barceló.

*   *   *

Governor Romero Barceló failed to take full advantage of Section 936 and even downplayed tax exemption in Fomento's mainland advertising. "We were throwing away a golden opportunity," Moscoso believed. When Romero attempted to carry out his political crusade against tax exemption, Moscoso decided to go public. Testifying before an insular senate committee in 1978, he gave a scathing critique of Romero's views.[3] Instead of decreasing tax exemption, he said, Puerto Rico should increase all its promotional incentives and even consider the repeal of the tollgate tax on Section 936 funds. Removing the tax exemption for tourist hotels, Moscoso continued, was also a grave mistake. He ended his emotional presentation by quoting a letter from a Fomento promoter in Los Angeles, a young man who was resigning so as not to witness the total collapse of the Fomento program.

But as the Romero administration pushed to cut the exemption drastically, resistance within his own party surfaced. Romero's head of Fomento, Manuel Dubón, a wealthy lawyer with considerable real estate holdings, skillfully convinced the governor to lessen the magnitude of the proposed changes. In the end, tax exemption was cut to 90 percent and further reduced after five or more years, depending on the plant's location. Moscoso recognized that Dubón's expert surgery saved the Fomento program from being emasculated. But the result was an overly complex tax exemption bill that no Fomento promoter, not even the tax experts, could understand, much less sell to an investor. "The bill," Moscoso said, "attempts to carry water on both shoulders—a tax exemption bill [or so it wants to be] but also a tax collection bill."

Although battered, Operation Bootstrap survived the Romero Barceló administration. In spite of the governor's hostility, the reduction of tax exemption, and the loss of minimum wage flexibility, 936 was so powerful an incentive that Fomento overcame the setbacks. The pro-commonwealth Rafael Hernández Colón was returned to the governorship in 1984 after running exclusively on reviving the island's economic development. The campaign's slogan consisted of one word, "Jobs." But for Moscoso and the Fomento people, there was no time for celebration. Simultaneously with the election results, Puerto Rico received still another economic shock, this time from the Reagan administration. The U.S. Treasury Department came out for the repeal of Section 936 and its substitution by a credit system.

*   *   *

When Congress first approved Section 936, it ordered the Treasury Department to submit an annual assessment of its impact on the island economy and particularly on unemployment. This placed Treasury and Puerto Rico on a collision course. Congress approved 936 as a development tool, but the U.S. Treasury Department saw it as a loophole and as forgone revenue. In its first report to Congress, Treasury used what became its principal argument against Section 936: that the rush of giant pharmaceutical companies that came to the island to take advantage of Section 936 proved that these firms only wanted to take advantage of the loophole. The tax credit for the pharmaceutical industry, Treasury added, was $35,000 per worker, or approximately three and a half times the employee's total compensation.[4] Responding to this argument, Congress amended Section 936 in 1982 but did not eliminate it. As anticipated, though, Treasury's opposition remained. Its fourth report, issued in February 1983, was even more critical. It declared that the pharmaceutical tax savings had climbed to $59,000 per employee. The most dramatic statistic was the tax benefit per employee in the ten largest 936 corporations: $168,270—an astronomically high percentage of the average employee compensation of $20,122.[5]

Puerto Rico was now in a catch-22 situation: the more it succeeded in attracting 936 corporations, the greater the alarm in the U.S. Treasury over the magnitude of the forgone revenue.

The Reagan administration now was hitting Puerto Rico from two directions. The island was hurt by the reduction of welfare programs, mainly the Comprehensive Employment and Training Program (CETA) and also the food stamp program, which was cut by $100 million (from $870 to $770 million a year). This contributed toward pushing up Puerto Rico's unemployment, which was already reeling from the renewed energy crisis. However, the drop in jobs further convinced the Treasury Department that the "costly" 936 experiment had failed. After all, wasn't 936 meant to resolve Puerto Rico's joblessness? Now President Reagan and the Treasury Department went for the jugular: the president requested Congress to entirely eliminate Section 936.

Governor Hernández Colón wrote to Treasury Secretary James A. Baker that "the proposal for its [Section 936's] repeal would be a disaster for the United States and Puerto Rico."[6] A study performed by Dr. Norman B. True, a former undersecretary of the Treasury for tax and economic affairs who supervised the preparation of earlier Treasury reports on 936, stated that there was "a gross understatement of the employment gains attributable to the response to Section 936 and a gross overstatement of the revenue cost to the Federal government."[7]

The Treasury Department's calculations failed to include the indirect jobs generated by the 936 firms. Additionally, they assumed that corporations would continue to operate on the island and pay taxes to the U.S. Treasury once Section 936 was repealed. This, True declared, is "misleading in concept and measurement." Many, if not most of these corporations, would eventually move to other sites with operation costs significantly lower than in Puerto Rico. "Compared with virtually any other job-creation program of the Federal government, the possessions tax provisions have been more cost effective. Indeed, the Puerto Rican experience under Operation Bootstrap and the possessions corporations provisions should be seen as overwhelming evidence of the effectiveness and low cost of relying on tax incentives for the private sector as the principal vehicle for energizing the process of economic development and growth."

* * *

Meanwhile, convinced that Section 936 could not survive the unrelenting attack by the Treasury Department, Hernández Colón asked a young Washington lawyer, Richard Copaken, to develop a new strategy to save it. Copaken conceived the idea of changing the focus on 936 from a tax issue to a national security issue. He wanted to bring into play President Reagan's concern about Soviet-Cuban penetration in the strategically vital Caribbean region, highlighted by the pro-Cuban Sandinistas' inroads in Nicaragua and by the American invasion of Grenada in 1983.

Copaken urged Hernández Colón to include in his January 1985 inaugural speech a dramatic proposal: if Section 936 were kept intact, Puerto Rico would channel hundreds of millions of dollars in 936 funds into Caribbean and Central American development. This would revive President Reagan's previously announced Caribbean Basin Initiative, which allowed for one-way free trade between the region and the United States but had failed to make an impact in its economy.

The governor, Copaken, and Moscoso made reference to an old article written by then-presidential candidate Reagan and published in February 1980 in the *Wall Street Journal* that favored statehood for Puerto Rico. Reagan argued that the best response to Fidel Castro and the Soviet menace in the Caribbean was the success of American democracy in the Puerto Rico. Copaken extended the argument to include the Caribbean and Central American nations that had joined Reagan's Caribbean Basin Initiative.

Following Copaken's strategy, Hernández Colón decided to launch Puerto Rico's own 936 Caribbean Development Program during the president's visit to Grenada to commemorate the U.S. military intervention to prevent a pro-Castro takeover. The governor next wrote to Treasury Secretary Baker explaining that he had received firm commitments from four pharmaceutical firms to establish plants in Grenada: Johnson and Johnson, Smithkline Beecham, Schering-Plough, and Abbott Laboratories. (The four firms eventually did so.) To succeed as a national defense tool or strategy, Copaken had to move Section 936 out of the Treasury Department's control and into the hands of the State Department and the National Security Council, which would, they hoped, understand the value of reviving the president's CBI program. Puerto Rico's pro-commonwealth leaders usually were well received in the State Department because of their cooperation with the U.S. delegation before the United Nations Decolonization Committee. This joint effort defused the annual Cuban-Soviet attempt to have the United Nations declare the island a "U.S. colony."

Copaken turned to Michael Deaver, who was about to leave the White House. Contracted through the brokerage house of Smith Barney, Deaver obtained the support of Secretary of State George Shultz, Defense Secretary Caspar Weinberger, Commerce Secretary Malcolm Baldridge, and National Security Council Advisor Robert McFarlane. Deaver's effort, however, did not stop the Treasury Department from sending to Congress in May 1985 a proposal to repeal 936. But Copaken's effort succeeded in creating doubts among key congressional leaders. Ways and Means Committee Chairman Dan Rostenkowski, whose Chicago district included a large Puerto Rican population, delegated the issue to New York Congressman Charles Rangel, who also had a large Puerto Rican constituency. Rangel became the most consistent defender of 936 in Congress. With Copaken's help, the governor initiated negotiations with the State Department's and National Security Council's representatives to forge a memorandum of agreement in which Puerto Rico would "guarantee" an annual 936 investment in the Caribbean of $100 million. Because 936 funds are the profits of 936 firms deposited in Puerto Rico's financial institutions, this was a major commitment by the insular government.

The Copaken strategy finally succeeded. On November 20, speaking at the annual conference on the Caribbean in Miami, Vice President George W. Bush declared that President Reagan had decided to endorse Section 936 and that preserving the tax provision meant specifically that Puerto Rico would continue to benefit from U.S. corporate investment "under the terms of this law." More important, he added that the United States was strongly committed to the success of the Caribbean Basin Initiative and that the administration would seek to preserve the benefits of 936 into the future if Puerto Rico's plan to stimulate investment in the Caribbean region bore fruit as anticipated.

Congress approved the reform tax proposal that retained Section 936. The conference report declared that Puerto Rico would make a good faith effort to carry out the twin plant initiative outlined in the memorandum of agreement. The report also referred to a $100 million investment of 936 funds in CBI countries.

Again Puerto Rico had averted an economic disaster. It was not only a spectacular victory for Puerto Rico and the Caribbean nations but also for Hernández Colón's and Copaken's strategy. By the early 1990s, a total of fifty-eight twin plants were in operation throughout the region; additionally, more than $1 billion in 936 funds were lent to Caribbean nations for infrastructure development.[8]

*   *   *

There was scarcely a segment of the island economy that was not impacted by 936 firms. A 1990 study of twenty-four 936 companies found that they alone had spent $538 million as payments for local supplies and services—from accountants, lawyers, and insurance agents to packers, printers, janitors, and guards. Since all 936 employees had health insurance coverage, the financial impact extended to the island's medical and health care services.

Puerto Rico's tourism also benefited from Section 936. In the mid-1970s, the island's tourist industry was in danger of losing its ability to compete with the growing number of Caribbean destinations because, unlike Hawaii, Puerto Rico is surrounded by dozens of sun-drenched, beautiful islands. As the total number of first-class hotel rooms declined in Puerto Rico, its next-door neighbor, the Dominican Republic, undertook a massive hotel- and resort-building program that added more than ten thousand rooms at rates significantly lower than Puerto Rico's.

However, due to low-cost 936 funds, a tourism revival started in the late 1980s. American Airlines announced in 1985 that it was investing more than $200 million, in part using 936 financing, to establish a major Caribbean hub in San Juan. Other 936-related travel businesses such as car rentals and conference and convention organizers added to the tourism bonanza.

The island's central and municipal governments also benefited and became dependent on 936 funds. By early 1990, Section 936 corporations were contributing $600 million to the Puerto Rican treasury through a variety of fees and other assessments, including the tollgate tax.

Chapter 20

Summing Up

Moscoso rushed through life with the excitement of a child in an amusement park, so exhilarated in anticipation of the next attraction that he never seemed to relish what was before him. He never took time to stop and think about his accomplishments, how his program and his agency had transformed Puerto Rico and impacted Latin American history.

The closest he came to summing up Fomento's enormous impact was an article he painstakingly prepared in 1984 with his close friend, former Fomento economist Hubert Barton—a work titled *Commonwealth and the Economics of Development*. It was a bittersweet summation, as much about opportunities lost and errors made as about the successes of Operation Bootstrap.

The first crucial decision made by Puerto Rico in the 1940s, they wrote, was to use the $160 million unexpected rum tax windfall for investment in development and not "on the immediate consumption needs of an impoverished population. It was a hard decision for a young, populist government." The money was mostly given to nine public corporations, among them the Economic Development Company. This was a vital decision because these public corporations, in turn, were able to raise hundreds of millions of dollars through debt financing. By 1983, the public corporations had poured $6.3 billion into the island's infrastructure: water, sewerage, transportation, power, and agricultural development.

Public investment in government-built factories was not enough. The key was public investment to attract private capital. Puerto Rico went beyond the classic liberal-conservative debate of whether the government or the private sector should take the lead in economic development. The answer for the island's undeveloped economy was both—what Moscoso called "development politics." While the success of Operation Bootstrap after the initial stage was based on private investment driven by the profit motive, it was the result of aggressive and imaginative government action. Bootstrap, indeed, was driven by private investment, but it was a *government program*. Most important was the government's willingness, often at substantial political sacrifice, to continue to channel the scarce resources into developmental investment in Puerto Rico's infrastructure.

Defending themselves from the old charge that Fomento's industrialization was responsible for the decline of agriculture, Moscoso and Barton argued that Puerto Rico, responding to political and ideological pressures, had wasted *too much* of the island's scarce resources on agriculture. "Many critics of Puerto Rico's economic policy complain that government abandoned agriculture. They are wrong: it was killed with kindness."

Another crucial governmental decision, they wrote, resolved "the underlying conflict between the longer range development objectives of government and the shorter range objectives of organized labor." Puerto Rico partly resolved the conflict by selling the initial Fomento-owned factories (but not the hotels) and dedicating itself to the promotion of privately owned industries. Left unresolved, however, were the conflicts with the labor unions that represented workers in the public corporations (the power, water, and sewerage authorities, which were state monopolies). These unions exerted enormous pressure on the government and significantly affected the direction of the agencies, including their programs and policies.

The economic miracle depended on Puerto Rico's special relationship to the United States, but did not evolve spontaneously or exclusively from that unique association called commonwealth. It was the resolve and creativity of Puerto Rico's leadership and, in the final analysis, of its people that were responsible for the transformation.

A fundamental lesson learned was that the existence of incentives, however attractive, were not of themselves enough to attract industrial and tourism capital. When the island lost its labor and other cost advantages, it became increasingly difficult to promote Fomento. Additionally, there were more Fomento clones representing both state and regional governments as well as foreign countries competing for job-creating investments.

This was one of the principal causes of Moscoso's bittersweet summation. The more Fomento succeeded, the less the insular government was inclined to fund the agency. The tug-of-war in the allocation of resources between developmental and social goals became increasingly intense.

The political parties in power found it more and more difficult to resist greater social spending. Part of the reason was that development and industrialization created new social ills. The island's urbanization and the emergence of a massive middle class had also created a new political landscape dominated by a strong two-party system, leading to very close elections. This forced a mind-set geared to short-term political payoffs. Moscoso and Barton were convinced that in the 1950s and early 1960s, Luis Muñoz Marín and the Populares would not have made the long-range developmental, pro-Fomento decisions if they had not achieved the political dominance that assured victory in the next elections.

In the 1980s, Moscoso and Barton pointed out, Fomento received less than 1 percent of the total budget, while in 1953 it received 7.5 percent. "Neither its reputation for performance nor the basic importance of its function gained Fomento the financial support it needed after investment promotion became more difficult and much more expensive."

The Fomento program, Moscoso and Barton continued, was the victim of its success in another, paradoxical way:

> [U]nderlying much of [the] questioning and criticism was undue faith in the Fomento program, which appeared to have become automatic. It was pushing up the economy every year at a rate that would double income every decade . . . . [C]ritics with $10,000 a year incomes were already complaining about the consumerism of a $3,000 a year middle class. They could live well enough and even with "serenity" if only— Walden like—they would trim their wants to what they could now afford.
>
> Events were to prove otherwise. The year 1968 marked the end of the long period of booming economic growth that began 20 years earlier. It also marked the election of the first of the recent administrations that favored statehood for Puerto Rico.

Continuity, so essential in a developmental policy, was broken. Moscoso and Barton severely criticized the policy changes that took place after 1970. The loss of flexibility in federal minimum wages cost the apparel industry an estimated seventy-four thousand jobs: "even though we can never know the number, it seems likely that over zealous administration of the minimum wage legislation is responsible for most of the heavy unemployment burden we carry today." They criticized with equal vigor the changes made during the 1977 to 1984 administration of pro-statehood Governor Romero Barceló: "we could no longer offer '100 percent tax exemption,' our strongest appeal to new investors and most direct route to additional investment and increased employment . . . . The damage done to the [Fomento] program in 1977 by denouncing the flexible system of minimum wage and in 1978 by enacting a watered down industrial incentives act was far more fundamental and impossible to correct."

These changes made Section 936 still more crucial. "It is sheer profitability that has brought most of the high wage industries to Puerto Rico," Moscoso and Barton wrote. Puerto Rico found that other countries "that had learned much from our earlier development experience" and had modeled their industrial promotion after Fomento—such as Taiwan and Ireland—now were getting the better of the global competition for industrial investment.

Moscoso and Barton recognized that as a model for economic development, Puerto Rico was indeed a special case due to its unique political and economic relationship to the United States. "At no time," they wrote, "has a developing company had so favorable an institutional and political environment. This is one reason why many outsiders have denigrated the success of the Fomento program and the unprecedented rate of increase in employment and incomes that was achieved in the 50's, 60's and 70's." It was evident that without its unique association to the United States, Puerto Rico's economy would not be much better than those of neighboring Caribbean nations, such as the Dominican Republic, or of the small Central American countries.

So, Moscoso and Barton concluded: "The United States is not going to develop the economy of Puerto Rico." The United States could help by giving stability to such vital incentives as Section 936, but "the rest is up to us."

The summing-up article was never published. Two years later, a four-page excerpt was included in the book *The Political Status of Puerto Rico*, published by the Americas Society.[1] Hugh Barton, who remained the closest to Moscoso of all the old Fomento people, had died a year earlier, on July 27, 1985.

*　　*　　*

A small group of Moscoso's friends gathered on November 26, 1990, to celebrate quietly his eightieth birthday. Long gone and mostly forgotten were the ills besetting Puerto Rico when Moscoso began his public life in 1938. The wooden shacks so tightly packed together that it was nearly impossible to carry out the dead no longer existed; El Fanguito, San Juan's Little Mud Hole where Eleanor Roosevelt saw potbellied Puerto Rican children playing in the putrid cesspool that passed for streets, was now part of a distant past recalled only in gallery exhibitions of striking black-and-white photographs such as those taken by Rexford Tugwell to shake into action the president of the United States.

Also gone were many of the men and women who made possible Puerto

Moscoso's inspiration and mentor, Luis Muñoz Marín, gives Moscoso a framed photograph with the inscription: "To Teodoro Moscoso, architect of the industrialization, from his companion who desires (as he does) that from that industrialization will rise a wider and deeper social justice, a more Puerto Rican Puerto Rico, a culture of greater excellence. With all my affection, Luis Muñoz Marin. April 5, 1974."

Rico's economic miracle. On July 10, 1979, Moscoso and Gloria had traveled to Santa Barbara, California, to visit Rexford Tugwell on his eighty-eighth birthday. Two weeks later, Tugwell died. They were the last Puerto Ricans to see him alive. The following year, on April 30, 1980, Luis Muñoz Marín died—more than a million Puerto Ricans lined the streets and roads from San Juan to Barranquitas in silent respect for the funeral procession.

⁂

On March 6, 1992, Moscoso made an appearance at a ceremony celebrating the fiftieth anniversary of the founding of Fomento that was organized by the Chase Manhattan Bank. The usually prompt Moscoso was late in arriving. When it was his turn to speak, he was hardly audible. He had been battling cancer for fifteen years. In December, doctors informed the family that it had spread to his lungs and liver. A letter from David Rockefeller was read to him:

> Under Governor Muñoz Marín's leadership, you developed what has proven to be one of the world's outstanding programs for economic

development. Puerto Rico, indeed all of this hemisphere, stands in your debt. Following your distinguished service as the Ambassador of the United States to Venezuela, your service as the head of the Alliance for Progress set the agenda for a program of hemisphere-wide development that has continued to this day under President Bush's Enterprise for the Americas Initiative . . . . Well done, Ted. Your accomplishments are an enduring witness to what the vision and enterprise of one dedicated man can achieve.[2]

This was his last public appearance. Moscoso died on June 15, 1992.

*　　*　　*

On August 20, 1996, President Bill Clinton, in a sparkling ceremony on the South Lawn of the White House, signed the Small Business Job Protection Act, surrounded by jubilant lawmakers of both parties and a small army of smiling children. The bill raised the federal minimum wage from $4.25 to $5.15 in two years. The 90-cent increase would have a major impact on Puerto Rico's labor-intensive industry, such as textiles, already hard pressed by the competition from Mexico under the North American Free Trade Agreement.

But the bill meant much more to Puerto Rico. The Republican-controlled Congress, over the objections of the president, had amended the bill to eliminate Section 936. The battle over this vital tax incentive, going back to 1962 when the predecessor to 936, Section 931, was under attack, was over.

Among the lawmakers at the White House event was Puerto Rico's former governor Carlos Romero Barceló, who years earlier, as Mayor of San Juan, had spared with Moscoso, rejecting his passionate defense of Operation Bootstrap and the tax exemption incentive. Romero was a member of the U.S. House of Representatives, elected Puerto Rico's resident commissioner in 1992. Once in Congress, he renewed his lifelong crusade against Bootstrap and Section 936.

The pro-statehood leader now found powerful support from Senator David Pryor, who himself led a crusade against the country's pharmaceutical industry, accusing it of making "excessive profits" while milking the American consumer, specially the elderly, with overpriced medicines. The former Governor of Arkansas had been Clinton's political mentor and now was a major influence on the new President and his wife as they prepared their massive health care reform plan. For Pryor, the pharmaceuticals were getting away with murder in Puerto Rico using the 936 "loophole" to avoid paying billions of dollars in U.S. taxes.

Again Puerto Rico was faced with a battle to save its industrialization—a battle the island had won each time. The Puerto Rican business community as well as labor unions, the 936 corporations, the bankers and professionals, geared up once more to convince members of Congress how vital this tax incentive remained for the island economy and for the Caribbean. Island polls showed wide support for 936: massive demonstrations of manufacturing employees were held, the videotapes sent to members of Congress. But, as in the past, the battle had to be led by the Government of Puerto Rico. Members of Congress that supported 936, such as liberal New York representative Charlie Rangel, had always insisted that that tax incentive had been given to Puerto Rico in order to reduce its high unemployment. It was up to Puerto Rico to justify and defend it.

This time, however, the crucial support from the insular government was absent. By 1995, Puerto Rico's new governor, the young physician Pedro Rosselló, after initially supporting 936, joined Romero in attacking it as "corporate welfare." Rosselló proposed the retention of tax credits based on wages, while eliminating the exemption on corporate income. The House, however, driven by House Speaker Newt Gingrich, eliminated both, giving existing 936 industries on the island a ten-year period to phase out the benefits.

Puerto Rico, for the first time, was no longer able to offer federal as well as local tax exemption to new investment, what had been since 1948 the indispensable core of Operation Bootstrap. Further affecting the island economy, its financial institutions and infrastructure financing, the additional exemption given to 936 profits deposited in Puerto Rico, now totaling over $15 billion—the fund used to support the Caribbean Basin Initiative—was also eliminated.

The 936 battle, now conducted exclusively by the island's private sector, was lost. The always contentious 936 issue was caught in national presidential politics. When Clinton surprised Republican candidate Bob Dole and the GOP congressional leaders by sending the proposed increase in the minimum wage—a measure with strong popular support as well as the militant backing of organized labor—the Republicans reversed themselves and decided to approve the increase. With the governor of Puerto Rico and the resident commissioner now opposed to 936, the GOP leaders earmarked the expected additional tax revenue from Puerto Rican corporations to help American small business pay for the minimum wage hike.

Now the White House issued a statement recognizing that Puerto Rico was seriously hurt: "This legislation ignores the needs of our citizens in Puerto Rico, ending the incentive for new investment now and phasing out the incentives for existing investments." The president committed himself and called on Congress to seek new means to help Puerto Rico retain its economic development. But the historic impact of the signing of this bill on Puerto Rico was an almost totally overlooked footnote at the White House ceremony.

Back in Puerto Rico, one of Teodoro Moscoso's protégés, a new generation Fomentarian who worked himself up to run Operation Bootstrap during the 1980's, shook his head in disbelief and grief. Antonio J. Colorado had grown up in the shadow of Muñoz and Moscoso. His father, a member of Muñoz's inner circle, was the University of Puerto Rico professor who half a century earlier had jumped on top of a piano to rant against Moscoso's overly aggressive programs. In 1992, young Colorado ran for resident commissioner for the Muñoz-Moscoso party, hoping to continue the defense of 936 in Congress. He lost to Bootstrap nemesis Romero Barceló.

"It's the end," he commented now, "and Puerto Rico will suffer."

A new chapter in the never-ending battle for the Puerto Rican economy — going back to the landing of American troops on July 25, 1898 — had begun.

The era of Operation Bootstrap had ended.

Epilogue

Was it an economic miracle?

By the beginning of the 1990s, Puerto Rico had a $20 billion economy; its per capita income of $6,000, still twice as poor as the poorest state, was well ahead of the island's Caribbean neighbors—six times higher than the Dominican Republic or Honduras and three times higher than Costa Rica. The average family income, $1,495 in 1950, was now $22,000. Life expectancy increased from 61 years in 1950 to 75 years; where there was one doctor per 4,108 persons in 1950, now the ratio was one doctor per 335 persons. From 60,564 vehicles to 1.2 million; from 34,509 telephones to 1.2 million; from 12,500 students in universities to 150,000.

None of this would have happened without Moscoso's Operation Bootstrap. It was Fomento that, year after year, raised the Puerto Rican economy by contributing 15.9 percent to the gross product in 1950, 21.8 percent in 1960, 25.4 percent in 1970, 36.8 percent in 1980, and 40 percent in 1990. As *The Economist* described it, Bootstrap produced "one century of economic development . . . in a decade."[1]

*   *   *

Walter Joelson, the German-born economist recruited by Moscoso in 1949, left Fomento ten years later and joined the company he helped bring to Puerto Rico—the first blue chip of Operation Bootstrap—General Electric. There he rose to become GE's chief economist. He always followed his company's success and growth in Puerto Rico and Fomento's extraordinary accomplishments.

"Was it really an economic miracle?" he was asked during an interview on July, 12, 1991.

Joelson remained silent for a few seconds, then answered:

Looking back at things from my perspective today, I have to say this: the single most difficult aspect of economic development for any country is to change the process that is prevailing. Every country knows how to increase the money supply, how to use fiscal policies, call it supply-side economics or whatever. The real problem is how do you change the system? How do you interfere in the traditional way in which an economic system works? We have enormous problems today in America. We don't know what to do about our welfare system. We don't know about our homeless people. We do not know where to get the money for education purposes. We do know that we have an inadequate production of technical personnel relative to Japan. We don't know how to do it. We are not exactly a poor country, but politically it is impossible to change the institutional framework, make a breakthrough in terms of making funds available for fundamental issues of economic development, of rising productivity, of competitiveness and so on. We have zillions of groups and committees and task forces that study these things, and everybody comes up with ideas, and nobody can implement them. We're completely stymied.

The miracle is that you had a situation in Puerto Rico which economically was incomparably worse than the economic situation in which this country is in today. The enormity of the task was mind-boggling. You had . . . the *jíbaros,* a people that had been under a political system that had been corrupt. All of a sudden an honest group of people comes into government and generates the confidence among the populace, among the voters, that they could do things which on the surface looked outrageous: give money away to the fat cats in America, have them come in without paying taxes to the Commonwealth, and yet they get the political support . . . . That a people like the Puerto Ricans could do all that, and give their men in power in those days, men with enormous vision and integrity, the wherewithal to do all this, by hindsight, is incomprehensible. You can call it a miracle: you can call it whatever you want to. The point is that it involved the implementation of new types of fiscal policies, of new types of economic policy . . . . All this was terribly difficult. It involved the building of the infrastructure, a new transportation system, competitiveness among airlines, among shipping lines and all this kind of thing.

I don't know if it was a miracle. But it was an incredible job that was accomplished.[2]

Notes

Prologue

1. Salivia, *Temporales,* 242–43.
2. Ribes Tovar, *Historia Cronológica,* 391.
3. Ciriaco, a Christian, lived around 240 A.D. under Roman Emperor Dioclecian. He was tortured and beheaded along with nineteen other Christians for refusing to abjure his religion.
4. Perpiñá y Pibernat, *Sobre el Ciclón,* 12–13.
5. Gruening, *Many Battles,* 181.
6. Karman, *Abe Fortas,* 166.
7. Perloff, *Alliance for Progress,* 34.

Chapter 1: Moscoso's Conversion

1. *El Mundo,* November 7, 1940.
2. Moscoso, *Oral Memoirs,* tapes 16-B and 17-A.
3. Muñoz Marín, *La Historia,* 33.
4. Bothwell Gonzalez, *Cien Años,* 296.

Chapter 2: Rexford Tugwell's Call

1. Collo, "Puerto Rico and the United States," 71.
2. Tugwell, *Stricken Land,* 161.
3. Schlesinger, *Crisis of the Old Order,* 400.
4. Tugwell, *Stricken Land,* 151.

Chapter 3: The Idea of Fomento

1. Tugwell, *Stricken Land,* 254.
2. Carroll, *Report on the Island,* 43.
3. Clark, *Porto Rico and Its Problems,* 454.
4. Morales Carrión, *Political and Cultural History,* 213.
5. Ibid., 220.
6. Okuda, "Industrial Development Program," 93.

7. Perloff, *Puerto Rico's Economic Future*, 260.

8. Ibid., 334.

9. Moscoso, *Oral Memoirs*, tape 100.

10. Bothwell González, *Cien Años*, 3:223.

11. Ross, *Uphill Path*, 63.

12. Tugwell, *Stricken Land*, 256.

Chapter 4: Industrialize Puerto Rico?

1. Ross, *Uphill Path*, 61.

2. Arthur D. Little Co., *Industrialization of Puerto Rico*.

3. Chardón, *Puerto Rico Policy Commission*, 2.

4. Goodsell, *Administration of a Revolution*, 23.

Chapter 5: Despite the Odds

1. Notes found in original Arthur D. Little Co.'s *Industrialization of Puerto Rico*.

2. Tugwell, *Stricken Land*, 221.

3. The recollections of Mariano Ramírez in this chapter were recorded during his interview by the author in San Juan in December 1990.

4. Tugwell, *Stricken Land*, 218.

5. Taft, letter to Donald Nelson.

6. Ibid.

7. Ramírez, interview, December 1990.

Chapter 6: Muñoz's Conversion

1. *El Mundo*, July 7, 1945.

2. Morales Carrión, *Political and Cultural History*, 268.

3. U.S. Tariff Commission, *Economy of Puerto Rico* (Dorfman Report), 32.

4. Morales Carrión, *Political and Cultural History*, 267.

5. Ibid.

6. Muñoz Marín, "Development through Democracy."

7. Ibid.

8. *El Mundo*, June 28, 1946.

9. Bothwell González, *Cien Años*, 499.

10. Taylor, *Industrial Tax Exemption*, 20.

11. Barton, "Industrial Development," 17, 23.

Chapter 7: From Public to Private Ownership

1. Moscoso, memo to Luis Muñoz Marín.

2. *El Mundo*, July 3, 1948.

3. *El Mundo*, November 12, 1949.

4. José Trías Monge, interview by the author, San Juan, March 1992.

5. Moscoso, *Oral Memoirs*, tape 25-A.

6. Ross, *Uphill Path*, 116.

Chapter 8: From Operation Bootstrap to Operation Serenity

1. Muñoz Marín, testimony before the House Committee on Public Lands, in *Los Gobernadores Electos,* 34.

2. Muñoz Marín, *Memorias II,* vol. 2, 116.

3. De Jesús, "El Gobierno," 117.

4. Roberto de Jesús, interview by the author, San Juan, March 1992.

5. Wells, "Administrative Reorganization," 470–89.

6. Moscoso, "Industrial Development," 60–69.

7. Bhana, *United States,* 195.

8. Muñoz Marín, message to the legislature, February 23, 1949, in *Los Gobernadores Electos,* vol. 1, 27.

9. Ibid., testimony before the House Committee on Public Lands, 35.

10. Ross, *Uphill Path,* 122.

11. Ibid.

12. Descartes, *Government of Puerto Rico,* 9.

13. Moscoso, "Industrial Development," 69.

14. Muñoz Marín, message to the legislature, in *Los Gobernadores Electos,* vol. 1, 27.

Chapter 9: Industrial Promotion and Economic Research

1. Reid Weedon, interview by Carmen Casellas-Marcou, Cambridge, Mass., March 1992.

2. *Fomento Magazine,* July 1952, 5.

3. Hector Meléndez and John Trifileti, interview by the author, San Juan, April 1992.

4. Amadeo Francis, interview by the author, San Juan, May 1992.

5. Walter Joelson, interview by the author, Fairfield, Conn., July 12, 1991.

6. Chase, *Operation Bootstrap,* 34.

7. Joelson, interview.

8. Jerry Maldonado, interview by the author, San Juan, December 29, 1992.

9. General Electric Company, *Manufacturing Services Bulletin,* 16.

10. Ignacio Rivera, interview by the author, San Juan, January 5, 1993.

11. Rafael Fábregas, interview by the author, San Juan, May 8, 1992.

12. Taylor, *Industrial Tax Exemption,* 18.

Chapter 10: How to Change a Dismal Image

1. "An Unsolvable Problem," *Life,* March 8, 1943.

2. Muñoz Marín, letter to Antonio Fernós Isern.

3. Ogilvy, *Ogilvy on Advertising,* 51.

4. Moscoso, *Oral Memoirs,* tape 33-A.

5. Weedon, interview.

6. Moscoso, *Oral Memoirs,* tape 33-A.

7. Kirk, *Pablo Casals,* 456.

8. Moscoso, *Oral Memoirs,* tape 40-B.

9. Kirk, *Pablo Casals*, 492.

10. Ibid., 498.

11. Moscoso, *Oral Memoirs*, tape 40-B.

12. Ogilvy, letter to Carmen Casellas-Marcou.

13. "Democracy Laboratory in Latin America," *Time*, June 23, 1958.

14. Nixon, *In the Arena*, 180.

15. Moscoso, *Oral Memoirs*, tape 33-A.

Chapter 11: Tourism: The Fighting Word

1. Moscoso, *Oral Memoirs*, tape 40-B.

2. *El Mundo*, August 23, 1944.

3. Ramírez, interview, December 1990.

4. Hanson, *Transformation*, 289.

5. Moscoso, letter to Rexford G. Tugwell.

6. Tugwell, letter to Rafael Picó.

7. Moscoso, *Oral Memoirs*, tape 24-B.

8. *El Mundo*, August 17, 1949.

9. *New York Times*, December 18, 1949.

10. Ramírez, interview by the author, San Juan.

11. Perloff, *Puerto Rico's Economic Future*, 361.

12. Barton, "Industrial Development," 32.

13. Ross, *Uphill Path*, 103.

14. De Jesús Toro, *Historia Económica*, 459.

15. *El Mundo*, November 21, 1949.

16. Morales Carrión, *Political and Cultural History*, 273.

17. Scott Runkle, interview by the author, New York, February 15, 1991.

18. Moscoso, *Oral Memoirs*, tape 40-A.

19. *El Mundo*, January 31, 1951.

20. De Jesús Toro, *Historia Económica*, 458.

21. Moscoso, *Oral Memoirs*, tape 40-A.

Chapter 12: The Price and Wages of Success

1. Robert R. Nathan Associates, *Evaluation and Minimum Wage*, 202.

2. Muñoz Marín, speech at ILGWU convention.

3. Leo Suslow, interview by the author, Washington, D.C., February 16, 1991.

4. Robert R. Nathan Associates, *Minimum Wage Issue*, 21.

Chapter 13: Migration: To New York and Brazil

1. *Fomento Magazine*, October 1952, 18.

2. *Fomento Magazine*, January–April 1953, 7.

3. Moscoso, *Oral Memoirs*, tape 38-A.

4. Ramírez, interview, December 1990.

5. *Fomento Magazine*, July 1952, 28.

6. Senior, *The Puerto Ricans*, 87.

7. Ibid., 41.

8. Gunther, *Inside South America*, 30.

9. Muñoz Marín, letter to Getulio Vargas.

10. Fernández García, "Report on Puerto Rican Colony in Brazil"; personal papers, Rafael Fernández García, September 15, 1952.

11. Gunther, *Inside South America*, 31.

Chapter 14: Winds of Change

1. Baggs, "Puerto Rico: Showcase of Development," in *Britannica Yearbook*, 60.

2. Barton, "Industrial Development," 23.

Chapter 15: Moscoso in Venezuela

1. Moscoso, letter to Chester Bowles.

2. Schlesinger, *Thousand Days*, 192.

3. Moscoso, *Oral Memoirs*, tape 48-B.

4. *El Universal*, April 4, 1961.

5. *La Esfera*, May 15, 1961.

6. Moscoso, *Oral Memoirs*, tape 44-B

7. Ibid., tape 51-A.

8. José Teodoro Moscoso, interview by Carmen Casellas-Marcou, New York, March 24, 1992.

9. Moscoso, *Oral Memoirs*, tape 44-B.

10. Ibid., tape 49-A.

11. Rogers, *Twilight Struggle*, 39.

12. Rusk, cable to Teodoro Moscoso with message from President Kennedy.

13. Moscoso, *Oral Memoirs*, tape 58-B.

14. Ibid.

Chapter 16: The Alliance for Progress

1. Moscoso, *Oral Memoirs*, tape 52-A.

2. Levinson and de Onís, *Alliance That Lost Its Way*, 351.

3. Rogers, *Twilight Struggle*, 228.

4. Ibid., 192.

5. Moscoso, *Oral Memoirs*, tape 52-B.

6. Schlesinger, *Thousand Days*, 767.

7. Richard Goodwin, interview by Carmen Casellas Marcou, Concord, Mass., March 20, 1992.

8. Moscoso, *Oral Memoirs*, tape 53-A.

9. *New York Times*, March 13, 1962.

10. *Newsweek*, April 9, 1962.

11. Arnold Leibowitz, telephone interview by the author, April 15, 1993.

12. Moscoso, *Oral Memoirs*, tape 53-A.

13. *Vista,* November 19, 1988.
14. Moscoso, *Oral Memoirs,* tape 53-A.
15. Rogers, *Twilight Struggle,* 201.
16. Schlesinger, *Thousand Days,* 790.
17. Rogers, *Twilight Struggle,* 231.
18. Moscoso, *Oral Memoirs,* tape 54-A.
19. Rogers, *Twilight Struggle,* 199.
20. Moscoso, *Oral Memoirs,* tape 54-A.
21. Rogers, *Twilight Struggle,* 269–70.
22. Moscoso, *Oral Memoirs,* tape 57-A.
23. Guthman and Schulman, eds., *Robert Kennedy,* 385–86.
24. Goodwin, *Remembering America,* 245.
25. Rogers, *Twilight Struggle,* 226.
26. Moscoso, *Oral Memoirs,* tape 62-A.

Chapter 17: A Superport and a Confession

1. Moscoso, *Oral Memoirs,* tape 72-B.
2. Ibid., tape 36-B.
3. Barney Baus, interview by the author, San Juan, December 1993.
4. Moscoso and Barton, *Commonwealth,* 1984.
5. Moscoso, *Oral Memoirs,* tape 72-B.
6. Ibid., tape 75-A.
7. Lewis Smith, interview by the author, San Juan, February 5, 1993.
8. Yergin, *Prize,* 588.
9. Moscoso, *Oral Memoirs,* tape 75-A.
10. Ibid., tape 47-A.
11. Robert West, statement before the Federal Energy Administration, April 12, 1976, mimeographed.
12. Alex Regan, statement before the Federal Energy Administration, April 12, 1976, mimeographed.
13. Yergin, *Prize,* 659.
14. Moscoso, statement before the Federal Energy Administration, April 12, 1976, mimeographed.
15. Moscoso, *Oral Memoirs,* tape 73-B.

Chapter 18: From 931 to 936

1. Moscoso, statement before the House Subcommittee on Territorial and Insular Affairs, 1974.
2. S. Hohn Bund of Vokswagenwerk, letter to Moscoso, June 14, 1974. Fomento Library Files.
3. Moscoso, statement before the House Subcommittee on Territorial and Island Affairs, 1974.
4. Moscoso, letter to Rafael Hernández Colón, June 5, 1975, Fomento Library.

5. Ramírez, interview by the author, San Juan, January 12, 1993.

6. Fernós Isern, *Estado Libre,* 559.

7. Hernández Colón, "Section 931 and 332."

8. Resident Commissioner Jaime Benítez, memorandum, June 3, 1973, Fomento Library.

9. Salvador Casellas, interview by the author, San Juan, March 1991.

10. *Caribbean Business,* February 16, 1983.

Chapter 19: Bootstrap under Siege

1. Romero Barceló, *La Estadidad,* 42.

2. Moscoso, *Oral Memoirs,* tapes 76-A, 75-B, and 74-A.

3. Moscoso, testimony on Puerto Rico Senate Bill 537, 1978, mimeograph.

4. U.S. Treasury Department, *Operation and Effect,* First Report, 5.

5. Ibid., Fourth Report, 116.

6. Hernández Colón, "Analysis of Treasury Proposal," 1.

7. True, "Measuring the Benefits," 5.

8. Daniel Lebrón, testimony before Puerto Rico Senate Committee on Labor, February 16, 1993, mimeographed, 13.

Chapter 20: Summing Up

1. Moscoso and Barton, "Economics of Development," 49–52.

2. David Rockefeller, letter to Moscoso, March 6, 1992.

Epilogue

1. Moscoso, testimony before the U.S. Senate Finance Committee, April 1990, mimeographed, 2.

2. Joelson, interview.

Bibliography

The main sources of information for this book consist of taped and transcribed interviews with Teodoro Moscoso and other key persons involved with the economic development of Puerto Rico. These transcriptions can be located at the Luis Muñoz Foundation and Archives in Trujillo Alto, Puerto Rico.

Other important unpublished sources, such as congressional testimonies and reports, can be located in the Economic Development Administration Library, Hato Rey, Puerto Rico.

Books

Albuquerque Loréns, Francisco. *Raúl Prebisch*. Madrid: Ediciones de Cultura Hispánica, 1989.

Alexander, Robert J. *Rómulo Betancourt and the Transformation of Venezuela*. New Brunswick, N.J.: Transaction Books, 1982.

————. *The Venezuelan Democratic Revolution*. New Brunswick, N.J.: Rutgers University Press, 1964.

Ameringer, Charles D. *The Democratic Left in Exile: The Antidictatorial Struggle in the Caribbean 1945–1959*. Coral Gables, Fla.: University of Miami Press, 1974.

Araez Ferrando, Ramón. *Historia del Ciclón de San Ciriaco* (History of the San Ciriaco hurricane). San Juan: Imprenta Heraldo Español, 1905.

Arthur D. Little Co. *Report of the Industrialization of Puerto Rico*. Cambridge, Mass., August 1, 1942.

Barbash, Jack, ed. *Unions and Union Leaders: Their Human Meaning*. New York: Harper and Brothers, 1959.

Barton, Hugh C. "Puerto Rico's Industrial Development." Paper presented at a seminar of the Harvard University Center for International Affairs, Cambridge, October 29, 1959.

Bayron Toro, Fernando. *Elecciones y Partidos Políticos de Puerto Rico* (Elections and political parties in Puerto Rico). Mayaguez, P.R.: Editorial Isla, 1989.

Beisner, Robert L. *Twelve against Empire*. Chicago: University of Chicago Press, 1968.

Berbusse, Edward J. *The United States and Puerto Rico—1898–1900*. Chapel Hill: University of North Carolina Press, 1966.

Berle, Adolf A. *Latin America—Diplomacy and Reality*. New York: Harper and Row, 1962.

Betancourt, Rómulo. *Tres Años de Gobierno Democrático*—*1959-1962* (Three years of democratic government). Vol. 2. Caracas: Imprenta Nacional, 1962.

Bhana, Surendra. *The United States and the Development of the Puerto Rican Status Question.* Wichita: University of Kansas Press, 1975.

Black, Ruby. *Eleanor Roosevelt—A Biography.* New York: Duell, Sloan and Pearce, 1940.

Blank, David Eugene. *Politics in Venezuela.* Boston: Little, Brown, 1953.

Bothwell Gonzalez, Reece B. *Puerto Rico: Cien Años de Lucha Política* (Puerto Rico: One hundred years of political struggle). 4 vols. Río Piedras, P.R.: Editorial Universitaria, 1979.

Burns, James MacGregor. *Roosevelt—The Soldier of Freedom.* New York: Harcourt Brace Jovanovich, 1970.

Carbonell, Nestor. *And the Russians Stayed: The Sovietization of Cuba.* New York: Morrow, 1989.

Caribbean Business, February 16, 1983.

Carroll, Henry K. *Report on the Island of Porto Rico.* 1899. Reprint, New York: Arno Press, 1975.

Chardón, Carlos, et al. *Report of the Puerto Rico Policy Commission* (Chardón Report). San Juan, 1934.

Chase, Stuart. *Operation Bootstrap in Puerto Rico.* National Planning Association Planning Pamphlet No. 75. September 1951.

Clark, Victor S., et al. *Porto Rico and Its Problems.* Washington, D.C.: Brookings Institution, 1930.

Coffin, Frank M. *Witness for AID.* Cambridge, Mass.: Riverside Press, 1964.

Cohen, Warren I. *Dean Rusk.* Totowa, N.J.: Cooper Square, 1980.

Collo, Martin Joseph. "Puerto Rico and the United States: The Effect of the Relationship on Puerto Rican Agricultural Development." Ph.D. diss., University of Pennsylvania, 1986.

Davis, George W. *Report on Civil Affairs of Porto Rico.* Washington, D.C.: U.S. Government Printing Office, 1900.

———. *Report on Industrial and Economic Conditions of Puerto Rico for the War Department.* Washington, D.C.: U.S. Government Printing Office, 1900.

De Jesús, Roberto. "El Gobierno de Puerto Rico en 1949." In Marshall Dimock and Pedro Muñoz Amato, *La Reorganización de la Rama Ejecutiva.* Río Piedras, P.R.: Sociedad Americana de Administración Pública, 1951.

De Jesús Toro, Rafael. *Historia Económica de Puerto Rico* (Economic history of Puerto Rico). Cincinnati: South Western Publishing Co., 1982.

Dietz, James L. *The Economic History of Puerto Rico.* Princeton: Princeton University Press, 1980.

Dimock, Marshall, and Pedro Muñoz Amato, eds. *La Reorganización de la Rama Ejecutiva* (The reorganization of the Executive Branch). Río Piedras, P.R.: Sociedad Americana de Administración Pública, 1951.

Drier, John C. *The Alliance for Progress.* Baltimore: Johns Hopkins Press, 1963.

Dulles, Foster Rhea. *The United States since 1865.* Ann Arbor: University of Michigan Press, 1971.

Eastman, Samuel, and Daniel Marx. *Ships and Sugar.* Río Piedras, P.R.: University of Puerto Rico Press, 1953.

Economic Development Administration. *Minimum Wage Issue in Puerto Rico, 1975.* San Juan, 1975.

El Mundo (San Juan), November 7, 1940; August 23, 1944; July 7, 1945; June 28, 1946; July 3, 1948; August 17, 1949; November 12 and 21, 1949; January 31, 1951.

El Universal, April 4, 1961.

Falk, Pamela, ed. *The Political Status of Puerto Rico.* Lexington, Mass.: D.C. Heath and Co., Lexington Books, 1986.

Fernández García, Rafael. "Report on Puerto Rican Colony in Brazil." September 15, 1952. Personal papers.

Fernós Isern, Antonio. *Estado Libre Asociado de Puerto Rico* (Commonwealth of Puerto Rico). Río Piedras, P.R.: Editorial Universitaria, 1974.

Fomento Magazine (San Juan), July and October 1952; January–April 1953.

Foner, Philip S. *The Spanish-Cuban-American War and the Birth of American Imperialism 1895–1902.* New York: Monthly Review Press, 1972.

Freidel, Frank. *The Splendid Little War.* New York: Dell, 1962.

Galbraith, John Kenneth, and Richard H. Holton. *Marketing Efficiency in Puerto Rico.* Cambridge: Harvard University Press, 1955.

General Electric Company. *Manufacturing Services Bulletin,* August 1956.

Goodsell, Charles T. *Administration of a Revolution: Executive Reform in Puerto Rico under Governor Tugwell 1941–1946.* Cambridge: Harvard University Press, 1965.

Goodwin, Richard N. *Remembering America: A Voice of the Sixties.* Boston: Little, Brown, 1971.

Gordon, Lincoln. *A New Deal for Latin America: The Alliance for Progress.* Cambridge, Mass., 1963.

Goulden, Joseph C. *Meany.* New York: Atheneum, 1972.

Gruening, Ernest. *Many Battles—An Autobiography.* New York: Liveright Press, 1973.

Gunther, John. *Inside South America.* New York: Harper and Row, 1967.

Guthman, Edwin O., and Jeffrey Schulman, eds. *Robert Kennedy—In His Own Words: The Unpublished Revelations of the Kennedy Years.* New York: Bantam Books, 1988.

Hanson, Earl Parker. *Transformation: The Story of Modern Puerto Rico.* New York: Simon and Schuster, 1955.

Hanson, Millard, and Henry Wells, eds. *Annals of the American Academy of Political and Social Science* 285 (January 1953): 1–8.

Hernández Colón, Rafael. "Analysis of Treasury Proposal to Repeal Section 936." March 12, 1985. Mimeographed.

———. "Section 931 and 332 of the U.S. Tax Revenue Code and the Economy of Puerto Rico." Testimony before the U.S. House of Representatives Ways and Means Committee, May 31, 1974. Mimeographed.

Hudson, Rex A. *Castro's America Department: Coordinating Cuba's Support of Marxist-Leninist Violence in the Americas.* Washington, D.C.: Cuban American National Foundation, 1988.

Humphrey, Hubert. *Alliance for Progress.* Minneapolis: University of Minnesota Press, 1963.

Ickes, Harold L. *The Secret Diary of Harold L. Ickes.* New York: Simon and Schuster, 1954.

Johnson, Roberta Ann. *Puerto Rico: Commonwealth or Colony?* New York: Praeger, 1980.

Karman, Laura. *Abe Fortas: A Biography.* New Haven: Yale University Press, 1990.

Karnow, Stanley. *In Our Image—America's Empire in the Philippines.* New York: Random House, 1989.

Kennedy, Robert F. *The Enemy Within.* New York: Harper and Brothers, 1960.

Kesterman, Frank R. *Analysis of Puerto Rico's Role in Marine Transportation.* Washington, D.C.: International Service Corp., January 1974.

Keyserling, Leon H. *Minimum Wage in Puerto Rico: The Problem Reexamined After Two Years.* December 1967.

———. *Minimum Wages in Puerto Rico in the Setting of Economic Development.* Vol. 1. July 1965.

Kirk, H. L. *Pablo Casals.* New York: Holt, Rinehart and Winston, 1974.

La Esfera (Caracas), May 15, 1961.

Lawson, Don. *The United States in the Spanish-American War.* New York: Abelard-Schuman, 1976.

Levinson, Jerome, and Juan de Onís. *The Alliance That Lost Its Way: A Critical Report on the Alliance for Progress.* Chicago: Quadrangle Books, 1970.

Life, March 8, 1943.

Luque de Sánchez, María Dolores. *La Ocupación Norteamericana y la Ley Foraker y La Opinión Puertorriqueña* (The American occupation and the Foraker law and Puerto Rican opinion). Río Piedras, P.R.: Editorial Universitaria, 1979.

Mahan, Alfred Thayer. *Interest of America in Sea Power—Present and Future.* London: Sampson, Low, Marston and Co., 1897.

———. *Lessons of the War with Spain.* New York: Books for Libraries Press, 1899.

Martz, John D., and David J. Myers, eds. *Venezuela: The Democratic Experience.* New York: Praeger, 1977.

Mathews, Thomas G. *Puerto Rican Politics and the New Deal.* Gainesville, Fla.: University of Florida Press, 1960.

May, Herbert. *Problems and Prospects of the Alliance for Progress.* New York: Praeger, 1968.

Morales Carrión, Arturo. *Puerto Rico: A Political and Cultural History.* New York: W. W. Norton and Co., 1983.

Moscoso, Teodoro. "Industrial Development in Puerto Rico." *Annals of the American Academy of Political and Social Science* (January 1953).

———. Letter to Chester Bowles. Moscoso files, box 3, John F. Kennedy Archives, Boston.

————. Letter to Rafael Hernández Colón. June 5, 1975. Economic Development Administration Library, San Juan.

————. Letter to Rexford G. Tugwell. October 15, 1946. Tugwell files, Franklin D. Roosevelt Library, Hyde Park, N.Y.

————. Memo to Luis Muñoz Marín. July 8, 1947. Puerto Rican Collection, Documentos P-Agencias, Compañía de Fomento Industrial, Document Group 3, University of the Sacred Heart.

————. *Oral Memoirs*. Interviews by the author. Tape recordings and transcriptions, 1987–91, San Juan. Luis Muñoz Marín Foundation and Archives, Trujillo Alto, P.R.

————. Statement before the U.S. House of Representatives Subcommittee on Territorial and Island Affairs. June 19, 1976. Mimeographed.

Moscoso and Hubert Barton. *Commonwealth and the Economics of Development*. 1984.

Moscoso and Barton. "Puerto Rico and the Economics of Development." In Pamela Falk, ed., *The Political Status of Puerto Rico*. Lexongton, Mass.: Heath, 1986.

Muñoz Marín, Luis. "Development through Democracy." In Millard Hanson and Henry Wells, *Annals of the American Academy of Political and Social Science*, 1–8.

————. In *Los Gobernadores Electos de Puerto Rico*. Vol. 1. San Juan: Corporacion de Servicios Bibliotecarios, 1973.

————. *La Historia del Partido Popular Democrático* (History of the Popular Democratic Party). San Juan: Editorial Batey, 1984.

————. Letter to Antonio Fernós Isern. January 22, 1948. Luis Muñoz Marín Archives, Trujillo Alto, P.R.

————. Letter to Getulio Vargas. January 28, 1952. Personal papers of Rafael Fernández García's estate, to be donated to the Puerto Rican Collection of the University of the Sacred Heart, Santurce, P.R.

————. *Memorias—Autobiografía Pública 1898–1940* (Memoirs: A public autobiography). San Juan: Universidad Interamericana de Puerto Rico, 1982.

————. *Memorias*. Vol. 2. Universidad Interamericana, 1992,

————. Speech at ILGWU Convention, Atlantic City, N.J., May 18, 1958. Pamphlet.

New York Times, December 18, 1949; March 13, 1962.

Newsweek, April 9, 1992

Nixon, Richard M. *In the Arena*. New York: Simon and Schuster, 1990.

Nystrom, John Warren. *The Alliance for Progress*. Princeton: Van Nostrand, 1966.

Ogilvy, David. *Confessions of an Advertising Man*. New York: Atheneum, 1963.

————. Letter to Carmen Casellas-Marcou, February 17, 1992.

————. *Ogilvy on Advertising*. New York: Vintage Books, 1985.

Okuda, Kenji. "The Industrial Development Program in Puerto Rico. 1942–1953." Ph.D. diss., Harvard University, 1954.

Perloff, Harvey S. *The Alliance for Progress*. Baltimore: Johns Hopkins Press, 1969.

————. *Puerto Rico's Economic Future*. Chicago: University of Chicago Press, 1950.

Perpiñá y Pibernat, Juan. *Sobre el Ciclón del Glorioso San Ciriaco y Compañeros Mártires* (About the San Ciriaco hurricane and martyr companions). San Juan: A. Lynne Hijos de Pérez Morris, 1899.

Pueblo Supermarkets. *Annual Report*. San Juan, 1965.

Puerto Rico Development Co. *Annual Report*, 1943, 1944, 1945, 1946, 1947, 1948, 1949.

Puerto Rico Planning Board. *Economic Report to the Governor*. San Juan, 1960.

Ribes Tovar, Federico. *Historia Cronológica de Puerto Rico*. New York: Plus Ultra Educational Press, 1973.

Robert R. Nathan Associates, Inc. *Evaluation of Minimum Wage Policy in Puerto Rico*. Washington, D.C., 1955.

———. *Minimum Wage Issue in Puerto Rico, 1973: A Report Submitted to The Commonwealth of Puerto Rico*. Washington, D.C., May 1973.

Robinson, Albert Gardner. *The Porto Rico of to-Day*. New York: Charles Scribner's Sons, 1899.

Rogers, William D. *The Twilight Struggle: The Alliance for Progress and the Politics of Development in Latin America*. New York: Random House, 1967.

Romero Barceló, Carlos. *La Estadidad Es Para los Pobres*. First edition. N.p., 1973.

Roosevelt, Franklin D. *Public Papers and Addresses of Franklin D. Roosevelt*. Vol. 2. New York: Random House, 1938.

Roosevelt, Theodore. *Colonial Policies of the United States*. New York: Doubleday and Co., 1937.

Root, Elihu. *The Military and Colonial Policy of the United States—Addresses and Reports*. 1916. Reprint, New York: AMS Press, 1970.

Ross, David F. *The Long Uphill Path*. San Juan: Talleres Gráficos Interamericanos, Inc., 1966.

Rusk, Dean. Cable to Teodoro Moscoso. Personal papers of Teodoro Moscoso, Luis Muñoz Marín Foundation, Trujillo Alto, P.R.

Russell, Maud. *Men along the Shore*. New York: Brussel and Brussel, 1966.

Salivia, Luis Alfredo. *Temporales de Puerto Rico y las Antillas* (Storms of Puerto Rico and the Antilles). San Juan: Editorial Edil, 1972.

Scheman, L. Robert, ed. *The Alliance for Progress: A Retrospective*. New York: Praeger, 1988.

Schlesinger, Arthur M. *The Crisis of the Old Order*. Boston: Houghton Mifflin Co., 1957.

———. *The Politics of Upheaval*. Cambridge, Mass.: Riverside Press, 1960.

———. *A Thousand Days: John F. Kennedy in the White House*. Cambridge, Mass.: Houghton Mifflin Co., 1965.

Senior, Clarence. *The Puerto Ricans*. Chicago: Quadrangle Books, 1961.

Shield, Lansing P., et al. *Report of the Puerto Rico Food Advisory Commission*. January 5, 1954.

Sorensen, Theodore C. *Kennedy*. New York: Harper and Row, 1965.

Szulc, Tad. *Fidel: A Critical Portrait*. New York: Avon Books, 1986.

Taft, Robert A. Letter to Donald Nelson, March 12, 1943. Record Group 400, Appointments, Puerto Rico. Franklin D. Roosevelt Library, Hyde Park, N.Y.

Taylor, Milton. *Industrial Tax Exemption in Puerto Rico*. Madison: University of Wisconsin Press, 1957.

Time, June 23, 1958.

Torruella, Juan R. *The Supreme Court and Puerto Rico: The Doctrine of Separate and Unequal*. Río Piedras, P.R.: Editorial de la Universidad de Puerto Rico, 1988.

Trias Monge, José. *Historia Constitucional de Puerto Rico* (Constitutional history of Puerto Rico) Río Piedras, P.R.: Editorial Universitaria, 1981.

True, Norman. "Measuring the Benefits and Costs of Section 936." 1985. Mimeographed.

Tugwell, Rexford G. *Investigation into Administrative Responsibilities under the 500 Acre Limitation*. San Juan: Bureau of Supplies, Printing and Transportation, December 1941.

————. Letter to Rafael Picó. November 4, 1946. Tugwell files, Franklin D. Roosevelt Library, Hyde Park, N.Y.

————. *The Stricken Land*. Garden City, N.J.: Doubleday and Co., 1947.

U.S. Tariff Commission. *The Economy of Puerto Rico: With Special Reference to the Economic Implications of Independence and other Proposals to Change its Political Status* (Dorfman Report). Washington, D.C., March 1946.

U.S. Treasury Department. *The Operation and Effect of the Possessions Corporations System of Taxation*. First Report, June 1978, and Fourth Report, February 1983. Mimeographed.

Vallenilla, Luis. *Oil: The Making of a New Economic Order*. New York: McGraw-Hill Book Co., 1975.

Vista, November 19, 1988.

Von Lazar, Arpad, and Robert R. Kaufman, eds. *Reform and Revolution: Readings in Latin American Politics*. Boston: Allyn and Bacon, Inc., 1969.

Wagenheim, Kal. *Puerto Rico: A Profile*. New York: Praeger Publishers, 1970.

Watkins, T. H. *Righteous Pilgrim—The Life and Times of Harold L. Ickes*. New York: Henry Holt and Co., 1990.

Wells, Henry. "Administrative Reorganization in Puerto Rico." *Western Political Quarterly* 9 (1956).

————. *The Modernization of Puerto Rico*. Cambridge: Harvard University Press, 1969.

Wish, John Reed. "Food Retailing in Economic Developmment." Ph.D. diss., Michigan State University, 1967.

Yaeger, Arthur. *Twenty Years of Progress*. (Excerpt from 1918–19 Governor's Annual Report). San Juan: Bureau of Supplies, Printing and Transportation, 1919.

Yergin, Daniel. *The Prize: The Epic Quest for Oil*. New York: Simon and Schuster, 1992.

Zimmermann, Erich W. *Staff Report to the Interdepartmental Committee on Puerto Rico*. Washington, D.C., September 9, 1940.

Index

Page numbers in italics refer to illustrations.

Fair Labor Standards Act (U.S.), 137,
204
Faisal (king of Saudia Arabia), 199–
200
Farmacia Moscoso, 7, 9
farm workers: hopelessness of, 69; and
industrialization, 28–29, 76; and
politics, 3–5. *See also* agriculture;
workers
fascism, 15, 18–19, 21
Faulkner, William, 171–72
Federal Energy Administration, 201–2
federal excise taxes: rebate of car, 204;
rebate of rum, 37, 42, 45, 52, 222
Ferdinand (king of Castile), 22
Fernández García, Benigno, 13, 36
Fernández García, Rafael: background
of, 25, 35–36; and Fomento budget,
45; and glass plant development, 38,
42–43; and migration, 145, 150–53;
recommendations by, 26–27, 33–34,
44; and tax exemptions, 46
Fernós Isern, Antonio, 84, 207
Ferré, José (Joe), 65–68
Ferré, Luis A.: background of, 61;
criticism by, 63–68; as governor,
191–92; meetings of, 215; and
Puerto Rican culture, 132
Ferré Enterprises, 43, 65–68
Ferrer, José, 127
Ferrer, Miguel, 124, 133
Figueres, José, 163
Firfer, Alex, 101
Five-Hundred Acre Law, 12–13, 36
"Fomentarian Revolution," xiv
Fomento (Economic Development
Administration): administration of,
155–58, 191–93, 224–25; authority
of, 72; beneficiaries of, 76–77;
budget of, 37, 42, 45, 74, 205, 224;
Continental Operations Branch of,
81, 85–86; credibility of, 33, 82, 88;
criticisms of, 61, 63–64, 99–102,

124, 129; employment service of,
147–48; events organized by, 105–6;
goals of, 53; Industrial Services
Division of, 141; obstacles for, 37–
45, 103–5, 203–4; origins of, 25–28;
pins and signs of, 86–87, *100*, 100–
101; slogan for, 69; staff of, 35, 39,
81, 85–86, 193; summary of, 222–
25; Tourism Advisory Committee of,
124, 126, 130–31. *See also* industrialization; industrial promotion;
Office of Economic Research (OER);
Operation Bootstrap; tourism
food, distribution of, 89
Food for Peace program, 181
Foraker Act (1900), 37
Ford, Gerald, 201–2
La Fortaleza: description of, 17, 21–22;
events at, xi, 111–12; meetings at,
17–18; restoration of, 111
Fortas, Abe, xii-xiii, 41, 114, 179, 202
Francis, Amadeo: career of, 193; on
Fomento milieu, 86–87, 98; and IRS
code, 212; and tax exemptions, 99,
101; and Volkswagen negotiations,
203–4
Franco, Gen. Francisco, 18, 110, 112–
13
Frazier-Simplex Inc., 42
free trade: agreements over, 55, 219,
227; benefits of, 51–52, 57; need for,
56
Fullmer, Robert, 101

Galbraith, J. Kenneth, 89
gambling, 120, 124–26
Gándara, José, 4–5
Gándara, Raúl, 121
Gandhi, Mahatma, 135, 155–56
General Electric, 37, 91–96, 101, 230
General Electric Realty Corporation,
94
Gingrich, Newt, 228